Religion
and
Economic
Ethics

Religion and Economic Ethics

EDITED BY

Joseph F. Gower

THE ANNUAL PUBLICATION OF THE
COLLEGE THEOLOGY SOCIETY
1985
VOLUME 31

UNIVERSITY
PRESS OF
AMERICA

Lanham • New York • London

University Press of America®, Inc.
4720 Boston Way
Lanham, Maryland 20706

3 Henrietta Street
London WC2E 8LU England

Library of Congress Cataloging-in-Publication Data

Religion and economic ethics / edited by Joseph F. Gower.
p.   cm. — (The Annual publication of the
College Theology Society ; v. 31 (1985))
Papers from the annual meeting of the College Theology Society
held in 1985 at Salve Regina College in Newport, Rhode Island.
Includes bibliographical references.
1. Economics—Religious aspects—Christianity—Congresses.
2. Social ethics—Congresses. I. Gower, Joseph F.,
1945–   . II. College Theology Society. Meeting
(1985 : Salve Regina College). III. Series: Annual
publication of the College Theology Society ; v. 31.
BR115.E3R36   1990   241'.64—dc20   89–29058 CIP

ISBN 0–8191–7665–6 (alk. paper)
ISBN 0–8191–7666–4 (pbk. : alk. paper)

The paper used in this publication meets the minimum requirements of
American National Standard for Information Sciences—Permanence
of Paper for Printed Library Materials, ANSI Z39.48–1984.

CONTENTS

PREFACE

The fourteen essays presented in this collection, with the exception of one, were originally prepared for the thirty-first annual meeting of the College Theology Society which was held in 1985 at Salve Regina College, Newport, Rhode Island. "Religion, Economics and the Social Order" was the theme of that national convention. This volume continues the pattern of the annual publication series of selecting those papers which were most pertinent to the conference's theme.

The College Theology Society's officers and its president, William M. Shea of the University of South Florida, were grateful for the hospitality extended by Sister Lucille McKillop, R.S.M., president of Salve Regina College, and also for the excellent work done by Frank D. Maguire, the local chairperson, and Thomas J. Shanahan of Creighton University, the convention coordinator.

The editor expresses his special gratitude to those who advised and assisted in the preparation of this publication, particularly to Robert Masson of Marquette University, John McCarthy of Loyola University in Chicago, and Rodger Van Allen of Villanova University. Sincere appreciation also is extended to my colleagues at Saint Joseph's University, to Ruth Malinowski, our faculty secretary, and especially to Robin Aronstam for her caring support.

INTRODUCTION

Joseph F. Gower

I

Economic ethics is an underdeveloped specialization within the discipline of religious ethics. Contemporary commentators have lamented the still emergent status of economic ethics and recently some have begun to point out new directions for this important area of moral reflection. Part of the problem has been the historical fact that not many religious ethicists have taken the time to acquire specialized competence in economics, economic theory and history. Like medical ethics, economic ethics is a multidisciplinary undertaking that requires much technical knowledge.

Representing quite distinct approaches, two contemporary observers have commented on the marginality of economic ethics for theology and religious studies. Michael Novak has deplored how little advanced Christian theology is in this area, noting "that there exists no serious disciplined body of theological reflection on the history and foundations of economics."[1] Beverly Wildung Harrison has identified serious deliberation about the meaning of authentic economic democracy as the priority for social ethicists in our time. As she sees it, "to recover a capacity to long for economic justice as deeply as we desire political justice is the task of religious ethics today."[2]

In a sense, both Harrison's and Novak's observations may be read as responses to the urgent plea sounded by John C. Bennett in 1975, when he strongly challenged Christian social ethicists to focus their energies

---

[1]Michael Novak, *The Spirit of Democratic Capitalism* (New York: Simon and Schuster, 1982), p. 236.

[2]Beverly Wildung Harrison, "The Role of Social Theory in Religious Social Ethics: Reconsidering the Case for Marxian Political Economy," in Carol S. Robb, ed., *Making the Connections: Essays in Feminist Social Ethics* (Boston: Beacon Press, 1985), p. 80.

on the basic questions of economic justice which had been neglected, he felt, for too long. In *The Radical Imperative*, he asserts that "a new debate is needed about economic institutions, and on a much more fundamental level" than had been achieved in earlier periods.[3] Later, Bennett called for fresh work in this area among the rising generation of Christian ethicists just as American society was about to enter "a new phase of a long-standing struggle for economic justice."

The traditional inattention to economic ethics in Christian theology is not all that surprising when it is realized that the field of social ethics itself has only in the recent decades come of age as a major discipline among Catholic and Protestant ethicists. It is true that throughout Christian history particular economic questions have been addressed such as: the proper use of wealth, the vocation of the Christian in the world, the moral status of usury, the appropriate participation of Christians in commercial life, and the responsible stewardship of the goods of creation. But, generally speaking, moral theologians simply lacked sophistication about economics. Even in the modern period the churches did not demonstrate much understanding of the emerging new economics. Novak observed that "in no major sphere of life have the traditions of theology fallen further behind."[4]

The development of Christian social ethics has been greatly influenced by historical events. John Bennett points out that issues of economic justice became prominent among his generation of theologians because of the Great Depression. He notes that "the decade of the 1930s was probably the most radical period in the development of Christian ethics in this country with the possible exception of today's revolutionary theologies and social movements in the Third World."[5]

Serious and sustained Christian thinking about social and economic justice started to mature in the late nineteenth century. This maturity was clearly reflected in the Social Gospel Movement among Protestants and in the papal social teachings tradition among Catholics. In America leadership was assumed by Walter Rauschenbusch whose writings attempted to reinterpret Christianity as capable of responding to the social and economic conditions of modern industrial life. He proposed a socialist political economic program that was compatible with the religious doc-

---

[3] John C. Bennett, *The Radical Imperative: From Theology to Social Ethics* (Philadelphia: Westminster Press, 1975), p. 156.

[4] Novak, p. 18.

[5] John C. Bennett, "The Next Stage of Christian Ethics as a Theological Discipline," in Beverly W. Harrison et al., eds., *The Public Vocation of Christian Ethics* (New York: Pilgrim Press, 1986), pp. 1, 8.

trine of the Kingdom of God. Other Protestant socialists who also questioned the survival of capitalism were Paul Tillich, Reinhold Niebuhr and Emil Brunner.[6] After the Depression of 1929, Christian ethicists worked hard at coming to terms with the challenge of Karl Marx, and much of the ethical debate in the twentieth century has revolved around assessing morally the contrast between capitalism and socialism.

A significant shift in social ethics was signaled with the publication in 1932 of Reinhold Niebuhr's *Moral Man and Immoral Society.* His criticism of theological liberalism prompted the rise of Christian realism. While critical of the theological assumptions of the Social Gospel, the ascending neo-orthodox movement, nonetheless, kept alive the social ethical concern among Christians for justice and peace. Besides the writings of Niebuhr and Roger Shinn, it was the work of John Bennett himself that exhibited the most theological interest in economic questions.[7] The school of Christian realism has remained the dominant influence among Protestant religious ethicists throughout this century.[8]

Despite the historical antecedents associated with the Fribourg Union and Cardinal Gaspard Mermillod, the Roman Catholic tradition of social teachings was born in 1891 with Pope Leo XIII's *Rerum Novarum,* the first of the great social encyclicals. Pope Leo was responding to the plight of workers in Europe who were caught between the rise of Marxism and the growth of laissez-faire capitalism. The encyclical defended human dignity and the right of laborers to organize for just wages and decent working conditions. Also, it proposed the formation of voluntary associations and the intervention by the state as remedies for serious

---

[6] See Walter Rauschenbusch, *Christianity and the Social Crisis* (New York: Macmillan, 1907); Paul Tillich, *The Socialist Decision* (New York: Harper, 1933); Emil Brunner, *The Divine Imperative* (Philadelphia: Westminster Press, 1937); Reinhold Niebuhr, *Moral Man and Immoral Society* (New York: Charles Scribner's Sons, 1932), and *The Children of Light and the Children of Darkness* (New York: Charles Scribner's Sons, 1944).

[7] See Roger Shinn, "Theological Ethics: Retrospect and Prospect" in Edward LeRoy Long, Jr. and Robert T. Handy, eds., *Theology and Church in Times of Change* (Philadelphia: Westminster Press, 1970), pp. 117-41, and "Ethical Responsibility and the Corporate World: An Educational Experiment," in Larry L. Rasmussen, ed., *The Annual of the Society of Christian Ethics* (Dallas: Society of Christian Ethics, 1982), pp. 217-27. Also see John C. Bennett, *Christian Ethics and Social Policy* (New York: Charles Scribner's Sons, 1946) and, ed., *Christian Values and Economic Life* (New York: Harper, 1954).

[8] For a study of the relationship of Niebuhr's Christian realism to contemporary liberation theologies, see Dennis P. McCann, *Christian Realism and Liberation Theology: Practical Theologies in Creative Conflict* (Maryknoll, NY: Orbis Books, 1981).

social wrongs. The Catholic Church's moral engagement with economic matters continued in Pope Pius XI's encyclical *Quadragesimo Anno*, written in 1931 at the depth of the Great Depression. Capitalism and unregulated competition were condemned in this document as were communism and the promotion of class struggle. Pius XI advanced moral principles to build a new economic order governed by charity and justice.[9]

Among Catholics the outstanding social ethicist who mediated the papal teachings to the American situation was John A. Ryan, who was associated with progressive social reform. Ryan's moral theological objective was to apply the natural law ethic to twentieth-century social and economic problems. Charles Curran characterizes Ryan primarily as an economic ethicist chiefly concerned about the proper distribution of the goods of the world. John Ryan's comprehensive study of the distribution of the products of industry is found in his impressive book *Distributive Justice*. He advocated economic democracy as the "movement towards a more general and more equitable distribution of economic power, goods, and opportunities."[10] Social reform would be achieved by increased sharing by labor in management and profits but also through legislation. The moderation of the papal encyclical tradition promoted by Ryan was challenged by a more radical and more evangelical voice in the American church during the 1930s. The Catholic Worker Movement, through the essays of Peter Maurin and Dorothy Day, envisioned the romantic restoration of a communal society that recognized the supreme value of persons. Day and Maurin rejected communism but also industrialism and capitalism as well.[11] For the last three decades Roman Catholic life has been shaped by the Second Vatican Council. Preceded by John XXIII's social encyclicals—*Mater et Magistra* and *Pacem in Terris*—and followed by Paul VI's *Populorum Progressio* and *Octogesima Adveniens*, the years from 1961 to 1971 manifested a signifi-

---

[9] See Peter J. Henriot et. al., eds., *Catholic Social Teaching: Our Best Kept Secret* (Maryknoll, NY: Orbis Books, 1987).

[10] Charles E. Curran, *American Catholic Social Ethics: Twentieth-Century Approaches* (Notre Dame, IN: Notre Dame, 1982), p. 50. See John A. Ryan, *A Living Wage: Its Ethical and Economic Aspects* (New York: Macmillan, 1906), and *Distributive Justice: The Right and Wrong of our Present Distribution of Wealth* (New York: Macmillan, 1916).

[11] For the fullest presentation of Catholic Worker radicalism, see the writings of Paul Hanly Furfey, *Fire on the Earth* (New York: Macmillan, 1936); *Three Theories of Society* (New York: Macmillan, 1937); and, *The Mystery of Iniquity* (Milwaukee: Bruce, 1944).

cant evolution in the corpus of Catholic social teaching.[12]

Predictably, the bishops in the United States were inspired by this development to address public issues more boldly and more consistently. For instance, in 1975 the National Conference of Catholic Bishops issued a condemnation of economic injustice, unemployment and maldistribution of resources. Then in 1983 in their controversial pastoral letter, *The Challenge of Peace: God's Promise and Our Response*, the bishops presented a critical and comprehensive moral analysis of the arms race.[13]

Certainly, no Catholic document since the Council has had the impact of Pope John Paul II's *Laborem Exercens* which continued the tradition of Catholic social teachings yet also pointed it in original and creative directions. It is presented as a dialogue with Marxism, but it is also a commentary on capitalism. It calls for a new approach to the global economy that is built on international cooperation and Christian socialist principles. Gregory Baum sees this encyclical letter as the turning-point in Catholic economic ethics.[14] This Roman initiative prompted activity on the part of episcopal conferences. For example, the bishops of Canada issued an important statement in 1983, "Ethical Reflections on the Economic Crisis," which continued John Paul's theme of the priority of labor over capital.[15]

Then the Catholic bishops of the United States undertook the task of writing a pastoral letter on the U.S. economy. It was the publication of the first draft of this letter that inspired the theme for the College Theology Society's annual meeting in 1985. For that reason the papers in this collection focus on religious sources for economic ethics. This volume traces its inspiration to the November 15, 1984 draft of the pastoral letter

---

[12] See Michael Walsh and Brian Davies, eds., *Proclaiming Justice and Peace: Documents from John XXIII to John Paul II* (Mystic, CT: Twenty-Third Publications, 1984).

[13] See David M. Byers ed., *Justice in the Marketplace: Collected Statements of the Vatican and the U.S. Catholic Bishops on Economic Policy, 1891-1984* (Washington: U.S. Catholic Conference, 1985); especially consult "The Economy: Human Dimensions" (statement of November 20, 1975) and "Political Responsibility" (statement of February 12, 1976).

[14] Gregory Baum, *The Priority of Labor: A Commentary on "Laborem exercens"* (New York: Paulist, 1982).

[15] For the Canadian bishops' statements, see Gregory Baum and Duncan Cameron, eds., *Ethics and Economics: Canada's Catholic Bishops on the Economic Crisis* (Toronto: Lorimer, 1984).

"Catholic Social Teaching and the U.S. Economy."[16]

The letter has come to be seen as a landmark event. In John Bennett's judgment "in regard to the use of nuclear weapons and to the American economy, Catholics are giving the most courageous ethical leadership on issues of peace and justice."[17] The American bishops found themselves taking the institutional lead in reasserting the moral dimensions of the economy. In bringing theological and ethical values to bear on so important a topic, these bishops attracted the serious attention of scholars as well as leaders of government and business. Their efforts had an ecumenical and interfaith impact and served to stimulate discussion of topics that were widely neglected. The bishops hoped that their bold initiative, however controversial, would be seen as the starting-point for the needed renewal of ethical reflection on economic life within the religious communities of this country.[18]

---

[16] There were three drafts of the pastoral letter before the final text was approved in 1986. The First Draft—"Catholic Social Teaching and the U.S. Economy"—appeared in *Origins*, 14, nos. 22/23 (November 15, 1984), pp. 337-383. The Second Draft appeared in *Origins*, 15, no. 17 (October 10, 1985), pp. 257-296. The Third Draft was issued with a changed title—"Economic Justice for All: Catholic Social Teaching and the U.S. Economy"—in *Origins*, 16, no. 3 (June 5, 1986), pp. 33-76. The Final Text was published in *Origins*, 16, no. 24 (November 27, 1986), pp. 409-455.

[17] Bennett, "The Next Stage of Christian Ethics as a Theological Discipline," p. 2.

[18] For informed discussions about and lively reactions to the successive drafts of the pastoral letter, see these excellent collections: Oliver F. Williams and John W. Houck, eds., *Catholic Social Teaching and the United States Economy: Working Papers for a Bishops' Pastoral* (Washington: University Press of America, 1984); R. Bruce Douglass, ed., *The Deeper Meaning of Economic Life: Critical Essays on the U.S. Catholic Bishops' Pastoral Letter on the Economy* (Washington: Georgetown, 1986); Thomas M. Gannon, ed., *The Catholic Challenge to the American Economy: Reflections on the Bishops' Pastoral Letter on Catholic Social Teaching and the U.S. Economy* (New York: Macmillan, 1987); and, Douglas Rasmussen and James Sterba, *Catholic Bishops and the Economy: A Debate* (Bowling Green, OH: Social Philosophy and Public Policy Center, 1987).

There were two highly publicized reports from the Lay Commission on Catholic Social Teaching and the U.S. Economy. See *Toward the Future: Catholic Social Thought and the U.S. Economy* (North Tarrytown, NY: Lay Commission, 1984), and Michael Novak and William E. Simon, *Liberty and Justice for All: A Report on the Final Draft of the U.S. Catholic Bishops' Pastoral Letter "Economic Justice for All"* (Notre Dame, IN: Brownson Institute, 1986).

Also, for a recent consideration of political ethics, see Leslie Griffin, ed., *Religion and Politics in the American Milieu* (Notre Dame, IN: Review of Politics, 1986).

II

To appreciate the sort of renewed commitment to economic ethics that our situation demands, it might be instructive to examine what is happening today in the name of economic ethics and then try to ascertain what needs to be done. Such an overview will help indicate the contribution these collected essays may be able to make to the discipline of religious ethics.

In its present stage of development it seems that the discipline of economic ethics is distinguished by two principal types of work. One genre encompasses the general field of business ethics, while the other main type involves making comparisons and moral evaluations of economic systems. And under business ethics there is an important subdivision known as corporate responsibility ethics. There is also the newer refinement of ethical reflection which is concerned with moral activity in the non-profit and public sector. This specialty is called organizational ethics and is becoming a distinct form of business ethics. In the recent years organizational ethics has attracted a good deal of interest among younger ethicists.

The emergence of business ethics was closely associated with the rise of vocational or professional ethics during the 1960s. Unlike medical ethics which had included a number of religious ethicists from its inception, business ethics has primarily been practiced by those trained in philosophy. Under the heading of business ethics, careful attention is paid to the ethical problems raised in the conduct of business affairs. The emphasis is on analyzing the moral dilemmas which business managers were likely to confront. Rapidly increasing enrollments in business colleges and graduate schools of management accelerated the growth of courses which applied moral norms to specific business practices and controversies. At Saint Joseph's University, for example, such a course is called "Business, Society and Ethics." Its description reads: "A study of applied ethics; the value dimensions of management; corporate social responsibility; responsible decision making. A role analysis of the individual, corporation, union and government in relation to business policies and social conditions."

A sampling of moral problems examined in business ethics courses may include the following: students of finance might examine the moral issues in investment policy; students in marketing might look at questions of product liability or deception in advertising; management majors could study the moral values at stake in price fixing or industrial espionage, etc. Generally, these courses do not raise fundamental critical questions about the overall economic order or closely scrutinize the basic premises and ideology of American capitalism.

But the prominent subspecies of business ethics designated as corporate responsibility ethics does venture into the larger social questions. Usually, courses on corporate responsibility deal with the concrete behavior and policies of active corporations; they may cover moral topics such as culpability in environmental pollution, a corporation's responsibilities to a community where it closes a plant, or with an international corporation's response to apartheid, etc. Here matters of global justice, social policy and public interest are broached under the inclusive rubric of business ethics.[19]

The second major genre that has been pursued for some time is the ethics of economic systems, which entails making comparisons among and moral evaluations of the different economic systems. For much of this century theological ethicists have engaged in this form of ethical reflection, most commonly comparing socialism and capitalism.[20] John Bennett was an important participant in the "great economic debate" among social ethicists. Bennett looked for the political economy that would be most congruent with the values of human welfare, freedom, order and justice when judged by the Christian ideal of self-giving love. Early in his career he favored socialism but then later moved to approve a mixed economy form of capitalism. Yet, more recently, he has become more disapproving of capitalism finding "structural flaws in free enterprise systems." Now Bennett thinks the time has come for the new generation of Christian ethicists "to press the socialistic questions even though they do not accept ready-made socialistic answers."[21]

J. Philip Wogaman is another well-known theological ethicist practicing this form of economic ethics. His objective is to locate Christian normative criteria by which theories of political economy can be assessed. In *The Great Economic Debate: An Ethical Analysis*, he presents an ethical evaluation of five "generic kinds" of political economy: Marxist

---

[19] For representative work in this field, see the publications of the Notre Dame Center for Ethics and Religious Values in Business such as: Oliver F. Williams and John W. Houck, eds., *The Judeo-Christian Vision and the Modern Corporation* (Notre Dame: Notre Dame Press, 1982), and *Co-creation and Capitalism: John Paul II's "Laborem exercens"* (Washington: University Press of America, 1983).

[20] For an outstanding recent addition to this field, see Bruce Grelle and David A. Krueger, eds., *Christianity and Capitalism: Perspectives on Religion, Liberalism and the Economy* (Chicago: Center for the Scientific Study of Religion, 1986).

[21] Bennett, *The Radical Imperative*, pp. 150-51, 154.

socialism, laissez-faire capitalism, social market capitalism, democratic capitalism, and economic conservatism. In this as well as in his later work, *Economics and Ethics: A Christian Inquiry*, he affirms democratic socialism to be the system most consistent with Christian convictions. He bases this judgment on the six "entry points" which he derives from biblical faith, namely: 1) physical existence as God's creation; 2) the priority of grace over works; 3) physical well-being and social relationship; 4) vocation; 5) stewardship; and 6) original sin.[22]

Other recent theological defenders of the system of democratic capitalism are Robert Benne, Richard John Neuhaus and Michael Novak.[23] Novak understands his own contribution to economic ethics to reside on the level of moral comparison of the systems and practices of political economies. The principal systems he identifies are these: state-controlled mercantilist systems, democratic capitalism, various forms of socialism, and communism. His intention in *The Spirit of Democratic Capitalism* is to describe the actual moral and theological presuppositions of democratic capitalism as it now exists and to argue that it is "more consistent with the aims of Judaism and Christianity than the practice of any other system."[24]

Many political theologians, liberation theologians, black theologians and feminist theologians sharply diverge from that view and have issued severe condemnations of Western capitalism.[25] In commenting on the record of the "great debate" approach to economic systems, Beverly Wildung Harrison is struck by the way those who employ Weberian ideal analyses assume that ideal types of economic systems actually exist.

---

[22] See J. Philip Wogaman, *The Great Economic Debate: An Ethical Analysis* (Philadelphia: Westminster Press, 1977), and *Economics and Ethics: A Christian Inquiry* (Philadelphia: Fortress Press, 1986).

[23] See Robert Benne, *The Ethic of Democratic Capitalism: A Moral Reassessment* (Philadelphia: Fortress Press, 1981); Richard John Neuhaus, *The Naked Public Square: Religion and Democracy in America* (Grand Rapids, MI: Eerdmans, 1984); and, Michael Novak, *Freedom with Justice: Catholic Social Thought and Liberal Institutions* (San Francisco: Harper & Row, 1984).

[24] Novak, *The Spirit of Democratic Capitalism*, p. 242.

[25] For a critical discussion between Christian theology and Marxist theory, see José Míguez Bonino, *Christians and Marxists: The Mutual Challenge to Revolution* (Grand Rapids, MI: Eerdmans, 1976), and *Doing Theology in a Revolutionary Situation* (Philadelphia: Fortress Press, 1975); also see Juan Luis Segundo, *Faith and Ideologies* (Maryknoll, NY: Orbis Books, 1984).

For a serious treatment of Christian theology in dialogue with critical theory, see Matthew Lamb, "The Challenge of Critical Theory," in Gregory Baum, ed., *Sociology and Human Destiny* (New York: Seabury, 1980), pp. 183-213. Also see Marvin M. Ellison, *The Center Cannot Hold: The Search for a Global Economy of Justice* (Washington: University Press of America, 1983).

They fail, she claims, to acknowledge historical developmental patterns or the interrelationships of economic systems. In her view, what is evaluated is the formal presence or absence of bourgeois political rights, i.e., political ideology rather than the basic conditions of an economy. Indeed, she finds that "economic functions such as the production and distribution of food and housing or shelter, the eradication of illiteracy, the effectiveness of health care delivery, education, or other essential goods and services are irrelevant to this discussion." [26] She concludes:

> What some religious ethicists have been doing under the rubric of economic ethics is evaluating the political ideologies used to defend economic systems rather than assessing concretely the capacity of these systems to meet the physical needs of their people or evaluating their impact on the environment, other nations, or the longer-term prospects of life on this planet. [27]

In reviewing Novak's and Harrison's commentaries on the present state and future of Christian economic ethics, despite their significant differences, we find a convergence of dissatisfaction with the current stage of development. Michael Novak writes as a Catholic neoconservative. In 1982 he noted how little advanced Christian theology was in economic ethics, so he envisioned a new "theology of economics." Most theologians recognize that our field requires a new discipline—the sustained application of theological reflection to economic realities." [28]

This was seen as the next great systematic task awaiting the succeeding generation of ethicists who would be trained both in theology and in economics. At its minimal level, this theological undertaking would promote critical clarification while, at the same time, debunking ideological uses of religious language. At a more advanced level, the new theology of economics would also be able "to articulate more exactly the worldly import of religious ideals and the religious import of worldly innovations." [29]

Novak understands this theological programme as requiring three separate specializations. The first would be a general theology of economics consisting of the inquiry into "economic realities present in every economic system in every age." [30] The second specialization would involve both a moral-theological understanding and evaluation of

---

[26] Harrison, "The Role of Social Theory in Religious Social Ethics," p. 72.
[27] Harrison, p. 73.
[28] Novak, p. 239.
[29] Novak, p. 241.
[30] Novak, p. 239.

the different systems of political economy. It is on this second level that Novak places his own reflections on economic realities. Finally, the third specialization would consist of theological assessments of institutions, practices and special ethical dilemmas that occur within particular systems.

Beverly Harrison likewise envisions a new shape for Christian economic ethics. But the direction she points in is quite distinct from Michael Novak's. In her interpretation a major difficulty with the underdevelopment of economic ethics is found in some of the methodological decisions Christian ethicists have made vis-à-vis social theory. She writes:

> It is my basic thesis that we have employed social theories in our work that preclude a full reevaluation of economic life and a reorientation of our economic ethics. It is my further contention that radical or neo-Marxian social theory answers several important religious-ethical criteria in ways that other social theories widely used in our discipline do not and that failure to recognize this has precluded a more critical address to questions of economic justice.[31]

When surveying the field, Harrison charges that economic ethics is ideologically captive to the theory of neoclassical economics which governs the discourse of contemporary public life. Each form of economic ethics manifests this ideological determination. She dismisses business ethics as having only limited interest since it fails to scrutinize the assumptions of capitalist business theory, for which moral norms are irrelevant because profit-making is its fundamental value. By definition, morality is understood as "exogenous" to the economic system.

Harrison has a higher regard for the work of scholars in the area of corporate responsibility ethics who have traditionally pressed more significant questions about the corporate system. But even here the narrow norms of economic rationality prohibit genuine ethical reflection. Further, she critiques as unhistorical and unempirical moral evaluation of economic systems whose presupposition is that existing economic systems actually represent four ideal types: laissez-faire capitalist systems, democratic-capitalist systems, democratic-socialist systems, and Marxist or communist systems.

Speaking as a feminist liberation ethicist, Beverly Wildung Harrison's prescription for economic ethics requires the productive encounter of

---

[31] Harrison, p. 58.

radical political economic theory and the various subtraditions within
Christian theological ethics. For the discipline to have a vital future, it
must examine critically its ideological commitments and incorporate in
its thinking the neglected tradition of radical social theory. If religious
ethics is not to become moribund, it must return to John C. Bennett's
"socialist question" and make human economic well-being an animating passion of its work. Only in that way will it recover the capacity
of longing for economic justice as the precise task of Christian
economic ethics.[32]

III

As we approach the next century, there is good evidence that Christian
ethicists and theologians are responding to Bennett's prophetic sum-
mons to restore the centrality of economic justice. The sought-after
renewal of ethical reflection on economic life is underway within many
religious communities throughout the world. The boundaries of social
ethics have been greatly expanded by the intellectual activity of political
and liberation theologians. There has been significant movement
beyond professional business ethics, corporate responsibility ethics, and
the moral comparison of systems of political economy. The shifts in
direction within the discipline which Harrison and Novak argued for are
beginning to take place. Increased critical attention is being given to
methodological questions, to historical modes of discourse, and to
ideological alliances. At last, economic ethics is moving from the
margins of religious ethics and is undergoing a profound reorientation.

Although there is much multidisciplinary work yet to be done, enough
formal groundwork has been laid for the entry of economic ethics into its
next phase. The fourteen essays presented in this collection are contributions to that development. *Religion and Economic Ethics* is divided
into four sections—Ethical Considerations, Theological Resources,
Historical Studies, and Church Perspectives.

Part One, Ethical Considerations, contains essays from three social
ethicists. It begins with Douglas Sturm's plenary address which
represents a critical sample of the "great debate" genre of Christian
economic ethics. "Economic Justice and the Common-Wealth of Peoples"

---

[32] Harrison, p. 80.

conveys Sturm's severe critique of liberalism and democratic capitalism. Its starting-point is the serious tension between capitalism as a principle of private control and democracy as a principle of public governance. Democratic capitalism is judged deficient because of its inability to deal adequately with the basic features of economic life, such as the organization of production, the distribution of wealth, and the allocation of investment. In its place, Sturm advocates an alternative of social or participative democracy which would extend the principle of public determination to all modes of social and economic existence. He issues a reasoned call for a revised social covenant, a new common-wealth of peoples, as the best way to advance justice and secure the common good.

"Public Policy: Reflections on the Role of Ethics and Ethicists" comes as an affirmative response to the pastoral letters on the arms race and the economy. Leonard J. Weber follows the lead of the Catholic bishops in recovering the legacy of Christian social thought as a living resource capable of responsibly shaping the future. Weber's goal is to identify the major moral aspects of the public policy agenda in this country. By focusing on the principles of justice and human rights, he endorses the traditional Catholic position emphasizing the public nature of moral discourse. In the contemporary debate over the nature of social ethics, it is clear that Weber allies himself with ethicists like David Hollenbach and J. Bryan Hehir over against the views associated with John Howard Yoder and Stanley Hauerwas. Weber's own recommendation is that public policies ought to seek the greatest public good.

Stephen J. Casey's stated interest is to determine what power might mean when it is defined in light of the notion of the "preferential option for the poor." First articulated by the Latin American church, the concept of the option for the poor has emerged as a basic ethical norm in contemporary Catholic social teaching. In "A View from the Underside: Defining Power in Light of the Preferential Option for the Poor," Casey takes much care in clarifying typologically the definitions of power: coercive power, compensatory power, and conditioned power. The essay's principal aim is to explore the preferential option for the poor as a theological means of reconceiving power in terms of human relations, deliberately giving special regard for the position of the weak.

Just as religious ethicists must rely on the results of the social and behavioral sciences, they likewise need to consult the scholarship generated by specialists in theology and religious studies. The four essays in Part Two, Theological Resources, were written by two theologians, a philosopher of religion and an exegete. They indicate the sort of valuable research scholars in religion are contributing to the growth of economic ethics.

"Equality and Subordination in Christ: Displacing the Powers of the Household Code in Colossians" is an exegetical and methodological essay which addresses some of the central topics under discussion in feminist biblical interpretation. It opens by studying the tension between egalitarian and subordinatist positions in the Pauline corpus. Then, it moves to a formal examination of the methodology of feminist biblical interpretation. Here, in a notable way, Anne McGuire is in conversation with the riveting work of Elisabeth Schüssler Fiorenza. Departing from an external interpretative model driven by the criterion of "women's experience in their struggle for liberation," McGuire proposes an alternative model that appeals to an "internal critique of the text by the text."

McGuire's developed Christological insights bring about a reinterpretation of the ethics of Colossians. Based on her Christological reading, the theological strategy of renaming the principalities and powers is extended to embrace the pattern of domination and subordination found in the household code. Under the lordship of Christ, social arrangements are changed, and a new community of humanity is formed which repudiates dominance based on gender, race or class.

This essay is followed by Andrew Tallon's studied attempt to situate and justify the legitimate place of the "reasons of the heart" in moral decision-making. "Affectivity and Praxis in Lonergan, Rahner and Others in the Heart Tradition" is offered as an exploratory paper, yet it is an intricate philosophical elaboration of the neglected notion of knowledge by affective connaturality. The immense task Tallon sets is to forge a synthesis of Bernard Lonergan's and Karl Rahner's understandings of affectivity and incorporate them with pertinent insights from other authors in the "heart tradition" such as Emmanuel Levinas, Daniel C. Maguire and Robert Doran.

Andrew Tallon's reflections are presented in three stages. The first stage augments Lonergan's underdeveloped appreciation of affectivity and then integrates it into the general scheme of the structure of consciousness. The second stage reconstructs Rahner's understanding of "differentiated feeling" as a rehabilitated model for decision-making in ethics. Tallon's description of "the way of the heart" is considered to be the most appropriate passage from experience to action. The treatise's third stage is an elucidation of the two major themes that have become prominent in the current development of the heart tradition, namely, the priority of praxis and the feminization of human consciousness. Then

Tallon concludes by affirming the primacy of affectivity in ethics and by advancing affective connaturality as a new moral paradigm.

"Karl Rahner and John Paul II: Anthropological Implications for Economics and the Social Order" is the essay contributed by Ronald Modras. It is an exposition of the theological anthropologies which form the foundations of the theological achievements of these two thinkers who, in different ways, have dominated the Catholic intellectual world. Both theologians are preoccupied with grasping the meaning of human personhood and human dignity. Though Karl Rahner's writings do not directly attend to questions in social or economic ethics, Modras is able to sketch out elements of a political theology through an analysis of Rahnerian concepts such as transcendent freedom, historicity and sociality. For Pope John Paul II, this task is made easier due to his extensive writings on modern society, work, economic systems and social justice. Focusing on the philosophical personalism in Karol Wojtyla's early book *The Acting Person*, Modras uncovers the anthropological basis for much of the moral reasoning of his papal encyclicals, including *Laborem Exercens.*

Joseph La Barge's meditation on the correspondence between biblical norms and economic systems is found in "Economic Systems and the Sacramental Imagination." He is distressed that the recent Catholic social proposals, like the ones in the pastoral letter, are inadequate. They miss the mark not so much in their economic strategies and programs, but more importantly on the deeper level of symbolic imagination. La Barge's purpose here is to review how "root metaphors" give symbolic interpretations of historical periods. His hope is to reclaim the sacramental imagination at the heart of the Catholic tradition and to recover the sacramental vision as the fertile way to integrate Christian faith and economic life. Taking an illuminating clue from Gibson Winter, La Barge adopts the metaphor of artistic creativity as the means to redefine our cultural and moral horizon. The recovery of the sacramental imagination can result in a resymbolization capable of informing and empowering a creative praxis in these troubled times.

Historical Studies characterize the four selections in Part Three which were produced by religious historians and ethicists. A representative piece indicating what historical investigation can yield to economic ethics is the one by Paul Misner, "Adam Müller and Adam Smith: A Romantic-Catholic Response to Modern Economic Thought." Misner describes Adam Müller as the first Catholic thinker to take seriously classical economic theory. A German convert to Catholicism, Müller became a disciple of Adam Smith. Yet, his thinking was also greatly influenced by the anti-revolutionary sentiments of Edmund Burke.

Müller's *The Elements of Statecraft* is depicted by Misner as a Romantic-Catholic response to *The Wealth of Nations.* Observing intrinsic flaws in economic liberalism, Müller was suspicious of doctrinaire free-trade and was cautious about the emerging factory system. Moreover, he faulted Smith for neglecting what he called "spiritual capital." In Misner's estimation, Adam Müller deserves our attention as the premier Roman Catholic thinker of the early nineteenth century to confront the problems of industrial capitalism.

Using recently available research material, William L. Portier formulates a fresh appreciation of the life of John Richard Slattery, the gifted priest who from 1892 to 1903 was the superior-general of the Josephite Fathers (the U.S. off-shoot of the English Mill Hill Fathers). He eventually resigned from the ordained ministry and is remembered for being one of only three North American priests condemned as a "Modernist." Slattery is famous for his work among American blacks and his writings on the black Catholic apostolate. In "Missionary as Philanthropist: A Social and Economic Portrait of John R. Slattery," Portier's biographical project is to discover what in his social setting brought this Irish-American heir to a construction company fortune to dedicate himself to the evangelization of the African-American. Slattery's missionary career is thus characterized as a rare instance of "Gilded Age" philanthropy among American Catholics.

The 1926 U.S. Supreme Court case of *McCardle v. the Indianapolis Water Co.* becomes the historical stimulus for James F. Smurl to inquire how a heated legal controversy about a public utility company's rate increases can open up crucial questions for economic ethics. "Common Moral and Religious Grounds for Uncommon Economic Times" is an historical study of the similar reactions of John A. Ryan, Walter Rauschenbusch and Louis D. Brandeis to the legal and moral issues at stake in *McCardle.* Yet, this essay also is an articulation of how a moral and religious consensus can be reached in public policy disputes. Through a skilled examination of the moral reasoning of Brandeis, Ryan and Rauschenbusch regarding property and distributive justice, Smurl advances an argument for the priority of human goods over economic goods.

The fourth item in this section of the volume concentrates on the significance of Walter Rauschenbusch's application of biblical exegesis in social ethics. "Scripture and the Social Order: 'Paradigmatic Construals' of Walter Rauschenbusch" is to be taken as a demonstration of the important disciplinary linkage between biblical studies and theological ethics. Reminiscent of James M. Gustafson's Christ and the moral life motif, William McInerny's recommendation is that present-day ethicists have much to learn about the ways biblical images can enliven the moral imagination. By focusing on the relevant work of the leader of the Social Gospel Movement, McInerny highlights the historical value of Rauschenbusch's use of Scriptural paradigms for modeling the moral life and forming the Christian vision.

Church Perspectives is the heading for the remaining three essays in this collection which were written by a philosopher, a systematic theologian and an ecclesiologist. Part Four starts off with the remarks of Arthur F. McGovern who, from his broad background in studying Marxism and Christian theology, is quite prepared to examine the recent controversy springing from the Vatican Instruction criticizing the Latin American theology of liberation movement. This article, "Liberation Theology and the Vatican: An Assessment," is a measured appraisal of some of the controverted points, especially the charges that liberation theologians wrongly adopted concepts from Marxism and that they have reduced faith to politics. Believing that the Vatican document has misunderstood the mature work of Gustavo Gutiérrez, Leonardo Boff and Jon Sobrino, McGovern makes a convincing case for the deep faith and loyalty of these Catholic theologians of liberation.

Rebecca Chopp's arresting contribution takes the form of a revealing analysis of the intellectual inconsistency present in the pastoral letter on the economy. Of all the essays in this collection, "Making the Poor the Rich: Rhetoric vs. Strategy in the Pastoral Letter on the Economy" most directly connects with Beverly Wildung Harrison's demand for a reconsideration of critical theory in economic ethics. Chopp's telling point is that the radical rhetorical argument made by the bishops in their pastoral letter actually works to deconstruct the progressive reforms and correctivist social strategy they advocate. Her suggestion is to reread the document from a standpoint that reflects *"the option of the poor"* rather than the option for the poor. That would lead in the more revolutionary direction of a critical theory of American culture and a reconstructive social theory which would require a far more radical transformation of our social and economic institutions. So questioning an interpretation of the pastoral letter presents a genuine challenge to the tradition of Catholic social teachings.

A distinctly ecclesiological exposition of the Catholic understanding of the teaching authority of episcopal conferences closes this volume. "Episcopal Teaching Authority on Matters of War and Economics" conveys James Heft's research into the status of bishops' conferences. He explains why it still remains an open question whether episcopal conferences enjoy a *mandatum docendi*. This has been a question of theological debate ever since the Second Vatican Council, but that it has important pastoral consequences can be seen from the variety of reactions, including dissent, to the U.S. bishops' letters on nuclear warfare and on capitalism. With regard to specific teachings in economic and social ethics, Heft clarifies that neither the basic principles nor the particular norms of natural law have ever been infallibly defined. This balanced essay serves, moreover, to draw attention to an emerging appreciation of non-infallible church teachings, the reexamination of the *sensus fidelium*, and the expanding roles of lay persons in the Catholic community.

Part One

ETHICAL CONSIDERATIONS

ECONOMIC JUSTICE AND THE COMMON-WEALTH OF PEOPLES

Douglas Strum

Preface

The College Theology Society, in its wisdom, has designated as the central theme for its national convention this year, "Religion, Economics, and the Social Order." The immediate stimulus for the theme was no doubt the publication of the first draft of the U.S. Bishops' Pastoral Letter on Catholic Social Teaching and the U.S. Economy. But the frustrations giving rise to the theme are of long standing.

In the latest issue of *Dissent*, Peter Steinfels (1985), in a sympathetic article on the Bishops' letter, quotes at length from R. H. Tawney, lines presented initially in lectures delivered in 1922:

> the philosophy which would keep economic interests and ethical idealism safely locked up in their separate compartments finds that each of the prisoners is increasingly restive. . . . Religious thought is no longer content to dismiss the transactions of business and the institutions of society as matters irrelevant to the life of the spirit. . . . The line of division between the spheres of religion and secular business . . . is shifting. . . . By common consent the treaty of partition has lapsed and the boundaries are once more in motion. . . . Rightly or wrongly, with wisdom or its opposite, not only in England but on the Continent and in America, not only in one denomination but among Roman Catholics, Anglicans, and Nonconformists, an attempt is being made to restate the practical implications of the social ethics of the Christian faith, in a form sufficiently comprehensive to provide a standard by which to judge the collective actions and institutions of mankind. . . . As in the analogous problem of relations between Church and State, issues which were thought to have been buried . . . have shown in our own day that they were not dead, but sleeping (Tawney, 11-13).

As Steinfels remarks, these "observations could have been written yesterday—which makes them both exhilarating and discouraging." I suggest we take them as indicative of the troubling character of modern times and as instructive of the need to make ever more explicit the conjunction between theory and praxis in religious faith.

That, I take it, is a fundamental point of the Bishops' Pastoral which, in general terms, illustrates the economic crisis we are experiencing and announces a religious vision out of which that crisis is understood as such. Thus, on the one side, the Bishops write the following:

> The U.S. economy has been immensely successful in providing for the material needs and in raising the living standard of its citizens. Our nation is one of the richest on earth. Despite this great wealth the country has recently gone through a severe recession with the highest unemployment rates since the Great Depression of the 1930s. In the recovery from this painful period the situation has improved, but very serious doubts remain about the future. The rate of poverty has risen sharply in recent years and is now at the highest level since 1965. Unemployment is exceptionally high even in the midst of recovery, especially for minorities and youth. Some regions have been especially hard hit and their economic futures are in doubt. Farmers with moderate-sized holdings, workers in aging heavy industries, owners of vulnerable small businesses, and the poor and minority populations in many central cities are often tempted to despair (U.S. Bishops, ¶ 18).

That is a statement of the problem—as experienced and understood in an ordinary, everyday sense. In the midst of national economic affluence, large classes of people are suffering economic pain and deprivation. Something, the Bishops declare, is wrong. Something is twisted, tortuous. These things should not be. The persistence of poverty in the presence of plenty is contradictory. But against what kind of background are these experiences understood as contradictory?

That is the other side of the Bishops' affirmation. The background against which these experiences are understood as contradictory is a communitarian social ontology. Expanding on the principle of economic justice, the Bishops announce:

> The basis for all that the church believes about the moral dimensions of economic life is its vision of the transcendent worth—the sacredness of human beings. The dignity of the human person, realized in com-

happen to our total nature such that our habits of response can be transformed. Under these circumstances, even the criteria we envisage as being designative of the good may undergo radical change (Meland 1953, 124).

Against that background, I intend to advance three theses for consideration: first, that, particularly at this point in the world's history, the common good is the first virtue of social institutions; second, that capitalism and democracy, although long associated historically, are in tension with each other; and third, that social democracy is an alternative institutional form more directly ordained to the common good than what has been traditionally called democratic capitalism. In developing the first thesis, I shall suggest that social interpretation and social ethics are, in their deepest dimension, ontological or cosmological. That is, they at least presuppose and sometimes deliberately articulate a vision of the world and they portray human agency as an expression of that world. In presenting the second thesis, I shall distinguish two interpretations of capitalism, orthodox and heterodox, and two sides of democracy, protective and paticipative. The tension between capitalism and democracy is evident even in instances where they seem most compatible. In stating the third thesis, I shall urge the need for a new social covenant in which concern for economic growth and distribution, while not ignored, is subordinate to the interests of commonwealth.

I
The Common Globe

God, desiring not only that the human race might be able by their similarity of nature to associate with one another, but also that they might be bound together in harmony and peace by the ties of relationship, was pleased to derive all persons from one individual (Augustine, *City of God*, XIV, 1).

Franklin I. Gamwell in an unpublished paper annunciates that "the peculiar task of religious ethics is to defend on humanistic grounds a comprehensive principle of evaluation, where 'comprehensive' is used in the strictest sense to mean a principle in terms of which the worth and importance of all things may be assessed." Two criteria are indicated by this statement. First, comprehensiveness is a criterion specifying the religiousness of an ethics. Second, defense of an ethics on humanistic grounds is a criterion, though perhaps not the only criterion, of the adequacy of an ethics, whether religious or not.

While these criteria are onerous, I intend to suggest that the common good is a principle of religious ethics which, while having roots deeply within the tradition of Christian faith, is justifiable on humanistic grounds. On the one hand, the common good is a principle which, while applying with particular force to social practices, is a measure for assessing "the worth and importance of all things." Moreover, the common good is a humanistic principle because it is expressive of the meaning of being a self within the world.

We begin with an examination of the meaning of "social practice," remembering that our topic, democratic capitalism, is a king of social practice. In ordinary life, we engage in many social practices ranging from conversations and CTS conventions to economic exchange and war. Some social practices are occasional and casual, such as in the greeting of a stranger. Others are periodic and, by intent, transformative, as in religious ritual. Still others are constant in their presence and far-reaching in consequence, as in the political and technological systems of the modern world.

But the idea of a social practice, which may seem obvious on the surface, is a matter of controversy. On one level the issue is methodological. What, the question is asked, constitutes the fundamental unit of social analysis? But the controversy is more than methodological. Methodologies are not divorceable from other aspects of social analysis and interpretation. They bear with them normative implications and ontological presuppositions. Thus, at another level, the controversy bears on the subject of social ethics. How the methodological question is resolved sets the conditions for determining what kinds of principles of social ethics are appropriate. And at still another level, the controversy is cosmological; it is a contention over the character of the kind of world within which practice takes place. To persuade you of the point, I ask you to consider Aristotle, Hobbes, and Marx in a round-table discussion over the meaning of social practice. The interplay in social analysis of questions of method, ethics and cosmology would, I suspect, be evident in the discussion.

Among parties to the controversy, three positions are dominant:

organic, individualist, and relational. Each position conveys something of importance about the character of experience which explains its persuasiveness, but the third, I suggest, is the most adequate in its comprehension of the conditions as well as the problems of human existence.

Within the framework of the organic position, a social practice has the character of a whole, a totality. The social practice is itself the unit of social analysis. Those who enact the practice are its members. Their identity is a function of the inner world of the practice itself. From this perspective, loyalty as devotion to the group and as willingness to perform one's role in its life is a primary virtue. Within local circumstances, the bonds of kinship and the compulsions of family are evidence of the sense of this position. Class consciousness and the urge to press for class interests manifest the strength of an organic understanding of social practice. So do the strong pull of ethnic and racial ties and the mysterious attractions of nationalism. We do seem, at certain times and under certain circumstances, to give credence to the idea of social totalities.

The opposite to the organic approach is the individualistic. According to methodological individualism, only individuals think, feel, and act. Nations and states, classes and ethnic groups are but collective concepts or metaphorical constructs. Such normative ideas as the public interest, the general welfare, the common good are mystical nonsense. As Murray N. Rothbard remarks,

> All these concepts rest on the implicit premise that there exists, somewhere, a living organic entity known as "society," "the group," "the public," "the community," and that that entity has value and pursues ends. Not only are these terms held up as living entities; they are supposed to exist *more* fundamentally than do mere individuals (Rothbard, 15).

But, insists Rothbard, there are no such entities. The fundamental axiom of social analysis is that only individuals exist, only individuals possess consciousness, only individuals have values and desires. This axiom is not without roots in human experience, for indeed experience is always that of a subject, even if the fact of subjectivity cannot without further argument be transmuted into a theory of subjectivism. Individuals, not classes or groups, suffer and wonder why, have desires and yearn for their satisfaction. But individuals conflict with each other, creating a problem of adjudication. From this perspective, the task of ethics lies in the resolution of conflicts whether through principles of utility maximization or distributive justice.

The third position is more complex, but more complete in its reflection of the relational character of our experience. In social theory, the position is represented in Anthony Gidden's concept of structuration which he intends to articulate the point of creative integration between the agency of individuals and the structures of society (Giddens, 49–96). Agents are individuals, but they are not individuals in total isolation from each other. They inherit and they enact social practices. In their identity, they are consitituted out of long traditions of understanding and sensibility. In their actions, they reproduce, in some form, a world of social practices. A social practice is a complicated mixture of several structural features. It is a shared knowledge by means of which agents explain their actions to each other and to outsiders. It is a set of expectations, of principles and purposes, through which agents assess what is desirable and correct and justify their responses when forced to do so. It is a structure of power, which both constrains and facilitates. That is, given an asymmetry in the distribution of power throughout a practice, its organized resources are structures of domination and limitation. But, at the same time, they are structures of transformative possibility. Giddens' concept of structuration thus affirms that agents are individuals, but in their agency they draw together, more or less intentionally and creatively, understandings, norms, and resources of social structure. As they do so, they set the conditions for all future agency. The focus for social analysis, from this perspective, is not social totality as such. Nor is it the individaul as such. It is the manner in which agents can and do bear forward through their action the features of social structure.

On the ontological (and theological level, this position is represented in Bernard Meland's principle of internal relations according to which there is a depth within our experience that connects all we are as unique individuals with all existent events and, ultimately, God, "that sensitive nature within the vast context of nature, winning the creative passage for qualitative attainment" (Meland 1953, 111–112). It is also represented in Philip Hefner's ontology of belonging which formulates the sense of

(1) our belonging to our fellow human beings, across all barriers—racial, sexual, economic, geographical, national, and age; (2) our be-

longing to the ecosystem of which we are a part, the natural environment which is the womb of our emergence and the support system for
everything human; and (3) our belonging to the matrix of evolutionary
development out of which our total ecosystem has unfolded (Hefner,
162).

In moral philosophy, the third position is stated in a limited way
in Michael J. Sandel's critique of John Rawls's theory of justice as
neglecting, save in so far as Rawls presupposes it unknowingly, an
understanding of community as basically constitutive of the meaning of selfhood. We live, Sandel asserts, as encumbered selves. To be
a self is to be in relation, to have loyalties and allegiances, responsibilities and associations which, taken altogether, enter into our
individuality. This means that at least "to some I owe more than
justice requires or even permits, not by reason of agreements I have
made but instead in virtue of those more or less enduring attach-
ments and commitments which taken together partly define the
person I am" (Sandel, 179). Sandel invokes friendship as an elemen-
tary case of what he intends, but he refers as well to family, tribe,
city, class, nation, people. If Sandel is correct, the first virtue of
social institutions is not, as Rawls contends, distributive justice
(Rawls, 3). It is the good of the community. The good of the community is a version of what Alasdair MacIntyre calls an "internal
good" (MacIntyre, 175–189), that is, a good that is realized only in a
practice but that is for all those who participate in that practice.
MacIntyre cites the instance of chess-playing.

Relying on Meland's principle of internal relations, I would violate
the strictures MacIntyre has placed on the concept to suggest we
consider our entire life a practice in which all entities are engaged.
This is the sense of Roberto Unger's theory of the self as consisting
in a wide-ranging set of relationships to nature, to other persons,
and to one's own work and station (Unger, 191–235). The self is
separate from these three worlds, yet engaged in them. The dynamic
interplay between separation and engagement is, in effect, the generic practice of being human. The ethical problem is to determine
what quality of relationship will redound to the good of all parties
in it and therefore to the good of the self.

The traditional language for this ethical concern is the common
good. The traditional locus of its responsibility is the political
association, for the function of the political association is to concern
itself directly and deliberately with the quality of relationships

throughout the community as a whole. What I am proposing therefore is that a relational approach to social analysis conjoined with a
principle of internal relations implies that the common good is the
first virtue of social institutions and that the public-regarding association has priority over those which are private.

What, then, is the common good? In focus, it is the goodness *of*
the community, but it is a goodness *for* all its participants. Thus it
is common in a double sense. As Jacques Maritain expresses it.

> The common good of the city is neither the mere collection of private
> goods, nor the proper good of the whole which like . . . the hive with
> respect to its bees, relates the parts to itself alone and sacrifices them
> to itself. It is the good *human* life of the multitude . . . ; it is their
> communion in good living. It is therefore common to both *the whole
> and the parts* into which it flows back and which, in turn, must benefit
> from it (Maritain 1947, 40–41; ital. in original).

In scope, the common good is local and global. Again, in Maritain's
words,

> The common good in our day is certainly not just the common good of
> the nation and has not yet succeeded in becoming the common good of
> the civilized world community. It tends, however, unmistakably to-
> wards the latter. For this reason, it would seem appropriate to consider
> the common good of a state or nation as merely an area, among many
> similar areas, in which the common good of the whole civilized society
> achieves greater density (Maritain 1947, 45; see also 1951.)

In content, the common good is procedural and substantive. The
procedures through which a community sets its policies and con-
ducts its work are not merely instrumental. In a significant manner,
they constitute the quality of the community. Procedures are ways
of living together through time. As a community endures, but
changes, its basic character is manifest in large part in the structure
of its public forum. Procedures are marked by varying degrees of
openness and exclusion, access and denial, participation and domination. Precisely because a common good is intended as common,
its procedural features are those of openness, access, participation.
Absent those features, the common good can be but deficiently
present.

On its substantive side, the common good is more readily specifi-
able by negative instance than by affirmative criteria: the rapid

deterioration of the environment, the depth and extent of poverty throughout the world, the persistence of discriminatory patterns against whole classes of persons, the escalating threat of nuclear holocaust, the stifling of free expression of the artistic impulse in ways direct and indirect. But negative instances are the reverse side of affirmative principles: in the material dimension, physical well-being; in the economic dimension, meaningful work; in the social dimension, civic friendship; in internatioanl relations, peaceful modes of conflict resolution; in the dimension of the human spirit, creative openness. I do not mean this as an exhaustive definition of the substantive content of the common good, but as an indication of its qualitative meaning.

Because of the nature of the self as relational, the common good, so construed, is not only the first virtue of social institutions. It is requisite to the flourishing of the individual and is an expression of the deepest meaning of freedom in its material sense.

II
Capitalism and Democracy

A Great Society has nothing to do with, and is in fact irreconcilable with 'solidarity' in the true sense of unitedness in the pursuit of known common goals (Hayek. 111).

Democracy is not founded merely on the right or the private interest of the individual. This is only one side of the shield. It is founded equally on the function of the individual as a member of the community. It founds the common good upon the common will, in forming which it bids every grown-up, intelligent person to take a part (Hobhouse, 115).

The second thesis I would advance is that capitalism and democracy are in tension with each other.

In their modern manifestations, capitalism and democracy have been associated together as part of the emergence of the modern world. As modern science and philosophy broke through the dogmatisms of medieval theology, so modern economic and political systems shattered the strictures of medieval society. All these movements bore the promise of a new age in which freedom—freedom of thought and freedom of action—was the centerpiece. Capitalism and democracy, in particular, even where these exact terms were not employed to refer to the movements, were expressions of a new class of persons, the bourgeoisie, coming into a place of prominence. Thus capitalism and democracy would seem to belong together as social practices promoted by the new class as instruments for the realization of liberty. That association of movements and ideals has long been a fixture, at least in the American mind. Joyce Appleby discerns it as central to the republican vision of the Jeffersonians in the late eighteenth century (Appleby, 1984). In a radically different version, Louis Hartz identifies it as underlying the interests of the New Whigs in the middle of the nineteenth century (Hartz, 1955). And it is a position espoused by Nichael Novak (1982) and Robert Benne (1981) at the present time.

But however accurate the historical thesis in some sense or other, it begs an important but extraordinarily difficult question of interpretation. How are capitalism and democracy to be identified? The possibilities in the case of capitalism, for instance range from the axiomatic approach of Ludwig von Mises (1960) to the massive historical studies of Immanuel Wallerstein (1974, 1980–1983). The resultant differences are striking.

For our purposes, I would contrast two understandings of capitalism, one more orthodox, the other more heterodox. For the former, I rely on Adam Smith and Friedrich Hayek. Adam Smith, to my knowledge, never used the word, "capitalism," but his treatise on *The Wealth of Nations* (1937/1776), is properly considered a classic statement of its meaning. Smith was impressed by the emergence in the modern world of a new form of organizing human relations, the commercial society, a system, in his judgment, of perfect liberty. The central institution of commercial society is the market, the genius of which is that, if unconstrained, it will produce, out of the self-interested actions of a myriad of persons a social order of benefit to all. Moreover, through it, the wealth of the nation, that is, the annual flow of its goods and services, will increase. As Hayek depicts the central idea of the system, "The chief cause of [its] wealth-creating charater . . . is that the returns of the efforts of each player act as the signs which enable him to contribute to the satisfaction of needs of which he does not know, and to do so by taking advantage of conditions of which he also learns only indirectly through their being reflected in the prices of the factors of production which they use" (Hayek, 115). Resource allocation, capital investment, consignment and division of labor, distribution of products are all questions to be determined by the concerns and pressures of the marketplace. Political interference is held undesirable as infringing on the liberty of individuals to act as they please and as, most likely, resulting in an inefficient allocation of capital. Government is thus limited to a supportive and supplementary role, e.g., protecting infant industries and providing a national defense.

The idea of a self-regulative social mechanism possessed of an inherent drive toward economic growth and efficiency and oriented toward an equilibrium between supply and demand and between cost and price is an elegant conception, however faulty may be its realization in practice. At its heart, it is an individualistic conception in which questions of moral purpose and the exercise of social power are taken as essentially private. Capitalism is pluralictic or, more bluntly, agnostic about the ends of human life. Hayek states this with characteristic clarity.

> Many people regard it as revolting that the Great Society [i.e., the market society] has no common concrete purposes or, as we may say, that it is merely means-connected and not ends-connected. it is indeed true that the chief common purpose of all its members is the purely instrumental one of securing the formation of an abstract order which has no specific purposes but will enhance for all the prospects of achieving their respective purposes (Hayek, 110).

From the standpoint of the market, depending on the structure of demands placed upon it at any given time, pushpin is as good as poetry (Jeremy Bentham) and cavier as tasty as carrion (Lionel Robbins). The market is in itself a neutral instrument whose sole governing function is the maximization of utility.

From a more heterodox perspective, however, capitalism, discerned historically and contextually, shows a distinctively different kind of face. It is not simply a benign mechanism for increasing the wealth of nations. To some, capitalism is a total culture—rationalistic, atomistic, ahistorical, quantitative in character—that comprises a threat to traditional societies and, more generally, to those ties of social cohesion that hold human civilization together. So Bruno Hildebrand in the 19th century (1848), and George F. Will (1983) in ours.

From a different angle, Joseph Schumpeter (1950) argues that capitalism is an evolutionary reality, expressive originally of the interests of the commercial and industrial bourgeoisie, but driven by the forces of its own success to its transformation and, ultimately, to its demise. The competitive marketplace has become an oligopo-

listic system. The entrepreneurial function has given way to the
managerial role. Older meanings of property and contract, essential
to the market system, have become essentially different kinds of
legal relationships. The values and motivational drive of the early
bourgeoisie are replaced by a consumer mentality (See Bell, 1976).

Within the Marxian tradition, as well, capitalism is viewed historically, but governed in its transmutations by internal tensions and
contradictions. All history at least heretofore consists in class struggles. According to Marx, in capitalism as a form of production, the
struggle is between those who control the means of production and
those whose labor power, secured through contract, produce the
results. Marx, particularly in his earlier writings, designated the
structure of this relationship as alienation. That is, in Bertell Ollman's compact summary:

> Persons are separated from their work (they play no part in deciding
> what to do or how to do it)—a break between person and life activity.
> Persons are separated from their products (they have no control over
> what they make or what becomes of it)—a break between person and
> material world. Persons are separated from their fellows (competition
> and class hostility have rendered most forms of cooperation impossi-
> ble)—a break between person and person. In each instance, a relation
> that distinguishes the human species has disappeared and its constit-
> uent elements have been reorganized to appear as something else
> (Ollman 1976, 133–134).

Moreover, according to Immanuel Wallerstein, a contemporary
socialist historian, capitalism is a movement driven toward self-
expansion, toward the endless accumulation of wealth, resulting in
the "commodification of everything" (1983, 13–43). The movement
has become a global system, involving an intricate division of labor
functionally and geographically. The consequence is a complex
commodity chain in which not all exchanges are equal as between
classes or geographical zones. In the struggle among groups for
benefits, the state is, as it always has been, despite orthodox capitalist doctrine, a critical factor of control and distribution. Furthermore, capitalism is linked inextricably with a scientific and technological culture which it advances throughout the world.

We must acknowledge that both orthodox and heterodox interpretations purport to be describing the meaning of capitalism. They are
both, by intention, concerned to specify its identity. But the differ-

ences are appreciable. At some points they are irreconcilable: the character of exchange relations (are parties to exchange in a strictly capitalist system by definition equal or is there an inherent tendency toward patterns of domination?); the status of labor (is labor genuinely free in its contractual relations or forced ineluctably into a condition of alienation?); the role of the state (is the function of the state peripheral or critical?); the quality of capitalist culture (is the market culturally neutral or does it propagate an instrumentalist, technologist morality?)

These variances are not merely empirical. They are rooted in divergent understandings of the world and methods of social analysis. But for our immediate purposes, it is sufficient to note that at one important point, orthodox and heterodox perspectives seem to converge, a point at which capitalism is in tension with democracy. According to both, capitalism is a kind of social system in which the principle of private governance is preeminent. Capitalism is not simply a synonym for market. Markets of various sorts and sizes may exist, even be encouraged, in a wide range of social systems (See Lange, 1938). But, from the orthodox perspective, a capitalist society is governed dominantly (in the strictest sense of that term as lordship) by the interplay of private interests and the result, if there are no artificial constraints, is a spontaneous order which Hayek calls the "Great Society." The role of the political association is supportive (it enforces basic laws of the system) and supplementary (it remedies occasional defects and failures), but clearly secondary. From the heterodox perspective as well, capitalism is viewed as a social order governed by private interests, but in the sense that, at its foundation, capitalism rests on private control of the means of production. In a classical formulation out of the socialist tradition by Marx and Engels, "modern bourgeois private property is the final and most complete expression of the system of producing and appropriating products, that is based on class antagonisms, on the exploitation of the many by the few" (1978/1848). Thus from both perspectives, capitalism intends a principle of private governance, which, in turn, means it intends that the political association shall not be supreme. On this issue, the central idea of democracy diverges. At stake is the question of authority. Most simply put, democracy means a people as such shall have authority for the quality of its own life as a people.

Within the history of political thought from ancient times to the present, there is an extensive range of theories of democracy. Even within the modern period, the spectrum runs from the direct congregationalist democracy of those whom A. D. Lindsay calls the "Puritans of the Left" (1943, 117–121) to Joseph Schumpeter's influential theory of democracy as competitive leadership (1950, 269–284) and Robert Dahl's polyarchy (1956). At times the theories are constructed out of special concern. Schumpeter, for instance, ponders whether democracy and socialism are compatible. And Dahl intends a theory susceptible to techniques of empirical research.

For our immediate purpose, I suggest that there are two sides to the meaning of democracy and that understandings of democracy differ according to which side is conceived as primary. The two sides are the protective and the participative. In protective democracy, participation is secondary to protection. In participative democracy, protection is secondary to participation.

Modern democracy, it is customarily argued, began with the bourgeois revolutions in England, America, and France. In each instance, tyranny was identified as the enemy and liberty exalted as the cause. The differences among these three revolutions and their resultant forms of democracy are of utmost significance and can be discerned even yet in their respective styles of political life. But in one pertinent respect at least they are alike. In Lindsay's words, "Democratic theory in its modern beginnings reflected a society in which men thought it more important to say what the state should not do than to say what it should do. The main emphasis of this early theory is negative" (1943, 116). Democracy was, in a sense, anti-governmental, but, in this context, government meant, first of all, the monarch and therefore the prospects of trampling on the rights and expectations of the people, or at least the class of people most interested at the time with acquiring the facilities and resources for pursuing their own life in their own way. At this juncture, the bourgeoisie, struggling against the constraints of mercantilism, found common interest with republicanism (which we nowadays, without attention to the niceties of differentiation, tend to call democracy). New forms of political association were thus concocted for protective or defensive purposes.

In the tradition of John Locke, for instance, rights were annunciated, the rights of life, liberty, and property, or, in Jefferson's amended version, life, liberty, and the pursuit of happiness. Rights were understood as claims against a government. Congress shall make no law, it was declared, prohibiting freedom of speech or the right of the people peaceably to assemble. Rights constituted a preserve for the freedom of the citizenry. In the tradition of James Madison, on the other hand, institutional restraints were designed out of the shrewd observation that tyranny is a disease not reserved for monarchs. It may infect popular government as well. The remedy is structural: separation of powers, checks and balances, dispersal of rule throughout the governing system, a multiplicity of factions.

To comprehend the full implications of this version of democracy in principle (granting the miserable character of its historical record in practice), we must distinguish its purpose, procedures, and presupposition. Its purpose is protective, to negate whatever forces threaten the privately determined life activity of the citizenry. Its procedures—its legally defined rights and its institutional arrangements—are designed to promote that purpose. At this point, democracy is individualistic. But the procedures have another, more positive side. They are means for participating in the public forum. Rights enable persons to speak and to act. Institutions, especially where their functions and powers are divided, facilitate access to the formulation of policy. Participation may be for purposes of protection, but at the procedural level it is, as well, a form of cooperation with others in the conduct of public business and, more importantly, it articulates a basic presupposition of the entire system: consent.

Procedures constitute a method of consent (see Gewirth, 1962), but consent itself is the primordial act of forming a public. It is the determination to live together, to share in a common destiny, to form a common life. Consent, however difficult it may be to construe what precisely that means theoretically or practically, is the beginning of a people. In that sense, it is the deepest authority of social existence. But what is authorized out of consent may be unauthorized. This is the reason for affirming that, within democracy, even of the protective kind, a people as such has authority for the quality of its own life as a people. What the people form for the sake of their living together, they may, with whatever wisdom they possess, reform or transform. There is thus a tension between democracy, which rests on a principle of consent, and capitalism, which intends a principle of private governance, even though, given the purpose of a protective democracy, a market system may be widely supported and encouraged within the economic realm.

The tension is more evident and more acute between capitalism and the version of democracy in which protection is secondary to participation. Where protective democracy, traditionally called "liberal democracy," serves a negative function, the role of participative democracy is affirmative. Moreover, where protective democracy is predominantly solicitous of the individual, participative democracy, more sensitive to the meaning of its grounding in consent, is concerned with the texture of relationship between personal and community life. This concern is the point of Eduard Heimann's affirmation that "The meaning of democracy lies in the liberty and dignity of the person and the community; or one may say that it lies in their dignity, which includes their liberty" (1961, 283). It is also the intent of Lindsay's statement that, "The function of the state . . . is to serve the community and in that service to make it more of a community" (1943, 245). But it is more amply depicted in John Dewey's formulation of "the nature of the democratic idea in its generic social sense":

> The idea of democracy is a wider and fuller idea than can be exemplified in the state even at its best. To be realized it must affect all modes of human association, the family, the school, industry, religion.
> . . . .
> From the standpoint of the individual, it consists in having a responsible share according to capacity in forming and directing the activities of the groups to which one belongs and in participating according to need in the values which the groups sustain. From the standpoint of the groups, it demands liberation of the potentialities of members of a group in harmony with the interests and goods which are common (1954, 143 and 147).

Participation, from this perspective, is not merely a procedure for conducting affairs or for protecting one's private interests. It is, more profoundly, expressive of the meaning of being a self within a community of selves. It is a good to be cherished, as exclusionary policies and practices demonstrate by contrast. But, the extension and deepening of democratic processes within a community require that the community through its public forum take deliberate control over its resources in a manner not to be expected in a system controlled by the capitalist principle.

The idea of participative democracy lies behind the complaint of those who insist that the traditional rights associated with democracy—rights of speaking, organizing, voting—are only formal without the economic and cultural conditions for their effective expression. As Joshua Cohen and Joel Rogers remark, "Both an unemployed worker and a millionaire owner of a major television station enjoy the same formal right of free speech, but their power to express and give expression to that right are radically different" (1983, 50–51). The idea of participative democracy also lies behind G. D. H. Cole's complaint that

> the answer that most people would give to the question 'what is the fundamental evil in our modern society?' would be the wrong one: 'they would answer POVERTY, when they ought to answer SLAVERY'. The millions who had been given the franchise, who had formally been given the means to self-government had in fact been 'trained to subservience' and this training had largely taken place during the course of their daily occupation. Cole argued that 'the industrial system . . . is in great measure the key to the paradox of political democracy. Why are the many nominally supreme but actually powerless? Largely because the circumstances of their lives do not accustom or fit them for power or responsibility. A servile system in industry inevitably reflects itself in political servility' (Pateman 1970, 38).

In both its versions, democracy means a people as such has authority for the character of its own life as a people. On that point alone, there is tension between democracy and capitalism, for one is fundamentally a principle of public governance, while the other is a principle of private control. But the tension is exacerbated in participative democracy because, since the basic questions of economic life—the allocation of investment, the organization of production, the distribution of wealth—bear directly on the quality of the life of a people as a whole, such questions are considered matters appropriate for public determination.

III
Social Democracy

> This interrelation of agents, which makes the freedom of all members of a society depend upon the intentions of each, is the ground of morality. . . . If we call the harmonious interrelation of agents their 'community', we may say that a morally right action is an action which intends community. . . . If the world is one action, any particular action determines the future, within its own limits, for all agents. Every individual agent is therefore responsible to all other agents for his actions (MacMurray 1961, 118–119).

To this point, I have proposed that the common good is the first virtue of social institutions and that capitalism and democracy as basic principles of social order are in tension with each other. The third thesis I would advance is that social democracy (an alternative expression for participative democracy) is more directly ordained to the common good than what has traditionally been called democratic capitalism.

Democracy (of the protective kind) and capitalism (understood in the orthodox way) are born in the modern world as parties of a general movement of liberation. The breakthrough of democracy is the effort of a people, or some classes of people, to gain control over their own lives. Civil liberty is among its primary concerns, the liberty to think, to speak, to act as one pleases. The emergence of capitalism is the effort to remove the limitations of restrictive legislation. Free contract is among its dominant interests, the right to associate, to negotiate, and to bargain as one wishes. Both are expressions in social practice of modernity's turn toward the subject. Sights are shifted from the heavens above to the earth beneath, from ultimate destiny to immediate circumstance, from final causes to what works. The shift is toward a world in which the solitary human agent, the subject, is central. Tradition is abjured as the dead hand of the past. Each of us, born as a *tabula rasa*, must ponder: what do *I* think, what shall *I* do, and what do *I* want? Democracy and capitalism are thus linked, granting the basic tension between them, in their avowed respect for individuality. Democracy promises an institutional context protective of open and free thought and action. Capitalism promises a system through which the wants of individuals, whatever they may be, can be satisfied.

The promises are attractive to anyone sensitive to the dignity of individual life. But for that very reason, the promises are easily transmuted into ideological explanations of practices that belie their stated intent, and appropriately provoke a hermeneutics of suspicion. It does not take a Marxist to discern that the language of modernity in general and of democratic capitalism in particular has been persistently used to justify institutions of domination. To cite but one prominent example, racism, in its various versions, has accompanied modernity from its beginnings to the present and has been built into its institutional forms, all of which have been justified in the name of freedom. Significantly, the mitigation of racism, where it has occurred, is attributable neither to capitalism (within which, it has been argued, racism is functional [Wallerstein 1983, ch. 2]) nor to liberal democracy (which treats such matters with benign neglect), but to a political struggle in which democracy is transformed into an agent of and for participation.

While charges of ideological confusion may be dismissed with the maxim, *abusus non tollit usus* (abuse does not eliminate use), they must not be dismissed too quickly for the confusion may be symptomatic of a flaw in the practices themselves, their structure or their theory. Thus, for instance, liberal democracy may be unable to honor its ultimate intention of protecting the liberty of the individual without an affirmative move toward the extension and deepening of the rights it professes to honor, in which case liberal democracy must make a move on the way toward social democracy. On the other hand, capitalism may be unable to support a thoroughgoing market system without an aggressive means of assuring the equality of all parties to all contracts, in which case capitalism must engage in the kind of intervention into the distribution of power and resources it abhors. In sum, to honor its own promises, democratic capitalism, understood as the historical conjunction of liberal democracy and capitalism in its orthodox interpretation, must be prepared to transform itself in the direction of the common good but away from capitalism's principle of private governance and liberal democracy's negative orientation.

Moreover, we must pose, at this point, a question of historical interpretation. The structures of social life change over time. While change may be relatively imperceptible to those engaged in it, there are moments of radical transition, of passage from an old world to a new. It is a matter of settled judgment, for instance, that the forms of life we distinguish as medieval and modern are appreciably unlike each other though the transmutation may have been gradual. Now, during recent decades, some interpreters claim to discern signs of a new epoch, a post-modern age, emerging, not in all cases one they cherish (e.g. Heilbroner 1976, Unger 1975, Habermas 1975, Bell 1976). Granting the methodological problem of determining the point at which an epochal change has been effected, the evidence of structural transformation in the life of peoples over the past two hundred years at least in the Western world is compelling.

The industrial revolution transformed methods of production and the social relations of those engaged in the productive process. The allied movement of urbanization shifted the center of life for most of the population from village to megalopolis. Continuous developments in technology introduced both gigantic alterations in means of production and shifts in the expectations and character of daily life. The automobile, for instance, completely altered residential patterns and cultural sensibilities. Furthermore, it simultaneously enhanced the private life of individuals and increased their dependency in extensive ways on the organized economic and political life of the nation.

The emergence of the large corporation in the 19th century and its developments in the 20th century (the managerial revolution, diversification of holdings, globalization of operations) have, among other things, complicated structures in the division of labor, changed the distribution of organizational power in society, and completely reversed patterns of work from self-employment to employment in a productive process controlled by others. The effects of periodic business cycles, culminating dramatically in the Great Depression, demonstrated convincingly the national, if not the global, scope of economic interconnections. The nation-state system, with its militaristic propensities and its increasing reliance on developments in military technology particularly beginning with World War I, has promoted the formation of a military-industrial complex. Struggles by the working class during the 19th and 20th centuries to improve working conditions led to organized labor as an important economic and political power in the social order.

In short, the actual structure of economic production and distribution in the Western world, throughout the globe, is a far cry from Jefferson's "vision of a free society of independent men prospering through an expansive commerce in farm commodities" (Appleby 1984, ix) or Adam Smith's pin factory (Smith, 1937). We are enmeshed in a complicated "material web of interdependence" (Winter). Even if ours is not yet strictly a new epoch, it would seem an anachronism to equate the prevailing structure of our political economy with either Smith's capitalism or Jefferson's democracy.

More importantly, a range of public policies has been instituted in America over the past century which, taken together, manifest a move away from the capitalist principle of private governance toward social democracy. My concern is less with the detailed administrative arrangements of the policies which may be altered from time to time than with the principles they are intended to effect. Principles of public regulation (e.g. FDA, FTC), workmen's compensation, collective bargaining, public employment, social insurance, national economic accounting and control (e.g. Unemployment Act of 1946), equal employment opportunity, and environmental protection are all part of a limited but remarkable tradition demonstrating the felt need of a people through its public forum to gain some degree of deliberate control over the quality of its life as a people. They represent an affirmative effort to extend the rights of citizens beyond those of liberal democracy and to expand the participation of citizens in the control of their common life beyond the matter of voting in elections. Their overall concern I would argue is with the quality of the community as a whole, that is, with the common good. They represent the judgment that at least in present social circumstances, democratic capitalism as traditionally understood is less able to secure the common good than social democracy.

However, at its deepest level, the difference between democratic capitalism (in its traditional sense) and social democracy lies in their respective understandings of self and world. That issue is at the heart of all social thought. In the relationship between self and world, there are three possibilities. First, the self exists for the sake of the world, whether the world of nation or race or class. This understanding is characteristic of political romanticism (see Tillich 1977, Part One) and of the historical school of economics (see Hildebrand 1848).

Second, the world exists for the sake of the self. This position, I would contend, underlies liberal democracy, orthodox capitalism, and their historical conjunction. The intent of democratic capitalism is to construct institutional conditions conducive to satisfying the interests and life plans of separate selves. These interests and life plans may have nothing to do with each other, but that does not matter. What matters is to design arrangements enabling persons to get on with their lives, whatever they may may be, with as little conflict as possible. Within this broad tradition, diverse ethical principles have been constructed to deal with questions of resolving conflict: from Locke's natural rights theory and Bentham's concept of utility maximization to Rawls's two principles of justice and Nozick's entitlement theory. Differences among these principles should not be ignored, but neither should their convergence. All are anthropocentric; all are individualistic; all are agnostic about ends. Underlying all is a view of the world as resource, but as, in itself purposeless and senseless.

In the third possibility, self and world exist for each other. The self is not first of all subject or consumer, but friend, neighbor, citizen. Friendship is, in the relation between persons, a goodness in itself: "It gives us an experiential taste of that wholeness to which as persons we are called" (Johann 1966, 46). Friendship is an

analogue for neighborhood, civil society, even cosmopolis (see Moltmann 1977, 114–121, 314–317). The ethical expression of this
understanding of self and world is the common good. As we have
already noted, the common good is a quality of community life
composed of two interpenetrating dimensions. Procedurally, it
means participating in the deliberations and decisions of a community by its members. Substantively, it embraces several qualities—in
material life, physical well-being; in social life, civic friendship; in
group relation, peaceable means of interaction; in cultural life, an
open spirit—whatever, that is, conduces to the enhancement of the
life of its members. The reverse side of the common good is alienation. This is the sense of G.D.H. Cole's exclamation that the fundamental evil of modern society is not poverty as such, but slavery. It
is also the sense of Gustavo Gutierrez's designation of dependency
or domination as the primary social problem in the Third World and
his projection of liberation as the immediate aim and solidarity as
the governing purpose of political and economic action (1973).

The institutional implication of the common good, at least at this
point in history, is, I would suggest, social democracy. Social democracy, as I have construed it, means the extension of the democratic principle, the principle of public determination, into all
modes of social life, including the economic. It means therefore
incorporating public determination into the functions of allocating
investment, organizing production, and distributing wealth with the
governing intention of enhancing the quality of relationships
throughout the community of life. It does not mean that markets are
inappropriate mechanisms within the economy or that no forms of
administrative control are ever acceptable. But it does require explicit structures of public accountability and control. And it does
require explicit attention to the governing intention and specific
consequences of programs and policies. Among recent proposals for
the transformation of the political economy which, while taking
account of historical reality, its limitations and possibilities, at least
approximate the idea of social democracy, I would cite Carole
Patemen's participatory democracy (1970), Daniel Bell's public
household (1976), Roberto Unger's theory of organic groups (1975),
Alec Nove's feasible socialism (1983), Michael Harrington's democratic socialism (1980), Martin Carnoy and Derek Shearer's economic democracy (1980, 1983) and Robert Dahl's latest book, A
Preface to Economic Democracy (1985). Once again, then, I am led
to affirm the thesis that social democracy is more directly ordained

to the common good, the first virtue of social institutions, than what has traditionally been meant by democratic capitalism.

Given the three theses I have advanced, I propose the need for a new social covenant. The language is intentional. At the beginning of the modern age, we were instructed to acknowledge a social contract as the foundation of our common life. The idea of a social contract bespeaks a world of individuals, a state of nature, out of which persons come to effect a *modus vivendi,* for they must live together even if they do not belong together. Each gains some benefit from the arrangement, else the bargain will not long be kept. The bottom line is commodity.

But the idea of social covenant invokes an alternative tradition of thought and action, religious in its expression but ontological in its claim. The idea of a social covenant bespeaks a world in which we already belong together but are called repeatedly to acknowledge that fact anew and to determine what the forms of our life together shall be. As Bernard Meland reminds us, the idea of covenant is a myth both of identity and of dissonance, for covenants are often broken. But even when broken, they remain covenants and compel us to their reaffirmation (Meland 1976, 97–98). In its theological meaning, the idea of covenant is grounded in that God who intends a universal community of being and to whom each self is related in and through all other relationships (Johann 1966, 49–66; Hartshorne 1953, 29–43). In its meaning for social practice, the idea of covenant implies that what is most to be cherished in our associations is not the commodities that derive therefrom, but the commonwealth that is created therein.

Works Cited

Appleby, Joyce, 1984, *Capitalism and a New Social Order: The Republican Vision of the 1790's.* New York: New York University Press.

Augustine, 1950, *De civitate Dei.* Transl. Marcus Dods. New York: Modern Library.

Bell, Daniel, 1976, *The Cultural Contradictions of Capitalism.* New York: Basic Books.

Benne, Robert, 1981, *The Ethic of Democratic Capitalism: A Moral Reassessment.* Philadelphia: Fortress Press.

Carnoy, Martin and Shearer, Derek, 1980, *Economic Democracy.* Armonk, N.Y.: M. E. Sharpe.

———, 1983, With Russell Rumberger. *A New Social Contract: The Economy and Government After Reagan.* New York: Harper & Row.

Cohen, Joshua and Rogers, Joel, 1983, *On Democracy.* New York: Penguin Books.

Dahl, Robert, 1956, *A Preface for Democratic Theory.* Chicago: University of Chicago Press.

————, 1985, *A Preface to Economic Democracy.* Berkeley: University of California Press.

Dewey, John, 1954, *The Public and Its Problems.* Chicago: The Swallow Press. Original publication: 1927.

Gewirth, Alan, 1962, "Political Justice." Richard B. Brandt, ed. *Social Justice.* Englewood Cliffs, N.J.: Prentice-Hall, 119–169.

Giddens, Anthony, 1979, *Central Problems in Social Theory.* Berkeley and Los Angeles: University of California Press.

Gutierrez, Gustavo, 1973, *A Theology of Liberation: History, Politics and Salvation.* Transl. Sister Caridad Inda and John Eagleson. Maryknoll, N.Y.: Orbis Books.

Habermas, Jurgen, 1975, *Legitimation Crisis.* Transl. Thomas McCarthy. Boston: Beacon Press.

Harrington, Michael, 1980, *Decade of Decision: The Crisis of the American System.* New York: Simon & Schuster.

Hartshorne, Charles, 1953, *Reality As Social Process.* Glencoe, Ill.: The Free Press.

Hartz, Louis, 1955, *The Liberal Tradition in America: An Interpretation of American Political Thought Since the Revolution.* New York: Harcourt, Brace and World.

Hayek, Friedrich A., 1976, *Law, Legislation and Liberty.* Vol. 2: *The Mirage of Social Justice.* Chicago: The University of Chicago Press.

Hefner, Philip, 1976, "The Foundations of Belonging in a Christian Worldview," Philip Hefner and W. Widick Schroeder, eds. *Belonging and Alienation: Religious Foundations for the Human Future.* Chicago: Center for the Scientific Study of Religion, 161–180.

Heimann, Eduard, 1961, *Reason and Faith in Modern Society: Liberalism, Marxism, and Democracy.* Middletown, Conn.: Wesleyan University Press.

Heilbroner, Robert, 1976, *Business Civilization in Decline.* New York: W. W. Norton & Co.

Hildebrand, Bruno, 1848, *Die Nationaloekonomie der Gegenwart und Zukunft.* Frankfort.

Hobhouse, L. T., 1964, *Liberalism.* London: Oxford University Press. Original publication: 1911.

Johann, Robert, 1966, *The Pragmatic Meaning of God.* Milwaukee: Marquette University Press.

Lange, Oskar, 1938, "On the Economic Theory of Socialism." Benjamin Lippincott ed. *On the Economic Theory of Socialism.* Minneapolis: University of Minnesota Press.

Lindsay, A. D., 1943, *The Modern Democratic State*. London: Oxford University Press.

MacIntyre, Alasdair, 1981, *After Virtue: A Study in Moral Theory*. Notre Dame: University of Notre Dame Press.

MacMurray, John, 1961, *Persons in Relation*. London: Faber & Faber.

Maritain, Jacques, 1947, *The Person and the Common Good*. Transl. John J. Fitzgerald. New York: Charles Scribner's Sons.

————, 1951, *Man and the State*. Phoenix Books. Chicago: The University of Chicago Press.

Marx, Karl and Engels, Friedrich, 1978, "The Communist Manifesto." C. B. Macpherson, ed. *Property: Mainstream and Critical Positions*. Toronto: University of Toronto Press, 61–64 (excerpts). Original publication: 1848.

Meland, Bernard Eugene, 1953, *Faith and Culture*. New York: Oxford University Press.

————, 1976, *Fallible Forms and Symbols: Discourses on Method in a Theology of Culture*. Philadelphia: Fortress Press.

Mises, Ludwig von, 1960, *Epistemological Problems of Economics*. Princeton, N.J.: Van Nostrand.

Moltmann, Jurgen, 1977, *The Church in the Power of the Spirit*. Transl. Margaret Kohl. New York: Harper & Row.

Novak, Michael, 1982, *The Spirit of Democratic Capitalism*. New York: Simon & Schuster.

Nove, Alec, 1983, *The Economics of Feasible Socialism*. London: George Allen & Unwin.

Ollman, Bertell, 1976, *Alienation: Marx's Conception of Man in Capitalist Society*. 2nd edition. Cambridge: Cambridge University Press.

Pateman, Carole, 1970, *Participation and Democratic Theory*. Cambridge: Cambridge University Press.

Rawls, John, 1971, *A Theory of Justice*. Cambridge, Mass.: Harvard University Press.

Rothbard, Murray N., 1979, *Individualism and the Philosophy of the Social Sciences*. Cato paper no. 4. San Francisco: Cato Institute.

Sandel, Michael J., 1982, *Liberalism and the Limits of Justice*. Cambridge: Cambridge University Press.

Schumpeter, Joseph A., 1950, *Capitalism, Socialism, and Democracy*. 3rd edition. New York: Harper & Bros.

Smith, Adam, 1937, *The Wealth of Nations*. New York: The Modern Library. Original publication: 1776.

Steinfels, Peter, 1985, "The Bishops and Their Critics." *Dissent* 32/2 (Spring 1985), 176–182.

Tawney, R. H., 1947, *Religion and the Rise of Capitalism*. New York: Penguin Books (Pelican Books). Original publication: 1926.

Tillich, Paul, 1977, *The Socialist Decision*. Transl. Franklin Sherman. New York: Harper & Row. Original publication: 1933.

U.S. Bishops, 1984, "Catholic Social Teaching and the U.S. Economy."
    Origins: NC Documentary Service 14/22–23 (November 15, 1984), 337–
    383.
Unger, Roberto Mangabeira, 1975, Knowledge and Politics. New York: The
    Free Press.
Wallerstein, Immanuel, 1974, The Modern World System: Capitalist Agricul-
    ture & the Origins of the European World Economy in the 16th Century.
    New York: Academic Press.
————, 1980, The Modern World-System: Mercantilism and the Consolida-
    tion of the European World-Economy. New York: Academic Press.
————, 1983, Historical Capitalism. London: Verso.
Whitehead, Alfred North, 1961, Adventures of Ideas. New York: The Free
    Press. Original publication: 1933.
Will, George F., 1983, Statecraft as Soulcraft: What Government Does. New
    York: Simon & Schuster.
Winter, Gibson, 1970, Being Free: Reflections on America's Cultural Revo-
    lution. New York: MacMillan.

PUBLIC POLICY: REFLECTIONS ON THE ROLE OF ETHICS AND ETHICISTS

Leonard J. Weber

During the Presidency of Harry Truman, Secretary of State Dean Acheson once described a foreign policy discussion this way:

> Our discussion centered on the appraisal of dangers and risks, the weighing of the need for decisive and effective action against considerations of prudence. . . . Moral talk did not bear on the issue.[1]

I suspect that the actual conversations that take place in the highest realms of the Federal Government are not significantly different today from what they were like in Acheson's day. What does seem to be somewhat different, though, is the willingness of public officials—and the public generally—to acknowledge a role for moral or ethical considerations. The ethical perspective is no longer considered quite as suspect and as irrelevant as it once was.

In the present context, those people who speak to public policy from the perspective of ethics are being given at least some hearing (which doesn't mean, of course, that they are being persuasive). The public attention given to the American Bishops' pastoral letters on the nuclear arms race and on the U.S. economy are examples of the willingness of many people to acknowledge a place for sustained and disciplined ethical talk about public policy.

There are still those who ask what ethics has to do with politics and public policies (much of the opposition to what the Bishops are doing in these pastorals involves a real concern about the appropriateness of religious leaders officially addressing political and economic issues), but, it seems to me, that that question may not be the

---

[1] Quoted in Amy Gutmann and Dennis Thompson (eds.), *Ethics and Politics: Cases and Comments* (Chicago: Nelson-Hall Publishers, 1984), p. xi.

one with which ethicists and religious leaders need to be primarily
concerned. There is a most important question that does need to be
explicitly raised and responded to, but the question is probably not
best expressed as *whether* ethics has anything to do with public
policy; rather, the question is a question of *what* ethical approach
should be used in addressing public policy issues, *how* ethics should
be related to public policy.

Those of us who may be inclined to speak to public policy issues
from the perspective of ethics or religious beliefs need to be very
clear about what we are trying to do. If we are going to have a role in
the public debate, we should think carefully about the nature of that
role. We need to understand what we are trying to achieve in the
public arena and what the implications are of the ways in which we
speak to public policy issues. It seems to me to be essential that we
reflect upon the nature of the contribution that ethics can make (and
of the limits to that contribution). We need to be aware of the level
of ethical sensitivity in American culture, of the impact of this
public policy role on the very way that we do ethics, and of the
possible dangers that face us as we assume this role.

This paper is an attempt to contribute to the discussion of the
proper role of ethics in public policy debate by identifying some of
the concerns that must be addressed. The concerns will be identified
under these headings: (1) the practicality of ethics, (2) political
ethics and the question of compromise, (3) the public philosophy,
and (4) ethics as advocacy. In each of these considerations, I will
make my own recommendations in the hope of stimulating further
consideration and discussion, but my major purpose is to identify
significant aspects of the agenda.

1. The Practicality of Ethics

Given the ways in which the term *practical* is frequently used in
discussions of political issues, it is easy for us to sometimes think
that being practical is undesirable. When we are urged to be practical
in the sense of accommodating ourselves to some injustice or of
abandoning our principles, being practical may be equated with
weakening our commitment to and our efforts for a more just society.
But there is another sense of practicality, a sense in which being
practical is essential for those who seek to bring ethical perspectives
to bear on public policy discussions. Public policy has to do with
shaping the public order; the discussion must be focused on the

impact that the policy will have on the world in which we live. Social ethics, the ethical perspectives brought to bear on the public policy debates, must be concerned with consequences, must be practical. The pursuit of justice and peace means that we must be committed to establishing real justice and real peace; our obligation to work for justice is a responsibility to take the world very seriously, to seek to be effective in achieving good results.[2]

There are many Americans (inside and outside the churches) who are convinced that the ethical ideals of the sort that have traditionally been accepted are not an adequate basis on which to build public policies. Those ideals may be of great importance in personal lives, but they are not workable in the real world and they should not be advocated. This approach is not opposed to the idea of ethics being practical (in fact, most individuals who have this outlook tend to be committed to being practical in regard to public policy), but clearly separates certain ethical ideals from the practical world.

There are also many people (especially in the churches) who are not at all comfortable in thinking about moral obligations as being obligations to be practical; they argue, in effect, that certain actions must be taken because they are "right," not because they "work." There is widespread opposition to consequentialism in religious ethics. Our obligation (for many) is to be true to the teachings of Scripture or of the Church or of the Spirit and not to be concerned about the consequences.

This, then, is the practicality dimension of the question of the role of ethics in public policy. We are faced with a twofold question: should we be concerned about consequences in our social ethical positions and, if so, can we adequately develop public policy positions within the framework of traditional ethical ideals? I want to focus on the question of consequences in this section and on the role of ethical ideals in politics in the next (though these two issues cannot be entirely separated). I do not intend here to attempt an adequate development of my position, but I do want to comment briefly on the reasons for resisting two temptations facing us: the "religious temptation" and the "dual ethic temptation."

The "dual ethic temptation" is the temptation to believe that the world—especially the political world—is not a moral world, that in that world we must speak the language of power rather than the

---

[2]See Leonard J. Weber, "Practical, Utopian, and Poor-Just Stewards." *Spirituality Today*, 33 (December, 1981), pp. 329–339.

language of morality, that we need one moral code for personal life
and another for the practices and policies of the state. Many political
theorists and religious leaders from the time of Machiavelli and
Luther have argued for the dual ethic and it has become widely
established in the accepted political wisdom. George F. Kennan has
expressed this position clearly:

> Morality, then, as the channel to individual self fulfillment—yes. . . .
> Morality in governmental method, as a matter of conscience and pref-
> erence on the part of the people—yes. But morality as general criterion
> for the determination of the behavior of states and above all as a
> criterion for measuring and comparing the behavior of different states—
> no. Here other criteria, sadder, more limited, more practical, must be
> allowed to prevail.[3]

It should be noted that an important part of rejecting the idea that
morality (in the usual understanding of the word) is a guide for
public policy is the conviction that morality is not practical. Max
Weber, in his important essay on "Politics as a Vocation," made the
distinction between "an ethic of ultimate ends" and an "ethic of
responsibility." Weber advocates the ethic of responsibility precisely
because it is concerned with the consequences of actions, whereas
the ethic of ultimate ends, as he describes it, is primarily concerned
with not being associated with evil or injustices (and is not concerned about the consequences of actoins).[4] Weber, with many of
those who are in the dual ethic tradition, insists upon our responsibility to be focused on the consequences of our actions in the real
world. And, even though I am not comfortable with the dual-ethic
orientation, I am fully supportive of the emphasis on being practical
and concerned with consequences.

The "religious temptation" (and I apologize if this term, as used
in this way, is offensive to anyone) is the temptation to be more
concerned with being "right" than with consequences of the positions taken; it is the temptation to focus more on personal morality
than on social consequences; it is the temptation to identify one
certain issue as a "touchstone issue" that determines by itself
whether a candidate should be supported; it is the temptation to ask

---

[3]Quoted in Erwin A. Gaede, *Politics and Ethics: Machiavelli to Niebuhr* (Lanham,
MD: University Press of America, 1983), p. 147.

[4]Max Weber, "Politics as a Vocation," in H. H. Gerth and C. Wright Mills (eds.),
From Max Weber: Essays in Sociology (New York: Oxford University Press, 1946).

whether any "good Catholic" (or "born-again Christian" or whatever) is able to support such and such a position. The religious temptation is the temptation to act politically in such a way that one avoids compromise with ethical principles rather than in such a way as to achieve greatest possible good in the circumstances.

The religious temptation and the dual-ethic temptation are closely related; they both hold that ethics and politics are incompatible (that ethics is not practical). A recent report from the Hastings Center very clearly indicates the two ways in which this understanding of the incompatibility of ethics and politics is found in our society:

> Some would argue that no realistic purpose is served by discussions of legislative ethics because legislators do—and must—respond single-mindedly to political pressures. According to the conventional wisdom, when push comes to shove legislators will not be moved by considerations of ethical duty but will inevitably act instead on the basis of feasibility and advantage. At the opposite extreme, some of the moral criticism leveled at legislators today is animated by an underlying hostility toward politics and politicians generally. Those who adopt this viewpoint understand that political life involves compromises, bargaining, and a willingness to forgo the ideal in order to achieve the possible. But they view these aspects of legislative politics as ethically dangerous at best or ethically corrupting at worst.[5]

What we need to achieve in our political discourse in this country, it seems to me, is a recognition that ethical perspectives have a very important role to play in that discourse, but that ethics cannot be understood to be an approach that is primarily concerned with the extent to which one can cooperate with evil. Ethics belongs in the public policy debate precisely because it contributes to a fuller understanding of what is involved in the choices we make. The understanding of ethics that we need to bring to these discussions is an understanding that insights from ethical and religious perspectives can contribute to a better understanding of the responsibilities of those seeking a more just society.

I think that ethical traditions and the study of ethics are very relevant for public policy discussions, but I need to acknowledge that what we often understand to be the role of ethics needs to change toward a more practical orientation. While I don't often agree

---

[5]The Hastings Center Staff, *The Ethics of Legislative Life* (Hastings-on-Hudson, N.Y.: The Hastings Center, 1985), pp. 7–8.

with James Schall in regard to particular political commitments, I
do agree with his emphasis upon the legitimacy of the political
realm, the emphasis on the practical:

> This practical realization which recognizes that an ostensibly noble
> and pure position can in fact lead to evil consequences places politics
> back at the center of the discussion. Politics is that discipline and
> action which must count for where things are most likely to go in fact,
> not merely in hope or in theory.[6]

In this discussion of the practicality of ethics, I have merely
touched on the issues to be explored and on the approach that I
would like to pursue at another time. But I have, I think, indicated
something of the agenda that has to be addressed by those concerned
about the relationship of ethics and public policy. John Coleman has
argued that Christianity has not adequately developed the concept
of citizenship as a moral ideal.[7] He is correct; the tension many
Christians (and many others concerned about morality) sense between moral beliefs and citizenship is obvious. Clearly one of the
tasks of ethicists is to continue to try to clarify the relationship
between ethics and public policy.

2. Political Ethics and the Question of Compromise

As I indicated earier, the "dual ethic" position (sometimes referred to as realism) is that traditional Christian ethical ideals are
not adequate for the world of politics, that the public arena must be
organized on the basis of a different system of ethical beliefs.

Where I differ from the so-called realist position is in regard to the
possibility of ethical ideals having desirable consequences if implemented in the political sphere. I differ in terms of underlying beliefs
about the possibility of justice in the real world. The "realist"
position is based on a belief similar to this one expressed by Irving
Kristol:

> I am not saying that capitalism is a just society. I am saying that there
> is a capitalist conception of justice which is a workable conception of

---

[6]James V. Schall (ed.), *Out of Justice, Peace and Winning the Peace* (San Francisco:
Ignative Press, 1984), p. 21.

[7]John Coleman, "The Christian as Citizen," *Commonweal* 110 (September 9, 1983),
pp. 457–462.

justice. Anyone who promises you a just society on this earth is a fraud and a charlatan. I believe that this is not the nature of human destiny. It would mean that we all would be happy. Life is not like that. Life is doomed not to be like that. But if you do not accept this view, and if you really think that life can indeed be radically different from what it is, if you really believe that justice can prevail on earth, then you are likely to start taking phrases like "social justice" very seriously and to think that the function of politics is to rid the world of evils: to abolish war, abolish envy, to abolish, abolish, abolish. We are not going to abolish any of those things. If we push them out one window, they will come in through another window in some unforeseen form. The reforms of today give rise to the evils of tomorrow. That is the history of the human race.[8]

My worldview is somewhat more idealistic. I believe that humankind is not fundamentally selfish or individualistic; we are social beings by our very nature. There are ways in which evil is deeply rooted in society, but it is also true that people do respond to calls to be generous and cooperative. The fundamental assumption of my approach to politics is that it is possible to build a more just society and a more peaceful world and that one does this by appealing to the best of human capabilities, the disposition to be cooperative and generous, at least at times.[9]

One of the major questions facing the ethical idealist in politics is the question of compromise. I have encountered individuals who are interested in "politics" and committed to taking an ethical approach to political issues but who hesitate to pursue an active career in public life because politics would mean a "compromise" of their ethical beliefs. They recognize that they will never be able to implement a full range of policies they reflect their ethical beliefs (we, after all, live in a morally pluralistic society); they will be intimately involved in a process that, at times, promotes or permits activities that they find to be ethically unacceptable. This fact causes them to hesitate; they do not want to compromise their ethical standards. Because they cannot achieve policies that do not have some element of evil in them, they hesitate to get involved in the day-to-day business of working out specific policies.

---

[8]Irving Kristol, "A Capitalist & Conception of Justice," in W. Michael Hoffman and Jennifer Mills Moore, (eds.), *Business Ethics: Readings and Cases in Corporate Morality* (New York: McGraw-Hill, 1984), p. 50.

[9]This "optimistic" view represents, I think, mainline Roman Catholic social thought. Andrew Greely summarizes this tradition succinctly in *No Bigger Than Necessary* (New York: New American Library, 1977), pp. 89–90.

It is possible for a Christian to pursue various ventures so long as those
ventures are not directly opposed to the life of the gospel and so long
as the actions of the Christian are not in opposition to the gospel. In
other words, it is possible (even noble) for a Christian to be in politics.
However, being Christian *first* and legislator *secondly* the Christian may
not act in opposition to the way of the gospel. Legislative positions
must give way to the norms of the gospel and equally give way to the
Christian's moral stance. Anything less than a boldly prophetic stand
(in or out of politics) in all aspects of a Christian's life is a lean toward
compromise.[10]

Raising the question of "compromise" of one's moral position in
politics is not, I think, a very useful way of considering the responsibility of conscientious citizens (or politicians). An adequate political ethics would mean, I think, that we have the responsibility to
choose (and support) that kind of political action that will do the
most good from among the real alternatives (keeping in mind the
ideal of a just society and working to make that ideal more realiza-
ble—this is where the idealism gets expressed). If we always choose
the best among the alternatives (that which most contributes to the
common good), then we are not compromising our moral standards
at all. (The concern about "compromising" one's moral position
appears to be based on a non-consequentialist understanding of
social ethics. There is, I think, no necessary connection between
idealism and a non-consequentialist approach in social ethics.)

One of the tasks of the ethicist is to attempt to establish priorities.
Sometimes, the choices that we are forced to make in policy decisions are choices between two or more possibilities, each of which
has something important to contribute; sometimes, the choices are
choices between policies none of which are entirely without undesirable consequences. The ethical decision is not usually the decision to do good and avoid evil (if that were the case, it *would* be
compromising to choose anything other than to do good); rather, the
ethical decision is to do the most good or the least evil in the
circumstances. The task of the ethicist, then, is to help persons
reflect upon how one establishes priorities, how we determine what
takes precedence over what in our national goals and policies. The
task of the ethicist is to reflect upon the social value systems that are
found in our society and critically assess the priorities that are found
there. This is, perhaps, the most important way in which the ethi-

---

[10]From a personal communication.

cists can contribute to raising the level of ethical discussion in regard to public policy.

During the 1984 Presidential campaign, much concern was raised about the "pro-choice" position taken by politicians like Geraldine Ferraro and Mario Cuomo (politicians who personally thought that abortion was morally unacceptable, at least in most cases). Much of the defense of their "pro-choice" position, especially by others, was based on the argument that individuals should not try to "impose their moral positions" on those who have different moral positions. That particular argument is not, I think, very satisfactory. What is needed is a better understanding of the moral basis for public policy decisions—the moral obligation to work for those policies that achieve the greatest possible good (after every effort has been made to identify and establish priorities in regard to the values involved). While it is true to say that personal morality is not the same as public policy, it is usually not enough to say that; we need to clarify further the nature of political ethics.

The political responsibility of the ethical person is much more complex and multifaceted than those who focus on "compromise" would tend to lead us to believe. But, I would argue, the task is not any less idealistic—we should seek nothing less than a more just and peaceful world.

3. The Public Philosophy

Ethicists will probably have their greatest impact on the public policies in this country, not by the specific policies that we recommend, but by the ways in which we are able to shape the public philosophy, the dominant social value system of the nation. Our policies, to a significant extent, reflect our social values. Any real changes in national policies are likely to occur only when the dominant social value system is changed (or replaced).

While it is not possible to describe here, in any detail, the dominant social value system,[11] it must be obvious to anyone who has studied American social philosophy that it is quite individualistic. The underlying assumption seems to be that we are all inclined to

---

[11]I have summarized some of the characteristics of the dominant American social value system elsewhere. See, for example, Leonard J. Weber, "Labor Unions and Two Concepts of Social Justice," in Adam J. Maida (ed.), *Issues in the Labor-Management Dialogue: Church Perspectives* (St. Louis: The Catholic Health Association, 1982), pp. 160–175.

seek our own self-interest and that the best system is one that allows
us to do just that. Perhaps one of the possible contributions of ethics
is to challenge the understanding of politics and public policy as
simply the regulation of interests. Richard Bishirijian calls for a
development of a more classical understanding of the purpose of
politics and policy.

> The classical political philosophers saw that political community is
> not only an alliance for the purpose of survival or of exchange. It is not
> a mere alliance for the resolution of conflicting interests, though that
> certainly is involved on the pragmatic level. It is possible after all to
> resolve conflicts of interest in a manner contrary to the common good.
> Politics is something more than deciding who gets what, when, and
> where. It includes that, but also the resolution of questions of a higher
> sort, such as what is good for the community as a whole.[12]

A more adequate social value system is one that is based on a
widely accepted understanding of a common good that transcends
individual self-interest. The special task of social ethics, then, would
seem to be to critique the dominant social value system and to
promote an alternative, more adequate social value system.

For religious leaders and religious ethicists, this role raises some
important questions. We need to think seriously, for example, about
the extent to which a specifically Christian ethic can serve as the
basis for contributing to an adequate public philosophy in a pluralistic society. We need to consider the question of whether the ethical
reflections that are made in regard to public policy considerations
should make use of religious concepts and symbols, should make
use of religious language.

At the heart of the question of Christian social ethics is the
question of the relationship of "Christ and culture" (to use the terms
found in the classic study by H. Richard Niebuhr).[13] This is the
question that I have already raised in regard to the "practicality" of
ethics: the extent to which we can expect Christian ethical ideals to
be workable in the real world. Many of the ethicists who argue for *a
specifically Christian ethic* (a specifically Christian social ethic)
appear to be convinced that the public order of politics and econom-

---

[12]Richard J. Bisharjian, *A Public Philosophy Reader* (New Rochelle, N.Y.: Arlington
House, 1978), p. 18. See also Robert B. Reich, "Toward a New Public Philosophy,"
The Atlantic Monthly, 255 (May, 1985), pp. 68–79.
[13]   H. Richard Niebuhr, *Christ and Culture* (New York: Harper, 1951).

ics is always going to be at odds with Christian beliefs and, therefore, the responsibility of Christians should be to maintain their witness in an unaccepting world; they should not expect that their values can actually be incorporated in public policy. Christ and culture, in this perspective, are not compatible.

The understanding that we have of the possibility of "Christianizing" society (of building a society based on our ethical beliefs regarding the meaning of justice) determines the nature of our contribution to the discussion about ethics and public policy. Stanley Hauerwas clearly recognizes the importance of this fundamental question and argues that religious ethics should not be directed to seeking to build a just social order:

> Surely in social ethics we should downplay the distinctively Christian and emphasize that we are all people of good will as we seek to work for a more peaceable and just world for everyone. Yet this is exactly what I am suggesting we should not do. I am in fact challenging the very idea that Christian social ethics is primarily an attempt to make the world more peaceable or just. Put starkly, the first social ethical task of the church is to be the church—the servant community. The church must learn time and time again that its task is not to make the world the kingdom, but to be faithful to the kingdom by showing to the world what it means to be a community of peace.[14]

As I have already indicated, I strongly disagree with this particular orientation. I have a more optimistic understanding of the possibility of achieving a somewhat more just society and a more optimistic understanding of the compatibility of finding a common ground between Christian ethical ideals and ethical ideals that arise from human reasoning. I do not think that religious ethicists can make significant contributions to public policy debates if they are constantly stressing the specifically Christian nature of our ethical beliefs.

This does not mean, of course, that religious leaders and ethicists should not be explicit about the extent to which their understanding of justice has been influenced by their religious beliefs. But, in the public policy discussions, they should stress, it seems to me, the values and principles that they can share with others, with those who do not adhere to their religious beliefs. I am very attracted to

---

[14]Stanley Hauerwas, *The Peaceable Kingdom* (Notre Dame: University of Notre Dame Press, 1983), pp. 99 and 103.

the approach that has been taken by the drafting committee of the American Catholic Bishops in the development to the Pastoral Letter on the U.S. Economy. Acknowledging and explaining their own religious perspectives, they then go on to state their ethical norms in ways in which they can be incorporated into the American public philosophy even by those who do not accept their religious staring point (for example, the stress on recognizing human rights in the economic sphere). Quite frankly, unless we recognize that a Christian understanding of social responsibilities is not significantly different from the understanding of social responsibilities that can be arrived at from other starting points, I fail to see an important role for religious ethicists in public policy debates and in the shaping of the public philosophy. What we would be doing in that case is separating ourselves from the most important element of life and leaving the field to others. It seems to me that the very concept of a public philosophy and the very intent to contribute to the shaping of public policy (something that I believe is a fundamental ethical responsibility) require a focusing on values that can be shared by individuals of very different religious beliefs or of no religious beliefs.

In addition to being more effective in contributing to public policy debates, an approach to social ethics that builds on values that can (potentially, at least) be accepted by others regardless of religious beliefs also has the advantage of being open to learning from "secular" wisdom. Ethicists need to be in constant dialogue with others in the effort to understand the social policies that can best promote justice and peace. An openness to "natural" ethics facilitates this dialogue.

There is a great concern in this country about "separation of church and state." And much of the discussion regarding the proper relationship between those two institutions is confusing and not very helpful. I do not want to be associated with those who think that individuals must put their religious values aside when they take positions on public policy issues. One of the most important recent studies of the role of religion in American democracy is Richard Neuhaus' *The Naked Public Square*.[15] There is much in Neuhaus' work that is valuable, especially his assessment of some of the more extreme separation of church and state rhetoric. He is also

---

[15]Richard John Neuhaus, *The Naked Public Square: Religion and Democracy in America* (Grand Rapids, MI: William B. Erdmans, 1984).

helpful in recognizing a need for a public philosophy that transcends various self-interests. But I do not follow Neuhaus in his emphasis on the need to have the public philosophy be religiously based. And I strongly disagree with him on what the content of that public philosophy should be (Neuhaus' fear of totalitarianism is not appropriately balanced, I think, by a commitment to meeting the needs of the poor and disadvantaged).

My model is neither that of Hauerwas nor Neuhaus but instead the implied position of the Economic Pastoral Letter. What is needed at this point, I think, is careful elaboration and defense of that approach.

4. Ethics as Advocacy

I have indicated above that the most important role that can be played by those interested in bringing ethical perspectives to bear on public policy issues is to attempt to shape the public philosophy or the social value system on which most policies are based. That would mean that a primary focus must be on underlying issues, on shaping the vision of what constitutes a just society. We need to be concerned, for example, with the understanding that we as a society have regarding economic/social human rights, regarding the right to private property, regarding the proper role of government in meeting human needs. We are to be involved in trying to shape the public understanding of social responsibilities—that much seems to be clear. The role of ethics and ethicists includes advocacy of a particular vision, of a particular understanding of the meaning of justice in a society like the one in which we live.

What is not so clear and what is much more the center of a debate today is the question of the extent to which those who are speaking to public policy questions from the perspective of religion or ethics should advocate particular policies. This is a very difficult question, I think, because there is probably only a fine line between the dangers that can be fallen into by going too far in either direction.

There has long been a discussion among religious ethicists about ethics as advocacy,[16] but the key focus of the discussion today seems to be in regard to documents being published by religious leaders (like the pastoral letters of the American Catholic Bishops). There

---

[16]See Joseph C. Hough, "Christian Social Ethics as Advocacy," The Journal of Religious Ethics, 5 (Spring, 1977), pp. 115–133.

are those who argue that church leaders should be promoting ethical principles, not advocating "partisan" policies (it is interesting, but not surprising, that those who take this position most often are those who disagree with the specific policy proposals found in some of these church documents)[17]. The concern is one that must be taken very seriously. There is a very real danger, in a society that understands politics to mean compromise among a variety of competing "special interest," to identify anyone who advocates particular policies as simply another special interest among others that can be accommodated or ignored (depending upon their clout).

There is no doubt in my mind that the primary focus of the ethical task of influencing public policy is the task of trying to shape the public philosophy by promoting ethical principles and a vision of the just society. This is the primary task; this the task that ethicists, philosophers, and religious leaders are the most qualified to undertake; there is the greatest need for this to be done, if we ever expect to improve the ways in which we as a society meet our justice obligations. One of the things that the Catholic Bishops are trying to do in their Pastoral Letters is to make a contribution to the public debate about nuclear policy and economic policies. They will be able to do that, if they are able to do that at all, by having an impact on the social value systems in this country.[18] I am convinced that, despite the focus of attention in the public media, that Part I of the draft of the Economic Pastoral (Ethical Norms) is much more important than Part II (Policy Recommendations).

The question remains, though, whether ethicists and religious leaders should be advocating specific public policies at all. The dangers are significant. I have already indicated that the key danger is the danger of being just another "special interest" that can be dealt with as other "special interests" are dealt with. It would seem that we need to be very careful not to identify the ethical perspective that we are trying to promote with a particular piece of legislation. There is always the possibility that when a particular legislative proposal is rejected in the political arena (sometimes for legitimate practical reasons) the reasoning and the convictions that led to support for that particular policy will be lost because of too close identification with the legislation. In those cases, where a particular

---

[17]See J. Brian Benestad, *The Pursuit of a Just Social Order* (Washington: Ethics and Public Policy Center, 1982).

[18]Leonard J. Weber, "Economics Pastoral: Contribution to American Social Ethics," *Groundwork for a Just World* (February, 1985).

ethical perspective could have enriched the discussion of other policy proposals, that perspective was lost when the bill was defeated. (Note, please, that most of the time support for particular *policies* is not the same as support for particular *pieces of legislation.*

There is another danger in becoming too closely associated with a particular policy. This is the danger of losing the larger, long-range perspective that is so important in bringing ethical considerations to bear on public policy issues. Individual polices are usually supported not because they are the full answer to the problems that are facing us as a society but because we believe that they are capable of moving us part of the way in the right direction. Becoming too closely tied to partial solutions can lead us to forget the proper relationship between the means and the end, to identify with policies that, if we kept the long-range perspective, we might need to separate ourselves from at some point in the future.

The above considerations are good reasons for being very careful about the ways in which ethics and ethicists are identified with specific public policy approaches. They do not mean, though, that specific policies should not be advocated; in fact, there are serious dangers associated, as well, with not advocating particular policies. One danger of articulating only the general principles is, quite simply, that one is not likely to be given any hearing at all if there is not some clarity regarding what the principles would lead to in terms of policy (assuming, as I do, that ethicists want to influence policies). There is, more importantly, a fundamental obligation for ethicists to be ethically responsible themselves, to propose only the visions and the principles that they have tested somewhat in terms of the applications. We are not really holding ourselves accountable for the impact of the ethical systems that we are promoting if we do not, in at least some suggestive ways, indicate the possible policy implications of what we are saying. The relationship between ethics and public policy is an aspect of applied ethics; we owe it to those to whom we are speaking or for whom we are writing to begin to work out some of the policy implications. Principles alone are not sufficient (just as, historically, ethicists have not considered it sufficient to propose only general principles when talking about personal behavior).

While we need to be very careful in the ways in which we advocate particular policy recommendations, I cannot support the position of those who argue that we have no justification for such advocacy. We should not tie ourselves too closely to particular candidates and bills, but not to promote the types of policies required is to do only part of the job.

Conclusion

What I have attempted to do in this brief paper is to address the agenda of "ethics and public policy," to identify some of the key questions that need thorough discussion as it becomes more common for explicit ethical perspectives to be given a hearing in public policy debates.

The agenda includes everything from clarifying our own understanding of the ethical basis for public policy (the dual ethic question) to determining whether we should support specific public policies. I have indicated some of my responses (briefly) and I hope to contribute more substantially to the discussion in the future. I invite you to join me in this enterprise.

A VIEW FROM THE UNDERSIDE:
DEFINING POWER IN LIGHT OF THE PREFERENTIAL
OPTION FOR THE POOR

Stephen J. Casey

The dream of reason did not take power into account. The dream was that reason . . . would liberate humanity from scarcity and the caprices of nature, ignorance and superstition, tyranny . . . [b]ut reason is no abstract force pushing inexorably toward greater freedom. . . . Its forms and uses are determined by the narrower purposes of men and women. . . . Medicine is . . . unmistakably a world of power where some are more likely to receive the rewards of reason than others.

The dominance of the medical profession . . . goes considerably beyond this rational foundation. Its authority spills over its clinical boundaries into areas of moral and political action. . . . [T]he profession has been able to turn its authority into social privilege, economic power and political influence.

> *The Social Transformation of American Medicine*
> by Paul Starr[1]

The root of these problems lies in faulty definitions. Power, being not a thing but a process of interaction among human beings, is simply not 'divisible' according to some static principle.

The power to define guarantees that the stereotypes . . . are created by the powerful and reflect only their view of life.

[The] view of power from below has been largely nonverbal. . . . The analytical view of power . . . has been directed to matters that concern the powerful: how to rule, how to seize a partrimony, how to justify a revolution. . . . But it's only half the story, it's the eagle's view from above, sharp and definable but separated from ordinary processes of living. To be content with this view alone is to agree that power belongs to the powerful as an attribute. . . .

> *The Power of the Weak* by Elizabeth Janeway[2]

---

[1]Paul Starr, *The Social Transformation of American Medicine* (New York: Basic Books, 1982), pp. 3–4.

[2]Elizabeth Janeway, *Powers of the Weak* (New York: Alfred A. Knopf, 1980), pp. 11, 14, 21.

A paper attempting to define *power* ought to begin with the note that power is seen from two perspectives—that of those who rule and that of those who are ruled. Even before the era of the sociology of knowledge and the "hermeneutic of suspicion," most people recognized that definitions give cognitive legitimacy to specific power relations. In this paper an attempt shall be made to describe the reality of power in a fashion that takes into account the "option for the poor."[3] This exercise, then, is an attempt to revitalize the perspective that sees power in terms of human relations with special emphasis on the position of the weak. It is opposed to the vision of power as an instrument.[4] Those exercising power instrumentally act as if power were their prerogative or possession; these people ignore the deep level of human relatedness in which creatures establish their own identities.

Economics, Politics, Power, Values: Interactions

In a contemporary secular society questions about power, economic status, relative distribution of wealth and political leverage are often dismissed as themes of theological reflection. It is clear, however, that answers to such questions reflect values which form our social reality and thus are appropriate objects of reflection from the perspective of Christian theology.

The issue of the values confronted here has been present since the

---

[3]See: Donal Dorr, *Option For the Poor* (Maryknoll, New York: Orbis Books, 1983) for a full development of the meaning of this expression. See also: Joseph Gremillion, *The Gospel of Peace and Justice* (Maryknoll, New York: Orbis Books, 1976) for documents and context.

[4]The use of the word *instrument* in this context could be misunderstood. It is used in the same way that Hannah Arendt uses it in her description of violence. See: Hannah Arendt, *On Violence* (New York: Harcourt, Brace and World, 1970). Violence has an "instrumental character. . . . [L]ike all other tools [it is] designed and used for the purpose of multiplying natural strength until . . . [it] can substitute for it" (p. 46). "[Violence] . . . like all means . . . always stands in need of guidance and justification through the ends it pursues . . ." (p. 51). In her approach peace and power are absolutes, i.e., they are ends in themselves and need no justification. This position separates her from those who see violence and power as identical; in this paper those identified as viewing power instrumentally do not. This conflictual approach to politics which denies any reason for obedience to rulers other than violence, will be treated later.

formation of the United States constitution; there has been a fundamental tension present between efforts to balance the demands of equality and liberty. In current terms the dispute is between equality of condition and equality of opportunity; others call it the dispute between fair share and fair play.[5] The conflict between those advocating one or the other of the poles noted results from the fundamental realization that it is impossible to separate economic and political equality.[6] In the United States "one can spin gold into influence; . . . the implicit political privilege enjoyed by business interests is by no means coincidental."[7] The United States regulates the use of private expenditure for partisan political purposes *less* than other democratic nations; we are virtually alone among democracies in permitting unlimited purchase of television ads by candidates.[8] These decisions favor liberty at the expense of equality.

Ironically recent attempts at reform designed to advance equality in the electoral process by increasing the representation of minorities and women have tended to increase class bias at the same time they were increasing distribution on the basis of age, sex and race. Those at lower levels of the socio-economic scale lost further ground in the battle to be heard. When these factors are added to the fact that there is a disproportionate representation of the more affluent and better educated among the politically active one can easily see why expenditures for programs such as education are supported over other, redistributive programs, despite the fact that education can begin anew a cycle of inequality.[9] In theory and practice Americans approach liberty in a more positive fashion than they approach

---

[5]It is not totally appropriate to segregate domestic situations from a global perspective when discussing power. However, for the sake of clarity one can illustrate the issues in an American political and economic context where relations are easily seen and can be clearly documented. Sidney Verba & Gary Orren, *Equality in America*, (Cambridge, MA: Harvard University Press, 1985), discuss the dilemma of equality; see their second chapter entitled "The Two Hundred Year's War" for a brief recapitulation of the history of this battle. The latter expression is from William Ryan, *Equality* (New York: Random House, 1981), pp. 3–36.

[6]See: Verba and Orren, pp. 1–20, as well as Dennis Wrong, *Power* (New York: Harper Colophon Books, 1979), Chapter 8, pp. 197–217, for interesting developments of what, it can be assumed, is a prereflective knowledge of most people not engaged in the social sciences.

[7]Verba & Orren, p. 15.

[8]The reporting of Elizabeth Drew on Washington politics has accented the role of purchased influence. See her *Politics and Money* (New York: Collier, 1983) for particulars about campaign money.

[9]Verba & Orren, pp. 15–17; Wrong, chapter 6, "The Bases of Power: Who Gets Mobilized?" pp. 146–196; both segments cover political participation in mass democracies.

the gap in political and economic equality. The poor and thus the powerless appear to have fallen into this gap.

It is possible to ignore the disjunction between our belief in equality and the economic realities.[10] Appeals can be made to the formal political equality that is part of the American political structure; however in a highly inegalitarian society formal political equality can favor those with the most advantages![11] Such an anomaly will require an elaborate ideology of defense that places the blame on those who "lose out."[12] Some current social science models such as what Verba and Orren call the dominant standard market economic model ignore this disjunction and in doing so ignore the role of values or beliefs. To do so is to employ an ideological perspective of reality masked as value-free inquiry.[13] Ironically Marxism, the oft-proposed alternative to the market ideology, does virtually the same thing. Neither perspective is adequate for those operating from within the prophetic stance of the Jewish and Christian traditions.[14]

---

[10]A brief discussion of this can be found in Verba & Orren, pp. 1–20, and in Ryan, chapter 1: "The Equality Dilemma," pp. 3–36.

[11]Wrong, pp. 198–9.

[12]See: William Ryan's classic *Blaming the Victim* (New York: Random House, 1976), and Philip Green's *The Pursuit of Inequality* (New York: Pantheon, 1981). Ryan develops his thesis in *Equality* as well.

[13]The way that the term *ideology* is defined is often confusing. The term is important to the critique used by the authors cited; further, its use here makes clarification crucial. The term has a long history of use before Marx, but most authors cite him as the key proponent of the idea. Karl Mannheim's *Ideology and Utopia* (New York: Harcourt, Brace and World, 1936) revived the non-Marxist use of the word. Mannheim's use of the concept is central to this paper; Peter Berger and Thomas Luckmann's *The Social Construction of Reality* (Garden City, New York: Doubleday, 1966) was also used. An ideology is not merely a set of ideas; it represents ideas that have been distorted by the interests of a ruling group so as to reinforce the status-quo and the interests of those who benefit from it. This distortion is unconscious; Berger and Luckmann work out the connections between it and false consciousness. Ideologies are a product of the institutionalization present in our social order. They create the rationale for an institution but in turn are created by it. Berger and Luckmann develop this dialectic in terms of alienation. Remy Quant in *The Phenomenology of Social Existence* (Pittsburg: Duquesne University Press, 1965) suggests that ideology can be thought of in the context of the category of "rationalization" in moral theology. Two reasons have been suggested for *not* using the term. The first is the Marxian use of it in the critique of religion; this is handled well in Werner Post's article "Ideology" in *Encyclopedia of Theology: The Concise Sacramentum Mundi*, ed. Karl Rahner (New York: Seabury Press, 1975), pp. 679–682. The second is the suggestion that its use relativizes all knowledge; a good critique of this position appears in Hans Barth's *Truth and Ideology* (Los Angeles: University of California Press, 1976).

[14]Verba & Orren (p. 2) comment on current perspectives that ignore values; these comments are familiar and repeated elsewhere frequently. For development of the issue of religion, see: Stephen J. Casey, "Definitions of Religion: A Matter of Taste?" *Horizons*, 11 (Fall 1984), 86–99.

Recent themes in some Third World, European and North American theologians have reflected this concern; their theologizing begins with a "critique of ideology" and is *value* oriented. A specific commitment to the poor is present.[15] It is necessary that we present, assess and critique definitions of power in this political context with these theological values.

Definitions of Power: A Typology

A definition of power is at once both simple and problematic. Dennis Wrong in his book *Power* adopts the following definition as his starting point. "Power is the capacity of some persons to produce intended and foreseen effects on others."[16] The problematic element occurs when we discuss the intentionality, the effectiveness, the latency, and the direction of power. It is difficult to discuss power without discussing its effects and then one must ask whether covert as well as overt results are to be admitted to the discussion. To extend the issue further Wrong suggests we cannot ignore the extensiveness (or range of areas in which power is exercised), the comprehensiveness (or fullness of power in the area applied) or the intensity (or strength) of power.

The problematic elements of such a definition were focused most clearly in the Sixties when the schools of the conflict and consensus theorists debated the nature of power; two key figures in this debate were C. Wright Mills and Talcott Parsons. Wrong's book is a synthesis of this debate designed both to cover the perennial elements and to advance the issue. Elements of these debates are of major importance in establishing a definition "from the bottom," but without clarity of context we will be able to see little of this. For clarity, therefore, I would like to present the major elements of definition in Wrong's synthesis within the context of a framework adapted from John Kenneth Galbraith's book, *The Anatomy of Power*.[17]

Galbraith suggests three types of power and later three sources of power. His brevity and inclusiveness make his typology exemplary.

---

[15]A selection of works would include Gustavo Gutierrez's *A Theology of Liberation*, Juan Luis Segundo's *The Liberation of Theology*, and, from different perspectives, Dorothee Soelle's *Strength of the Weak*, Jurgen Moltmann's *The Power of the Powerless*, and Stephen Charles Mott's *Biblical Ethics and Social Change*.

[16]Wrong, p. 2.

[17]John Kenneth Galbraith, *The Anatomy of Power* (Boston: Houghton Mifflin Company, 1983).

When thinking about power most people think first, and often exclusively, about what Galbraith calls *coercive power;* Wrong calls this phenomenon *force.* Coercive power wins submission by the ability to impose an alternative to an individual's or a group's preference that is sufficiently painful or unpleasant so as to cause the preference to be abandoned.[18] When resources are unevenly distributed (as they are most often) one can see how and why people focus on this aspect of power. This does not make the perspective either correct or useful to those viewing power from the bottom. While coercive power is not exclusively physical most observers regard it as such; in doing so one can miss some very consequential elements of coercion.

The second type of power is *compensatory power;* it is exercised by those offering rewards, most often money, to achieve submission.[19] Wrong deals with this type of power in his section on "authority by inducement." There he points out what those on the bottom always know, i.e., that this form of power is often harsh and exploitative despite its more benign facade. What comes to mind when discussing compensatory power is a business exchange. Yet, when one party holds the means of subsistence needed by another, there cannot be a reciprocal or contractual arrangement; there is a situation of inequity and control.[20] Compensatory power can be viewed as the base of economic power and coercive power as the base of political power. However, it is undesirable to forget the interrelationships and disparities noted above. The two are not practically distinct. In state socialist societies disparities may appear to be less. Note, however, that the power of the government in such a system is both coercive and compensatory. The opportunity for exploitation is clear.

The third type of power, *conditioned power,* is exercised by changing/forming the beliefs of others; this is best done in a subtle fashion.[21] Indeed, if conditioned power is to be used effectively those submitting should not be doing so consciously. People submit by reason of tradition, moral appeal, socialization, or the appeal of reason, and also because they have been manipulated or persuaded by the media or charismatic individuals. People accept competent authority (which is based upon expertise or technical competence)

---

[18]Galbraith, p. 4.
[19]Galbraith, pp. 4–5.
[20]Wrong, pp. 44–9.
[21]Galbraith, p. 5.

and legitimate authority (which is based on an acknowledged right to command and a parallel obligation to obey) as well.[22] In a good deal of the literature emphasizing conflict there is a tendency to regard such submission with acute cynicism. Wrong suggests caution. Legitimation of a position of authority need not be mere camouflage for force. Legitimate authority is not always fraud rising out a desire of the ruler to advance the position of the dominant.[23] It is correct to suggest that people have followed their rulers by choice; it also true that their motives for doing so have been mixed. Despite suggestions to the contrary some regimes have ruled totally by force—at least for a limited time. To admit either does not preclude the possibility that there is consent to political power or that conditioned power is a *bona fide* political reality.

Galbraith suggests three sources of power: *personality, property* and *organization*.[24] It is germane to indicate that the first, personality, is less consequential in the age of bureaucracy than it once was. Currently it is to be viewed less as an independent source than as one related to organization and an appropriate social-economic setting. Without appropriate conditions there are few charismatic leaders. As Wrong notes, in a democratic state the issue is more one of numbers than personality. Clearly this does not preclude the disproportionate influence of a charismatic leader, but it does indicate a consequential limit on this form of power. The idea of property as power has an inherent limit as well. Property is finite and can be expended, especially when it is employed in a compensatory fashion for the masses. Power, then, is focused in organization; it appears that power resides in groups. Hannah Arendt suggests that "[p]ower corresponds to the human ability not just to act but to act in concert. Power . . . belongs to a group and remains in existence only as long as the group keeps together."[25] Organizations have greater ability to impose alternatives, greater resources to compensate and greater cognitive conditioning power than individuals. When one recognizes that the primary focus of politics is often the state, it is necessary to reinforce this point. Groups are necessary to control the administration of the state, the ultimate form of organization.[26]

---

[22]See: Wrong, pp. 21–83, for his development of subtle forms of power.

[23]Wrong, pp. 99–103.

[24]Chapters 4–7.

[25]Hannah Arendt, *On Violence*, p. 44. To quote further: "In current usage we when we speak of a 'powerful man' . . . we already use the word metaphorically. . . ."

[26]This point was made emphatically by Max Weber in his often quoted essay,

Reflections and Assessment

It should be apparent that we may possess *conceptual clarity* when discussing power; it is less certain that we can make clear distinctions in practice. The forms of power interrelate in practice since they are parts of a wider network of interactions and relations. Stable power relations are not the product of a single type of power; this is especially true when the power is extensive, i.e., is exercised over a wide area of interactions. Our concepts are *ideal types* in the tradition of Max Weber. They represent strategic abstraction, i.e., they are the result of a subjective ordering of reality and distort reality by simplifying in order to clarify it. There are no pristine examples of what we have defined. Perhaps the best illustration of this is the change that takes place in regimes that have won control by coercion and almost immediately begin to attempt to legitimatize their power. Legitimacy is definitely to be subsumed into the category of conditioned power. The result is a mixture of forms of power.

In the context of the disputes in the Sixties this conclusion is perplexing. The lines during that period were distinctly drawn between consensus and conflict interpretations. Wrong's explanations of key traditional disputes represent a synthesis and a critique of each interpretation. It is appropriate to explore several areas of dispute between these schools. This should allow us to see the difficulties inherent in the exclusive use of either interpretation.

By their heavy emphasis on violence in the political sphere conflict theorists create the situation where all political power is defined in terms of violence. Force may be the *ultimate form of power* (Max Weber's famous dictum), but we cannot deny the reality and the importance of other *nonviolent forms of power*. Political power *may* result from a monopoly of physical force exercised by the state (Weber—again) but a state can establish its legitimacy nonetheless. This legitimacy will ultimately be based on some factors other than force.[27] The extreme of this position, Machiavellian cynicism, lacks necessary subtlety. It suggests that all forms of power are coercive;

"Politics as a Vocation." This essay appears in the collection, *From Max Weber*, edited by H. H. Gerth and C. Wright Mills (New York: Oxford University Press, 1946), pp. 77–128.

[27]See: Wrong, chapter 4, "Forms and Interactions," and chapter 5, "The Interaction of Coercion and Legitimation." These factors include: a need for order, and a desire to believe in the benevolence of the ruler or an ideology. This can even be seen in situations that seem to contradict the assertion. Examples include the situation prevailing in slavery and the Holocaust.

any suggestion to the contrary is seen as fraud. As appealing as the cynicism of this approach might be to those critiquing the powerful, it is important to note that political legitimacy is ultimately based on more than coercion.[28] While fear can never be completely dissolved into love in a power relationship, it does no one any good to deny the reality of power beyond what we described as coercive power or force.[29] Emphasizing violence works to the detriment of those on the bottom. In situations of exploitation those at the bottom have a paucity of the instruments of violence and the means to secure them. When we define power and politics in these terms we ignore the subjugated as active agents.

The other "mainline" academic approach to the study of power has different problems. The classical approach to the study of politics found in the consensus school illustrates a limit of the approach. Hannah Arendt is a representative of this group and an uncommonly perceptive political critic. Her vision, drawn from Aristotle, starts with the premise that society is a given, i.e., passive material to be shaped. In analyzing classical texts as is customary in this tradition, we come to accept an

> . . . analytical vision of power, [which] from Aristotle through Machiavelli, Hobbes, and the philosophers of the Enlightenment, of revolution, of communism, has been directed to matters that concern the powerful . . . [this view,] the eagle's view from above [is] sharp and definable but separated from ordinary living.[30]

On the latter point Wrong correctly critiques Hannah Arendt for espousing such a view as it separates the "entire realm of materials inequities and social welfare from the proper concern of politics."[31]

---

[28]This characteristic cynicism of the proletariat was noted by Reinhold Niebuhr during the Thirties in *Moral Man and Immoral Society* (New York, Charles Scribner's Sons: 1960). He notes that this is related to a belief in the economic determination of all thought in Marxism; we shall return to this later.

[29]Weber, for example, suggests that nonviolence is part of the "ethics of ultimate ends" and thus is inappropriate in the political arena. See his "Politics as a Vocation," and Gene Sharp's more adequate model of the relationships between politics and violence in "Ethics and Responsibility in Politics," *Inquiry* (Oslo), 3 (1964), 306.

[30]Janeway, p. 21. It is interesting to note that the eagle is a bird of prey.

[31]Wrong, p. 287, n. 63. With careful documentation Wrong develops this point. Arendt's failure is disappointing as her brilliance has made her very insightful otherwise; the source of her insight, Aristotle, is her downfall in this case. An interestingly parallel case can be seen in the writings of Leo Strauss which are currently consequential in academia. See a review of his work that appeared while this paper was in process: M. F. Burnyeat, "Sphinx Without a Secret," *The New York Review of Books*, 32, No. 9 (30 May 1985), 30–36.

Other representatives of the consensus school are likewise guilty of this error. There is a conceptual clarity and an apparent rationality in the classical approach. The consensus for which the approach is named is reached by placing at the margin of study the conflict resulting from a lack of real equality. The bias against the poor and powerless in this "rationality" hardly needs special notice.

The study of politics in an empirical mode sometimes escapes the problems of the classicists only to introduce other problems. There are those who simply do not see beyond the institutions of power, especially those focused in the state. An empirical study with such premises creates several problems. One can focus on power elites since this emphasis provides a clear empirical focus (a desirable end). It is assumed that one can identify those who affect policy and thereby get to the center of the power question. In doing so one presupposes that the elites are the only group affecting political reality (an undesirable end). Politics becomes one dimensional, i.e., it is seen only in terms of the movement of ruler to ruled. This is no asset to those on the bottom. The same holds true of the emphasis on the study of hierarchies and visible organizations. How misleading the picture produced can be is seen in a study of the leadership of the women's movement. One element of the movement, which is well organized, wants power *within* the system; it calls for redress of inequities. Another element challenges the system and its hierarchical presuppositions; clearly it does little good to try to identify the hierarchy in the latter. What one understands of the movement is heavily dependent upon what one studies.[32]

A view from the bottom would lead us to recognize that more occurs in politics than is apparent from the formal study of it. Wrong points out that politics certainly represents a struggle for power but is also an attempt to limit, resist or escape the power of others, especially that focused in the state.[33] Indeed it is appropriate to note, as Christian Bay does, that there are two sides of political action. One is power; the other is freedom. Says he, "the task of politics is to make oppressive realities *problematic*."[34]

---

[32]Verba and Orren see this clearly in their study of equality from the perspective of leaders (chapter 3). For an example of the first type of response see Judith Thurman, "All About Power," *MS.*, December, 1982, p. 32ff.; for the latter see Janeway, cited above.

[33]Wrong, p. 13.

[34]Christian Bay, *Strategies of Political Emancipation*, (Notre Dame, Indiana: University of Notre Dame Press, 1981), p. 3. Emphasis in the original is based on the desire to emphasize the reliance on Paolo Friere's concept of problem solving.

A precise statement about power from those on the bottom is difficult to get. It is important to remember that,

> the view of power from below has been largely nonverbal, a kind of subliminal awareness that's expressed in behavior rather than words. . . . The powerful, it appears, never study the weak; the weak are viewed as daydreamers who gratify their immediate wishes. . . . What the weak do not know about the processes of the power relationship is their own strength. The weak possess a latent appreciation of how power works in the everyday world, and especially of what happens when it works badly.[35]

It is our job to view the "option for the poor" at this juncture.

The Option for the Poor and Power

The expression, *the option for the poor*, is of recent origin; it dates from the Medellin conference in 1968. Taking a longer view the Catholic Church has had its tradition of social teaching articulated in papal documents for over one hundred years.[36] This tradition has been one of engagement on the side of the poor. It would be fair to say that from its inception the social teaching reflected in the encyclicals has been a response to perceived social/economic inequities that are self-perpetuating. The Church's current approach is marked by a hermeneutic of suspicion and an increasing partisanship, i.e., the Church has abjured "objectivity" for a commitment to the poor. There is a tendency to give greater respect to the grass roots analysis of the condition of the poor as well. This turn is not without controversy. The stress on solidarity and raising consciousness at both the grass roots and hierarchical level indicates a certain acceptance of, if not a wholehearted embracing of, a conflictual approach. As the "option for the poor" is based upon specifically religious commitments and warrants, there are and will be problems with conflict, social or physical.

In applying the idea of an option for the poor to the concepts of power we developed earlier, we can suggest several directions of exploration. The concept of power as instrumental will be rejected

---

[35]Janeway, pp. 21, 14.

[36]The work of Donal Dorr, *Option for the Poor* (Maryknoll, New York: Orbis Books, 1983), covers this history in a most illuminating fashion. This segment of the paper relies on Dorr's work for historical and substantive support.

at the outset. As Janeway suggested, this approach ignores the reality of human relationships and thus contributes directly to an alienated consciousness. Such a consciousness reinforces the status-quo and contradicts the interests of the downtrodden.

The emphasis on solidarity in the option for the poor fits well with the emphasis on the group nature of power; numbers constitute a formidable political resource, if organized. This is fortunate because in many cases the poor have little else than their numbers. There is already an emphasis on solidarity and equality in the morality of the proletariat that was noted by Reinhold Niebuhr; it is in marked contrast to the individualism of the privileged classes.

The option for the poor would appear to dictate the adoption of a conflict approach to power; the lack of a critical assault on the pretensions of the status-quo in the consensus approach should disqualify it. However neither the consensus nor the conflict theory is totally acceptable to Wrong; when approaching each from the perspective of the option for the poor we find that we, also, must take a dialectical path. The type of consensus thought represented by Arendt's classical approach reveals an elitism that is unacceptable; it reflects too little suspicion of the grounding of society and its ideology. It lacks some of the critical tools needed for penetrating moral analysis. At the same time the pervasive cynicism of conflict theory has the critical suspicion capable of unmasking "pretension and illusion" (Niebuhr). It also has a corrosive cynicism present in its critique of consciousness; this critique, which includes in its sweep religion, is based upon the assumption that all thought is determined by economics. The only escape in this view is "scientific" Marxism. This use of the term *science* is incompatible with religious thought and ultimately counterproductive to social change.[37] Further, as noted above, there is a tendency when thinking in this context to disregard all but force or coercive power. We are compelled to regard the competing visions of conflict and consensus as complimentary rather than separate realities; they interact at all levels. Specifically one must negate elements of either as well as affirm elements of both to be faithful to the option to the poor.

Flowing from this is a necessary caveat. Conservatives in attacking those on the bottom suggest that "if *they* would only . . . (work harder, study more, be more acculturated, etc.) *they* would succeed."

---

[37]See: Casey, "Definitions . . . ," pp. 90–91.

This is "blaming the victim."[38] Radical rhetoric emphasizes the "objective interests" of the classes (learned from scientific Marxism), and radicals say, "*if only* the oppressed would sacrifice and organize, the situation of oppression would be lifted." The problem is that organization is a long tedious task involving defeat and injury.[39] It should be the grass roots decision of the oppressed, then, as to whether and when action should be taken. A view from the bottom sees the necessity of the oppressed controlling their own destiny.

Thus far we have suggested that power is pluriform; for the poor there is less of a range of possibilities for the exercise of it because of a lack of access to compensatory power and to a lesser degree, to coercive and conditioned power. This lack of access to power is a logical result of the absence of property among the poor and the reduced value of personality as a source of power. What the poor possess is numbers, and with organization, not easily achieved, they have a means of altering their condition. This approach holds great potential for conflict; indeed some say violent conflict is the only way to a resolution of this situation of oppression.

The question of the powerless exercising conditioned power has to be addressed as this avenue has been *the* way that rulers maintain the status-quo. Conditioned power functions without being noticed by those affected. Sometimes conditioned power functions so subtly as to raise the issue of the latency of power.[40] In certain circumstances latency must be discussed as one is imputing power to those who do not seem to be exercising it. Thus certain parties, particularly those in power, appear to have greater control than merited by their actions. In some measure their power seems to flow from a perception by others that they possess resources they can wield if they wish; as a result others anticipate their wishes. This mechanism works against those lacking power for precisely the opposite occurs; they are assumed to be powerless and their wishes are ignored. The poor must begin the process of empowering themselves by recognizing the actual scope of the power of their rulers. Then to use conditioned power the poor need to establish a political reputation that will be credible. Even an indirect influence on affairs suggests the existence of a clearly articulated set of desires that can be anticipated in the context of bargaining. One cannot ignore the fact

[38]This is William Ryan's phrase and is the title of his book (noted above) which critiques the position well.

[39]See: Wrong, pp. 180–196, for an excellent development of this issue.

[40]See: Wrong, pp. 6–10 and 126–129.

that even indirect or negative exercise of power can be significant.

The ability to suppress an issue is a significant exercise of power; it suggests interaction between parties to establish a political agenda. When the powerless have entered into the establishing of a political agenda they are on their way to using the structures of society to bolster their position; they are active agents in the forming of their own destiny.

The ability to employ conditioned power is dependent on two conditions. As noted above, organization is necessary if numbers are to be consequential. In the situation of the oppressed there is a necessary link of consciousness, personal and political, with organization.[41] It is in the creation of solidarity rather than in mere formal participation in the rituals of politics that the oppressed will achieve control of their lives.[42] The second point is related to the first; a group must note that an exercise of conditioned power involves more than political action. Establishing power is an exercise in the sociology of knowledge and cultural criticism. Put in a somewhat different fashion one could say that the exercise of power will involve a critique of the vision we have of values and our social order. In addition it is the creation of a social order with its own legitimacy and values.

There are a number of issues which, while germane, are beyond the scope and length of this paper. The conflictual nature of power as developed here needs exploration. Does conflict necessarily mean violence? Is it necessary to accept a variation of the "just war" argument in the moral discussion of power and the emancipation of the oppressed? Can emancipation be achieved while preserving a standard of morality that is based upon a deliberate correspondence of means and ends? Can a conflict orientation fit into the Catholic social tradition, with or without violence? Can the Church play a role in the liberation of the oppressed? As the issue of emancipation cannot be purely theoretical, have we any models of organizations which, in practice, have had sustained effectiveness in organizing the poor to secure power?[43] These questions await answers in another context.

---

[41]This is the message of Paulo Freire in his books, *Pedagogy of the Oppressed* (New York: Seabury Press, 1970) and *Education for Critical Consciousness* (New York: Seabury Press, 1973).

[42]This point is developed well in an American context by Bay in *Strategies of Political Emancipation.*

[43]A name that has repeatedly appeared in reading about these issues is that of Saul

In conclusion it is appropriate to acknowledge that these reflections have been characterized by a paradox: we have discussed the
power of the powerless.[44] This paradox is best encapsulated by the
Apostle Paul in his second letter to the Corinthians (5:8–10):

> . . . on my own behalf I will boast not, except of my weakness. Three
> times I besought the Lord about this, that it should leave me; but he
> said to me "My grace is sufficient for you, for my power is made perfect
> in weakness. . . ." For the sake of Christ then, I am content with
> weakness. . . for when I am weak then I am strong.

Alinsky; a study of his work would be useful. Alinsky's works include: *Reveille for
Radicals* (New York: Random House [Vintage Books], 1969) and *Rules for Radicals*
(New York: Random House [Vintage Books], 1971); two older assessments of his work
are: Charles Silberman, *Crisis in Black and White* (New York: Random House [Vintage
Books], 1964) and Lyle Schaller, *Community Organization: Conflict and Reconcilia-
tion* (New York: Abingdon Press, 1966). A recently published biography is P. David
Finks, *The Radical Vision of Saul Alinsky* (New York: Paulist Press, 1984). For a
theological assessment that is highly useful in this regard see: Charles Curran, "Saul
D. Alinsky, Catholic Social Practice, and Catholic Theory," in *Directions in Catholic
Social Ethics* (Notre Dame, Indiana: University of Notre Dame Press, 1985), p. 171–
199.

[44]Special thanks are to be given to John McCarthy (Theology Department, Loyola
University of Chicago) and Ellen Miller Casey (English Department, University of
Scranton), for aid in editing; the remaining mistakes are mine.

Part Two

THEOLOGICAL RESOURCES

EQUALITY AND SUBORDINATION IN CHRIST:
Displacing the Powers of the Household Code in Colossians

Anne McGuire

In recent years, biblical scholars, historians, and theologians have begun to reassess the use of biblical texts in shaping the images and roles of women in the social orders of the Church, household, and world.[1] Several have shown that biblical texts have been used to support two divergent views on the relation of women and men in Christian tradition. One group of texts, including Gen. 1:26–27 and Gal. 3:28, has widely been used to claim scriptural authority for the full and equal partnership of women and men before God and in the social order. Another group, which includes Gen. 2–3, 1 Cor. 11–14, and the household tables of Colossians, Ephesians, and 1 Peter,[2] has been used in contrast to claim authority for the subordination of women and their exclusion from positions of leadership and authority in the Church, the household, and the world.[3]

---

[1]For useful studies see Krister Stendahl, *The Bible and the Role of Women* (Philadelphia, 1966); Rosemary R. Ruether, *Religion and Sexism: Images of Women in the Jewish and Christian Tradition* (New York, 1974); R. Ruether and E. McLaughlin, eds. *Women of Spirit: Female Leadership and the Jewish Christian Traditions* (New York, 1979); and Leonard Swidler, *Biblical Affirmations of Woman* (Philadelphia, 1979).

[2]The household codes, or *Haustafeln*, appear in Col. 3:18–4:1, Eph. 5:21–6:9, and 1 Peter 2:13–3:7. On the relation between Graeco-Roman and Christian codes, see David Balch, "Household Ethical Codes in Peripatetic, Neopythagorean and Early Christian Moralists," *SBL Seminar Papers* 11 (1977) 397–404. On the Christian adoption of the codes, see Elisabeth Schüssler Fiorenza, *In Memory of Her: A Feminist Theological Reconstruction of Christian Origins* (hereafter *IMOH*) (New York, 1983), 243–342, and D. Balch, *Let Wives Be Submissive: The Domestic Code in 1 Peter* (SBLM 26; Chico, 1981).

[3]Gen. 2–3, 1 Cor. 11, and the household tables are most often cited to support the subordination of women to men; to restrict women's roles, the texts most often cited are 1 Cor. 14 and the pastoral letters, where the bishop of the household of God is to be a *paterfamilias* in his own household. For further discussion see Fiorenza, *IMOH*, 335.

The conflict of such claims to scriptural authority derives in part from the divergent interests of the interpreters, but even more, from the diversity and tensions of the biblical canon itself.[4] In an effort to address the tension between equality and subordination in the Christian Bible and contemporary interpretation, this essay focuses on the development of Pauline notions of equality and subordination in the letter to the Colossians. *The first part* of the essay analyses the tension between egalitarian and subordinatist positions in the letters of Paul; *the second part* examines alternative models of feminist biblical interpretation; (and,) *the third part* applies one of these models to exegetical analysis, critique, and re-interpretation of the Christology and ethics of Colossians.

I. Equality and Subordination in the Letters of Paul

More than any other texts of the Christian Bible, the letters attributed to the apostle Paul embody the tension between egalitarian and subordinationist positions. It finds its sharpest expression among the letters most confidently attributed to Paul[5] in the "baptismal reunification formula" of Gal. 3:28, on the one hand, and in passages that restrict women's behavior, such as 1 Cor. 11–14, on the other. The later letters of the Pauline corpus, but especially Colossians, Ephesians, and the Pastoral letters,[6] give increasing emphasis to the subordinationist position, shaping a Church in which women are subordinate to men and excluded from positions of authority and leadership.

According to the baptismal formula quoted by Paul in Gal. 3:27–28, baptism inaugurates the believer's entry into the eschatological people of God, where distinctions of race, class, and gender are abolished in the unity of Christ.

> For as many of you as were baptised into Christ have put on (*enedusasthe*) Christ. There is neither Jew nor Greek, there is neither slave nor

---

[4]On contemporary evangelical use of biblical texts to support "egalitarian" and "traditional" views, see W. W. Gasque, "The Role of Women in the Church, in Society, and in the Home," *Crux* 19 (1983) 3–9.

[5]On the problem of authorship, see W. G. Kümmel, *Introduction to the New Testament* (Nashville, 1975) 315–87. Wayne A. Meeks, *The Writings of St. Paul* (New York, 1972), 1 presents 1 Thess., Gal., 1 Cor., 2 Cor., Rom., Phil., and Phlm. as the "undoubted letters of St. Paul . . . whose genuineness is beyond reasonable doubt."

[6]Meeks, *Writings*, 105, presents 2 Thess., Col., Eph., and the Pastoral letters (1 Tim., 2 Tim., Tit.) as "works of the Pauline school . . . the authenticity of which is disputed among modern scholars."

free, there is no male and female *(ouk eni arsen kai thélu)*, for you are all one *(pantes gar humeis heis este)* in Christ Jesus. And if you Christ's, then you are the offspring *(sperma)* of Abraham, heirs according to promise (Gal. 3:27–29).

Through baptism, Jews and Greeks, slaves and free, males and female "put on" Christ, the offspring or seed *(sperma)* of Abraham (Gal. 3:16), and thereby become heirs, regardless of race, class, or gender, of the inheritance given to Abraham by promise (Gal. 3:18).

Underlying these claims of unity and inheritance is the notion that the "putting on" of Christ in baptism overcomes distinctions of race (Jew and Greek), class (slave and free), and gender (male and female) that constitute human life in the cosmos, and establishes a new humanity,[7] the eschatological *ekklesia* of God "in which you are all one in Christ Jesus," all "heirs according to promise."[8]

Yet though distinctions of gender, race, and class do not apply to Paul's notion of inheritance in Christ, they do apply to his notions of order *(taxis)* in the Church.[9] These emerge most clearly in 1 Corinthians, where Paul is concerned to balance the Corinthians' perspective on their reception of spiritual gifts with a recognition of their incompleteness in the present world. Throughout the letter, Paul criticizes the Corinthians' claims to spiritual *charismata*[10] and urges them to do all things "for edification" and "in order" *(kata taxin)*.[11]

In his instructions, Paul reveals a definition of order in the cosmos

---

[7]Though Paul does not quote Gen. 1:26–27, the use of the terms "humanity" *(anthrōpos)* and "male and female" *(arsen kai thēlu)* supports the hypothesis that the pre-Pauline formula of Gal. 3:27–28 drew from traditions of its interpretation. Wayne A. Meeks, "The Image of the Androgyne," *HR* 13 (1974) 165–208, analyses the social functions of the image of the androgynous *anthropos* of Gen. 1:26–27 in early Christianity. Against his argument that Gal. 3:28 should be understood as the "eschatological restoration of man's original divine, androgynous image," see Fiorenza, *IMOH*, 205 and 235–36.

[8]W. A. Meeks, *The First Urban Christians* (New Haven, 1983) 107–110 discusses the social and theological senses of *ekklesia*; 150–57 on baptism as a rite of initiation.

[9]1 Cor. 14:39–40, for example, argues that "all things should be done decently and in order" when the Corinthians gather for worship.

[10]In 1 Cor. 4:8–21, Paul sarcastically contrasts the claims of the Corinthians ("Already you are filled!") with the state of the apostle ("We are fools for Christ's sake, but you are wise in Christ"). In 1 Cor. 13:11–12, he employs the images of the child and the mirror to emphasize the incompleteness of the *charismata* of prophecies, tongues, and knowledge.

[11]1 Cor. 14:26, 14:39–40, on the issue of Christian assembly. On the issue of meat offered to idols, Paul similarly urges the building up of the community (1 Cor. 8–10). For further discussion of 1 Cor. 11–14, see Fiorenza, *IMOH*, 226–236.

and the Church that builds upon the distinction and subordination
of persons by gender. In 1 Cor. 11:2–16, for example, even while
affirming the interdependence of woman and man in the new creation, Paul puts forward an argument based on a complex and ingen-
ious exegesis of Gen. 1–3 that distinguishes the wearing of veils as
appropriate to women but not to men, and subordinates women to
men. "For a man ought not to cover his head, since he is the image
and glory of God *(eikōn kai doxa theou)*, but woman is the glory of
man *(hē gunē de doxa andros estin)*" (1 Cor. 11:7).[12] In 1 Cor. 14,
Paul[13] continues to argue for a practice of distinction and subordination by gender.

> Women should be silent in all the assemblies, for it is not permitted to
> them to speak, but they should be subordinate *(hypotassesthōsan)*, as
> even the law says. If they wish to learn anything, let them ask their own
> husbands in the home *(en oikō)* (1 Cor. 14:34–35).

These passages show clearly the social limits of Paul's adoption,
or modification, of the pre-Pauline baptismal theology of unity and
equality in Christ. Though Paul himself was more concerned to
maintain the eschatological tension between the new and the old
than to restrict the involvement of women in the Church,[14] his
concern to restore social order to the Church in the world led him to
distinguish and subordinate in the terms of that world. As a result,
the spiritual and social implications of equality and unity in Christ
for Christian behavior in the Church and in the world reached their
limits in a theory and practice of distinction by gender.

In the household codes of Colossians and Ephesians, distinction
by gender supports a theory and practice of subordination that

---

[12]The subordination of women to men is also grounded in a pattern of descent from
God to Christ to man to woman: "The head of every man is Christ, the head of a
woman is man, and the head of Christ is God" (1 Cor. 11:3).

[13]Hans Conzelmann, *First Corinthians* (Philadelphia, 1975), 246, among many
others, argues that 1 Cor. 14:33b–36 is a non-Pauline interpolation. I agree with the
assessment of Fiorenza, *IMOH*, 230: "Since these verses cannot be excluded on
textual-critical grounds but are usually declared inauthentic on theological grounds,
it is exegetically more sound to accept them as original Pauline statements and then
explain them within their present context."

[14]Fiorenza, *IMOH*, 235–36 argues that "Paul's interests . . . are missionary and not
directed against the spiritual freedom and charismatic involvement of women in the
community." Yet that missionary concern leads Paul to distinguish the behavior of
women and men, and to subordinate the former but not the latter to the interests of
Christian mission.

virtually eliminates the tension between equality and subordination in Christ.[15] New Testament scholars have longed placed the adoption of these codes in the context of the historical development of early Christianity. Elisabeth Schüssler Fiorenza has recently given a feminist analysis of that development, placing the adoption of the household codes in a movement from a "discipleship of equals" in Jesus' ministry[16] to an ecclesiology that modified egalitarian traditions and restricted women's roles in Pauline Christianity, to the "patriarchal household of God" that replaces equality with subordination in post-Pauline Christianity.

> The post-Pauline and pseudo-Pauline tradition will draw out these restrictions in order to change the equality in Christ between women and men, slaves and free, into a relationship of subordination in the household which, on the one hand, eliminates women from the leadership of worship and community and, on the other, restricts their ministry to women.[17]

Such a feminist analysis provides an historical explanation for conflicting positions on the role of women in the Christian Scriptures. Even more important, the analysis of patriarchy and androcentrism in the development of Christianity and its Scriptures suggests a solution to the problem through Christian feminist critique and reinterpretation of biblical texts that sustain the patriarchal subordination of women to men in the contemporary Church, household, and world.

II. Alternative Models of Feminist Biblical Interpretation

Elisabeth Schüssler Fiorenza has developed a consistent program for such critique and re-interpretation in her widely discussed reconstruction of Christian origins[18] and in several essays on femi-

---

[15]As noted above (n. 5–6), the Pauline authorship of Col. and Eph. is disputed. The question of authorship, however, does not significantly alter the problem of the canonical authority of the texts. Both claim the authority of Paul, and were written either by Paul or by members of the Pauline school.

[16]Fiorenza, IMOH, ch. 4, esp. 140–153, offers a reconstruction of the Jesus movement as achieving liberation from patriarchal structures and the discipleship of equals.

[17]Fiorenza, IMOH, 236.

[18]The scholarly achievement of In Memory of Her has been widely recognized by scholars and scholarly organizations, including the CTS. Two review symposia of the book have appeared: P. Perkins, J. Koenig, R. Ruether, and B. W. Harrison, "Four Perspectives," Horizons 11 (1984) 142–53; and S. M. Setta, ed. "A Symposium on an Important Book," Anima 10 (1984) 95–112.

nist biblical interpretation.[19] As Fiorenza sees the task of feminist
biblical interpretation:

> a feminist critical interpretation of the Bible cannot take as its point of
> departure the normative authority of the biblical archetype, but must
> begin with women's experience in their struggle for liberation. In doing
> so this mode of interpretation subjects the Bible to a critical feminist
> scrutiny and to the theological authority of the church of women, an
> authority that seeks to assess the oppressive or liberating dynamics of
> all biblical texts. . . . As the church of women, we are not called to
> reproduce biblical structures and traditions, but to remember and
> transform our biblical heritage.[20]

The task of transformation is required, in Fiorenza's view, because
the androcentrism of the Church, its Scriptures, and biblical scholarship has concealed the presence of liberating traditions and wom-
en's voices in the Bible and the history of the Church. The solution
thus requires a method that can strip patriarchal traditions of their
authority and uncover traditions of equality and liberation that
remain hidden among the canonical texts or in tension with traditions of subordination.[21]

The model of feminist biblical interpretation that Fiorenza offers
is constituted by four elements:[22]

1. a *hermeneutics of suspicion* that starts from the assumption
that biblical texts are androcentric and serve patriarchal functions;

2. a *hermeneutics of proclamation* that assesses critically the
theological significance and power of biblical texts for contemporary
communities of faith, and denounces those that legitimate patriarchal oppression;

3. a *hermeneutics of remembrance* that seeks to adjust the andro-

---

[19]Elisabeth Schüssler Fiorenza, *Bread Not Stone: The Challenge of Feminist Biblical Interpretation* (Boston, 1984) (hereafter *Bread*) gathers together several of Fiorenza's previously published essays on feminist biblical hermeneutics.

[20]Fiorenza, "Women-Church: The Hermeneutical Center of Feminist Biblical Inter-pretation," *Bread*, 13–14. An earlier version of the same essay appeared as "Emerging Issues in Feminists Biblical Interpretation," *Christian Feminism: Visions of a New Humanity*, ed. Judith Weidman (New York, 1984) 33–54.

[21]Fiorenza, "Women-Church, *Bread*, 16 draws an illuminating connection between this search for lost traditions and the woman's sweeping the whole house in the Parable of the Lost Coin. In most of her writings, Fiorenza limits her search to texts of the Christian Bible, ignoring texts, such as the Acts of Paul and Thecla, that provoca-tively suggest alternative images of women.

[22]Fiorenza, "Women-Church," *Bread*, 15–22; "Emerging Issues," 47–54.

centric memory of biblical history by reconstructing women's history, recovering in memory both the positive remnants of women's equality and leadership in the earliest Christian communities,[23] and the struggles of women in the biblical and historical past;

4. a *hermeneutics of creative actualization* that is both critical of the structural sins of sexism, racism, or classism, and constructive of a new vision of Woman Church through a rediscovery of the biblical story, retold from a feminist perspective.

As indicated above, the point of departure and guiding criterion in this process of critique, recovery, and reinterpretation is not the normative authority of the Bible, or even those portions that affirm equality and liberation. What guides critical feminist interpretation instead is "women's experience in their struggle for liberation" under and against patriarchy. Under the terms of Fiorenza's model, biblical texts are subjected to critique from the perspectives of women's experience, feminist theory, and the historical prototype of the discipleship of equals achieved in the ministry of Jesus.[24]

> Just as Jesus according to the Gospels realized freedom toward Scripture and tradition for the sake of human well-being and wholeness (cf. Mark 2:27), so too a feminist critical hermeneutics seeks to assess the function of the Bible in terms of women's liberation and wholeness. It follows Augustine, Thomas, and the Second Vatican Council in formulating a *criterion* or *canon* that limits inspired truth and revelation to matters pertaining to the salvation, freedom, and liberation of all, especially women. But it derives this canon, *not* from the biblical writings but from the contemporary struggle of women against racism, sexism, and poverty as oppressive systems of patriarchy and from its systematic explorations in feminist theory. It can do so because it does not understand the Bible as perduring archetype but as historical prototype or as formative root-model of biblical faith and life.[25]

In this model of feminist biblical interpretation, biblical texts come "under the authority of feminist experience."[26] Those texts

---

[23]Fiorenza, "Women-Church," *Bread*, 20 argues that the remnants of a nonpatriarchal ethos indicate that "a 'patriarchalization' process was not inherent in Christian community but progressed slowly and with difficulty."

[24]Fiorenza, *IMOH*, 140–54, does not acknowledge as fully as she might the extent to which her "historical reconstruction" may idealize the social structure of the Jesus movement. Even under stringent historical-critical analysis, the gospels are problematic sources for the task of historical reconstruction.

[25]Fiorenza, "Women-Church," *Bread*, 13–14, emphasis is mine.

[26]Fiorenza, "Women-Church," 14: "It places biblical texts under the authority of feminist experience insofar as it maintains that revelation is ongoing and takes place for the sake of our salvation."

judged to be "historical prototypes" can inform the feminist vision
of liberation and salvation, but they do not constitute the criterion
or canon that makes such judgments and "limits inspired truth and
revelation to matters pertaining to the salvation, freedom, and liberation of all, especially women." It is only in combination with and
"under the authority of" perspectives drawn from women's struggle
against patriarchy and feminist theory that biblical texts, serving as
"historical prototypes" or "formative root-models" contribute to
formulating the criterion by which such judgments are made and
texts are re-interpreted.

   Fiorenza's articulation of the problem of androcentrism and proposal of a feminist hermeneutical method make important contributions to biblical scholarship and interpretation. Yet, as Fiorenza
herself would admit, her proposal cannot claim to be the exclusive,
authoritative model for feminist biblical interpretation. As in feminist studies more generally, those concerned with the same problems may develop alternative approaches from varying perspectives
to the task of feminist theology and biblical interpretation.[27]

An Alternative Model

   The critical feminist interpreter, for example, may, instead of
placing biblical texts under the authority of women's experience,
feminist theory, or reconstruction of historical prototypes, place the
texts, as well as the criteria of experience, theory, and historical
reconstruction, under the authority of the biblical texts themselves.
According to this model, literary and theological features of a particular text, critically discerned, provide the basis for an *internal*
critique of the text by the text. Through exegetical analysis, the
interpreter seeks to expose internal inconsistencies that subvert the
theological or ethical claims of the text. This exegetical analysis and
critique precede and control the external critique drawn from the
contemporary perspectives of feminist experience and theory, and
together they form the basis for critical feminist re-interpretation. In
this model, biblical texts are placed under the authority of biblical
texts, critically analysed and discerned from literary, theological,
and feminist perspectives.

---

   [27]Fiorenza, "Women-Church," 3, notes that "feminist studies articulate the feminist
paradigm in different ways and according to various philosophical perspectives. . . .
There exists not one feminist theology or *the* feminist theology but many different
expressions and articulations of feminist theology."

This alternative diverges from Fiorenza's model in at least two ways. First, it distinguishes internal exegetical analysis and critique from external critique and re-interpretation, but views them as integrated parts of the interpretive process, ordered to reflect the authority of the biblical text. Similarly, it distinguishes without separating literary, theological, socio-historical, and ethical features of a text, and views these features as interconnected parts of the textual whole. Second, this alternative acknowledges the role of the interpreter's contemporary feminist perspective in analysing the text, but restores greater authority to the biblical text. In this model, the text is also subjected to critique and re-interpretation, but the criteria and objects of such critique and re-interpretation are not feminist experience or theory, but theological, literary, and ethical features discovered within the text itself. Through critical exegesis informed by a feminist perspective, the interpreter exposes resources and inconsistencies within the text, subjects the inconsistencies to internal critique, followed by critique from the perspective of feminist theory, and in its re-interpretation suggests alternatives that remain hidden from, but bound to, the text.

The interpretations opened up by this approach, like the contemporary critical perspectives brought to the text, cannot be identified with the "original meaning" or "intention" of the text. They are, rather, contemporary feminist re-interpretations emerging from the Christian feminist concern to address critically the problem of authoritative biblical texts that continue, in diverse ways, to challenge and restrict the images and roles of women and men in the Christian tradition. With this understanding of the interpretive task, I turn now to apply the interpretive model outlined above to the issue of equality and subordination in Christ in the letter to the Colossians.

III. Exegetical Analysis, Critique, and Re-Interpretation of Colossians

The author of Colossians, whom I shall call Paul, writes to a community he had never met, but about whose problems he appears to be well informed.[28] He writes in order to retrieve the Colossians' "good faith" and "love of the Spirit" (Col. 1:4, 8) from the threat of

---

[28]Col. 1:7 identifies Epaphras, Paul's "beloved fellow servant" as founder of the Colossian church.

"philosophy" or "empty deceit" to which some in the community had turned,[29] and to return to "a life worthy of the Lord" (1:10), rooted and built up in the Lord.

> I say this that no one may delude you with beguiling speech . . . For though I am absent in body, yet I am with you in spirit, rejoicing to see your good order (taxin) and the firmness of your faith in Christ. As therefore you received Christ Jesus the Lord, so live in him, rooted and built up in him and established in the faith, just as you were taught, abounding in thanksgiving. Be on your guard that no one snares you by philosophy and empty deceit according to human tradition (kata tēn paradosin tōn anthrōpon), according to the elements of the cosmos (kata ta stoicheia tou kosmou) and not according to Christ (ou kata Christon) (2:4–8).

This passage builds on two oppositions: between the "philosophy" to which some have been seduced[30] and the tradition they had received;[31] and between the stoicheia of the cosmos and Christ. The two poles of these oppositions suggest at the same time a connection, on the negative side, between "philosophy," "human tradition," and the "stoicheia of the cosmos," and, on the positive side, the traditions that had been taught, baptism, and Christ.

To live a life rooted in Christ, he tells them, is not to "submit to regulations . . . according to human precepts and doctrines (kata ta entalmata kai didaskalias tōn anthrōpon)" (2:20–22), nor to adopt beliefs and practices "according to the stoicheia of the cosmos." It is, rather, to be faithful to what they received, to live "according to Christ. For in him the entire fulness of deity (pan to plērōma tēs theotētos) dwells bodily (sōmatikōs), and you have been filled (pe-

---

[29]Col. 2:8. The precise nature of this 'philosophy' is unclear, but most commentators agree that it involves beliefs and practices designed to establish a proper relation to the powers and principalities of the cosmos. For discussion see Fred Francis and W. A. Meeks, Conflict at Colossae (SBLSBS 4; Missoula, 1973); and Eduard Lohse, Colossians and Philemeon (Philadelphia, 1971), 2–3, and 92–99.

[30]Lohse, Colossians, 94 points out that the verb "to snare" or "capture and carry off booty" (sulagōgein) "indicates seduction but also points to the evil intent of those who are trying to gain influence over the community."

[31]See also 1 Thess. 4:1, Gal. 1:9, Phil. 4:9, 1 Cor. 11:2, and 1 Cor. 15:1–5 where Paul uses similar expressions (paralambanō, paradosis, didaskō) to remind his communities of the theological and ethical teachings they received from him and other apostles. Lohse, Colossians, 93 argues that "Christ Jesus the Lord" in Col. 2:6 refers not to teachings of Jesus, but to "the content of that which had been communicated to the community in the apostolic tradition," citing also Phil. 2:11, cf. 1 Cor. 12:3, Rom. 10:9.

plērōmenoi) in him, who is the head *(kephalē)* of every power and principality *(pasēs archēs kai exousias)"* (2:9–10).

This passage explicitly links the Christ they received (2:6) with the hymnic confession of Col. 1:15–20, according to which Christ the "image of the invisible God, the first-born of all creation . . . in whom all the fulness [of God] *(pan to plērōma)* was pleased to dwell" (1:15–20). At the same time, it reminds them that the Christ of this hymn, the Lord of creation and redemption, whom they received in the tradition of hymnic praise, they also received in baptism.

> You have to come to fulness of life in him, who is the head of every principality and power. In him also you were circumcised with a circumcision made without hands, by putting off the body of flesh in the circumcision of Christ, and you were buried with him in baptism, in which you were also raised with him through faith in the working of God who raised him from the dead (2:10–12).

In baptism, they began to share in Christ's death and his resurrection from the dead. Their submission to the principalities and powers of the cosmos, however, betrays their failure to understand. "If with Christ you died to the *stoicheia* of the cosmos, why do you submit to regulations *(dogmatizesthe)* as if you were still living in the cosmos?" (2:20). "If you have been raised with Christ, seek the things that are above *(ta anō)*, where Christ is, seated at the right hand of God. Set your minds on things that are above, not on things that are on earth *(mē ta epi tēs gēs)"* (3:1–2).

The Colossians' life of ascetic and cultic practices (2:16–18, 20–23) directs them not to the things that are above, with Christ, but to things of the cosmos, to human tradition and the *stoicheia* of the cosmos. This compromises the gospel and threatens to cancel out their transformation through baptism in Christ: "You, who once were estranged and hostile in mind in evil works, he has now reconciled *(apokatēllaxen)* in his body of flesh by his death to present you holy and blameless and irreproachable before Him, provided that you continue in the faith, stable and steadfast" (1:21–23). By adopting the "philosophy" which is, in fact, "empty deceit," the Colossians betray not only their own misunderstanding, but the gospel of Jesus Christ himself.

All of the passages cited above link baptism with the new life of faith and order *(taxis, 2:5)*, rooted in Christ. Yet unlike 1 Corinthians,

Colossians does not immediately link order in the community to distinctions of gender. Given the different problems he is confronting, the 'Paul' of Colossians focuses primary attention on the distinction between Christ and the *stoicheia* of the cosmos, between the things above and the things on earth. The issue of gender distinctions arises initially by its absence from Colossians' version of the baptismal formula.

> Put to death therefore the parts that are upon earth. . . . In these you once walked, when you lived in them. But now put them all away. . . . Do not lie to one another, seeing that you have put off *(apekdusamenoi)* the old *anthropos* with its practices and have put on *(endusamenoi)* the new anthropos, which is being renewed in knowledge after the image *(kat'eikona)* of its creator. Here there cannot be Greek and Jew, circumcised and uncircumcised, barbarian, Scythian, slave, free man, but Christ is all things *(panta)* and in all *(en pasin)* (3:9–11).

This version of the baptismal formula builds on the distinction between things above and things on earth, and joins it to the image of "putting on" *(endusamenoi)* found in Gal. 3:28. But in place of "Christ," the Colossians formula states that the baptized have put on "the new *anthropos*, which is being renewed after the image of its creator." To this it adds the complementary image of "taking off *(apekdusamenoi)* the old *anthropos* and its practices."

Like the pre-Pauline baptismal formula of Galatians, Colossians' version proclaims that baptism establishes a new relationship with Christ, in which "Christ is all things and in all," but it extends the idea of unity in Christ with the image of "the new *anthropos* renewed in the image of its Creator." Even more important, it eliminates the antithetical juxtapositions of Gal. 3:28 and omits male and female *(arsen kai thēlu)* from the series of distinctions that replaces it.[32] This omission suggests what the rest of the text confirms: that the author of Colossians was more interested in developing the cosmic and ethical signification of the relation between the new *anthropos* put on in baptism and the Christ of creation and redemption.

Yet while analysis of Colossians confirms and explains this inter-

---

[32]Lohse, *Colossians*, 143–44, argues that the differences were already present in the tradition, and fails to discuss the striking omission of male and female. Fiorenza, *IMOH*, 251–52, suggests that the author of Col. quotes Gal. 3:28 but changes it considerably.

est, at the same time it exposes the text's failure to develop the potential implications of its claims about Christ's reign over the principalities and powers of the cosmos for the new life of the baptized. In what follows, I want to develop this analysis of the relation between Christology and ethics in Colossians, and apply the model of feminist interpretation outlined above to the resources that are hidden in Colossians' Christology and betrayed in its adoption of a pattern of dominance and subordination in the household code of Col. 3:18–4:1.

Christology and Ethics in Colossians

According to the Christology of Colossians, Christ stands first, as Lord, ruler, and head over all things in creation and redemption. The Colossians hymn names him "the image (eikōn) of the invisible God, the first-born of all creation (prōtotokos pasēs ktiseōs), for in him were created all things (ta panta) in the heavens and on earth, visible and invisible, whether thrones or lordships (thronoi eite kuriotētes), or principalities or powers (archai eite exousiai)" (1:15–16). Christ is thus the head (kephalē) of the body, the Church (1:18),[33] and "the archē (the beginning, rule, or principality) and first-born from the dead that in all things (en pasin) he might be preeminent (prōteuōn) (1:18).

Through his death and resurrection, the world was reconciled and his rule over the principalities and powers established (1:19–20; 2:14–15).[34] In the image of the cosmic body, he is "the head of every principality and power" (2:10). All other forms of lordship, rule, or authority stand under the rule of the first-born of creation and redemption.

In baptism, Christians participate in this reconciliation and redemption. "And you, who were once estranged and hostile in mind, doing evil deeds, he has now reconciled (apokatēllaxen) in his body of flesh (en tō sōmati tēs sarkos autou) by his death" (1:21–22). The Christian participates in this death "with a circumcision made

---

[33]Lohse, Colossians, 42–43, 52–55, among others, views "of the church" as an interpretive addition to a tradition that originally referred to Christ as the head of the cosmos.

[34]The hymn of Phil. 2 similarly highlights the cosmic dimensions of the salvation brought in Christ; see esp. Phil. 2:9–10. F. F. Bruce, "Colossian Problems. Part 4: Christ as Conqueror and Reconciler," BiblSac 141 (1984) 291–302 illustrates the compatibility of the images of reconciler and conqueror in Colossians.

without hands, in the putting off *(en tē apekdusei)* of the body of flesh *(tou sōmatos tēs sarkos)* in the circumcision of Christ" (2:11). This anticipates the language of "putting off *(apekdusamenoi)* the old *anthropos* with its practices" in baptism, and points again to the relation between Christology, baptism, and ethics in the theology of Colossians.

The passage that follows builds on the connections between Christology, baptism, and ethics, but extends the discussion to the cosmological dimensions of the redemption brought through Christ.

> And you who were dead . . . God made alive together with him, having forgiven us all our trespasses, having cancelled the bond which stood against us with its regulations *(dogmasin)*, this he set aside nailing it to the cross. He stripped *(apekdusamenos;* disarmed or put off, cf. 3:9) the principalities and powers *(tas archas kai tas exousias)*, and exposed them publicly *(edeigmatisen)*, triumphing over them in him (2:13–15).

This text reminds the Colossians that God triumphed over cosmic powers by stripping them of their false claims to power in the death and resurrection of Christ.[35] By reminding them that they participated in Christ's death and resurrection through baptism, he assures them that they participate as well in this victory.

This assurance builds on a crucial, but unstated connection between the principalities and powers of the cosmos and the old *anthropos* put off in baptism. As the principalities and powers were stripped of their power *(apekdusamenos)*[36] on the cross, so the old *anthropos* and its practices were stripped *(apekdusamenoi,* 3:9) in baptism. On the positive side, it builds on the connection between the risen Christ, "the image *(eikōn)* on the invisible God" (1:15), and the new *anthropos,* "renewed in the image *(kat' eikona)* of its creator" (3:9–10). The connection of these two pairs (cosmic powers-old *anthropos;* Christ-new *anthropos)* corresponds in turn to the opposition of the first and second terms of each pair. The cosmic powers *(archai* and *exousiai)* are opposed to the true *archē,* Christ, as the old *anthropos* is opposed to the new.

The structural similarity between the terms of Christ's death and

---

[35]Lohse, *Colossians,* 112: "Though they brought Christ to the cross, God has exposed them on the cross in their powerlessness (cf. 1 Cor. 2:6–8). God has proclaimed publicly that he has divested them of their usurped majesty by putting them on public display and exposing them to ridicule."

[36]Against earlier interpretations, Lohse, *Colossians,* 11–112 notes that most exegetes rightly maintain that God is the subject of the entire section.

resurrection and Christian baptism reminds the Colossians that their stripping off the old *anthropos* and putting on the new in baptism draws its power from God's stripping the cosmic powers on the cross and raising Christ from the dead. Thus, baptism has already begun for them the displacement of the cosmic powers and the reconciliation of all things, on earth or in heaven (1:20) in the new reign of Christ.

Colossians' argument for the relation between Christology, cosmology, baptism, and ethics functions primarily to convince its readers to abandon their "philosophy and empty deceit according to human tradition *(kata tēn paradosin tōn anthrōpōn)*, according to the *stoicheia* of the cosmos, and not according to Christ (2:8)," and return to a life in Christ. Against false teachings that cosmic powers still rule, the text assures its readers that Christ now reigns over the principalities and powers as head of the whole cosmic body, and over the one body of the Church (1:18, 2:19), which "nourished and knit together through its joints and ligaments grows with a growth that is from God" (2:19). Since they became members of that body when they stripped off the old *anthropos* and put on the new, they should abandon the tradition of *anthrōpoi* with its ascetic and cultic practices (2:16–23). God has triumphed over the cosmic powers they serve, as they have "died to the *stoicheia* of the cosmos" (2:20) so they should live in Christ who now rules over all things, "rooted and built up in him and established in the faith, just as you were taught" (2:6–7).

As the argument of Colossians turns from proclamation to exhortation, it begins to define the life of the new *anthropos* as one "where there cannot be Greek and Jew, circumcised and uncircumcised, barbarian, Scythian, slave, free, but Christ is all and in all" (3:11). The omission of the pair "male and female" from this formula appears to suggest that the reconciliation and transformation effected through baptism does not involve a corresponding transformation in the structure of social relations. This suggestion is confirmed as the instructions on the life of the new *anthropos* take specific shape in Col. 3:12–4:1.

> Put on *(endusasthe)* . . . above all these love *(agapēn)*, which binds everything together in perfect harmony. And let the peace of Christ, to which indeed you were called in the one body, rule in your hearts, . . . And whatever you do, in word or deed, do everything in the name of the Lord Jesus, giving thanks to God the Father through him. Wives

(gynaikes), be subordinate (hypotassesthe) to your husbands (tois an-
drasin), as is fitting (hōs anēken) in the Lord (en kyriō). Husbands, love
your wives, and do not be harsh with them. . . . Slaves, obey in
everything those who are your earthly masters (tois kata sarka kyriois),
not with eyeservice, but in singleness of heart, fearing the Lord (3:12–
4:1).

As this passage moves from the image of love and peace in the body
of Christ to the structure of domestic relations, it suggests a connection between the life of the new anthropos renewed in baptism and
the household code.

This code of domestic relations establishes an order (taxis) or
pattern of dominance and subordination in which dominant and
subordinant positions are determined by distinctions of gender,
generation, and class. Within this order, wives, children, and slaves
are sub-ordinated to, or positioned under, their super-ordinated
husbands, parents, and masters (kyrioi). Colossians' adoption of this
code and omission of gender categories in its version of the baptismal formula recommend and legitimate this pattern of dominance
and subordination as "fitting in the Lord" and normative for the
Christian church.

The recommendation of the code as "fitting in the Lord" implies
a correspondence and harmony between the code's articulation of
social order and the divine order articulated in the Christological
hymn which proclaims Christ's lordship over all creation (1:15–18).
Since he is the "first-born of all creation" and "first-born from the
dead," Christ is the archē and Lord (kyrios) over all, including all
forms of lordship or dominion (kyriotētes). He is "head of every
principality and power, of every ruler and authority (pasēs archēs
kai exousias)" (2:10). The claim that the household code is "fitting
in the Lord," then, seems to imply that the pattern of dominance
and subordination in the household corresponds to this Christology
of dominion, that its pattern of rule and authority finds support in
Christ's rule and authority over all things. Thus, it seems to suggest,
worldly masters (hoi kata sarka kyrioi) and husbands stand in
relation to, or over, their slaves and wives as Christ the Lord stands
in relation to all things in heaven and on earth.

The recommendation that the household code is "fitting in the
Lord" does not imply that the super-ordinate position of earthly
masters (kyrioi) or husbands equals that of the Lord. Though earthly
masters take the super-ordinate and dominant position in household

relations, the last verse of the instructions reminds them that they take the sub-ordinate position in relation to Christ, who reigns as Lord of all creation. "Masters *(hoi kyrioi)*, treat your slaves justly and fairly, knowing that you also have a Master *(kyrion)* in heaven" (4:1). "As is fitting in the Lord" thus points to the similarity of language *(kyrios)* and structure in the relation of master to slave and Lord to creation, but preserves their utter distinction, as an earthly lord rules over his slaves only in the social cosmos of the household, but the heavenly Lord rules over the entire cosmos of creation. The ethical instruction of Colossians thus distinguishes the social cosmos of the household as a subset of the cosmos over which Christ reigns, but builds on their similarity to legitimate the pattern of dominance and subordination by gender (husbands-wives), generation (parents-children), and class (masters-slaves) in the household as "fitting in the Lord."

Colossians thus recommends and legitimates the order of the household code as fitting for the church by implying a correspondence and harmony between its Christology and its household ethics. From the perspective of Colossians and many of its interpreters, there is no tension between its Christology and the ethics of the household code. In their view, the social order of dominance and subordination, rule and subjection, in the household code stands under the divine order of Christ's rule, but conforms to its structure. Within the logic of the letter, then the code cannot be said to participate in the rule of the principalities and powers of the cosmos or to fall to their diplacement in the death and resurrection of Christ.

Viewed from another perspective, however, the text of Colossians undermines this strategy of legitimation, and its Christology subverts the ethics of the household code. As the exegetical analysis above has shown, Colossians' adoption of the household code does not merely "draw out Pauline restrictions," eliminate egalitarian traditions, and establish subordination as the normative position of women in the social order of household, Church, or world. More than that, it overlooks the potential resources and social implications of its own Christological claims, namely, that God stripped the principalities and powers of their power (2:15) and raised Christ from the dead (2:12) to be pre-eminent over all things (1:18).

Under an alternative reading which draws from these Christological claims, the earthly pattern of dominance and subordination and the text's own strategy of legitimation fall to critique and the text is opened up for re-interpretation. Against Colossians' legitimation of the household code, this strategy of critique and re-interpretation seeks to reclaim for feminist biblical interpretation the rich, but largely untapped force of the claim that God exposed the principalities and powers and stripped them of their power in Christ. Similarly, it seeks to extend this image to the conception of baptism as a stripping off the old *sarkic anthropos* with its false claims to power, and a putting on the new spiritual *anthropos* renewed in the image of the one who stripped the cosmic and *sarkic* forces of their power and established the rule of Christ the Lord.

This critique and re-interpretation is supported by exegetical, socio-historical, and feminist analysis, but gains its greatest force from their integration in an interpretive strategy of re-naming the principalities and powers of the cosmos to include the pattern of domination and subordination in the social cosmos of the household code. Each of these perspectives exposes critical problems in the text, as it illuminates its potential for re-interpretation.

Exegetical analysis of the letter as a whole exposes the text's strategy of legitimation and its failure to link the social cosmos of the household code to the *stoicheia,* principalities, and powers of the cosmos, or even to the practices of the old *anthropos* (3:9) and the precepts and teachings of *anthropoi* (2:22). It thereby illuminates the text's agenda and proposes an alternative drawn from the Christology of displacement and transformation in Christ.

Socio-historical analysis exposes the particularity of the household code as a first-century articulation of social relations and illuminates its participation in the things of this world. A sociology of knowledge perspective supports this further by exposing the social constructedness of the household code, like any social cosmos, and thereby illuminates its participation in the realm of cosmic authority, power, and rule stripped of their power in Christ.

A feminist analysis exposes the household code's pattern of dominance and subordination as oppressive for women, and illuminates the kinship between the claims to power of patriarchal sexism, racism, or classism, and those of the principalities and powers of the cosmos.

Integration of these perspectives suggests a re-naming of the principalities and powers to include the pattern of domination and subordination in the household code and Colossians' strategy of legitimation under the critique and displacement of the cosmic powers in Christ. The claim that God stripped the principalities and powers by exposing their false claims to power, can now be re-interpreted to include the claim that God stripped the pattern of dominance and subordination in the social cosmos by exposing its false claims to power. In place of these false claims to power, God established the lordship of Christ and the new community renewed after the image of its creator.

Under this reading of Colossians, the call to put off the old *anthropos* with its practices and put on the new becomes a call to be freed from patterns of domination and subordination in the cosmos, and conformed to new patterns, established in the image of the Lord. The vision of the new humanity to which this re-interpretation leads is not Fiorenza's *ekklesia* of women or a discipleship of equals. It is rather the community of new *anthropoi,* male and female, renewed and transformed in the image of creator, and knit together in the body of Christ with a growth that is from God (2:19).

This vision does not eliminate all patterns of dominance, empowerment, or subordination and replace them with a pattern of equality alone. Instead, it seeks to retain and re-interpret the notions of equality, dominance or dominion, empowerment, and subordination to apply in different ways to the relation of God and humanity, on the one hand, and the relation of human beings with one another, on the other. Under this vision, dominion, empowerment, and subordination apply more appropriately to divine-human relations; equality and subordination to human relations.

Subordination takes on different meanings in its respective pairing with dominion in divine-human relations, and equality in human relations, but both derive their form from the Christological claims of stripping the old *anthropos* and putting on the new. The pairing of equality and subordination in Christ applies to all human beings renewed according to the image of their creator. Under this pattern, all humans, male and female, masters and slaves, are equal among themselves not only as they stand before God, but in God's transformation of the social cosmos of Church, household, and world as well. They are, in turn, equally subordinate, first to the Lord, but also to one another.

Conclusion

The Christology of Colossians, therefore, as re-interpreted above, stands against a notion of subordination that supports human dominance and super-ordination by gender, race, or class. The displacement of the principalities and powers of the cosmos stands against human claims to dominance by gender, race, or class, even those that take the form of mutual subordination or revolutionary subordination in Christ,[37] if one gender, race, or class retains a position of superordination after its temporary abandonment in the name of Christ.

The Christological images of Colossians extend the definition of equality and subordination in Christ further. The identity of Christ as the image of the invisible God, and the notion of the new *anthropos* renewed in the image of its creator, supports the notion that all are equally created, equally renewed, and equally empowered in the Lord. The identity of Christ as both Lord over creation through whom God stripped the principalities and powers of their power further supports the notion that Christ is Lord over all things, so human beings are called equally to subordinate themselves to the Lord, but not to rulers and authorities of the cosmos that falsely claim power and dominion by gender, race, or class. Finally, the identity of Christ as one whose obedience and submission on the cross[38] brought the disarming of the principalities and powers of the cosmos supports the notion that those renewed in his image are called equally to subordinate themselves to one another, not from positions of dominance or subordination, as in the household code, but from positions of full equality in Christ.

The implications of this reading of Colossians for the contemporary debate on the role of women in the social orders of Church, household, and world now become clear. Exegetical analysis, critique, and re-interpretation of the letter to the Colossians opens the text up to an understanding of equality and subordination in Christ at odds with its own legitimation of the pattern of dominance and subordination in the household code. The image of Christ as one who stripped the cosmic powers of dominance and subordination displaces the pattern of dominance and subordination by gender and sets in its place a new notion of equality and subordination in Christ. The body of the new *anthropos* renewed in the image of its creator knows and effects the equality of all humans to one another

---

[37]John Howard Yoder, *The Politics of Jesus* (Grand Rapids, 1972), 167–192, for example, emphasizes the code's innovative notion of "revolutionary subordination." In his view, 181, "the *Haustafeln* do not consecrate the existing order; far more they relativize and undercut this order by then immediately turning the imperative (to be subordinate) around." This emphasis leads him then to argue that the code derives its shape and meaning and language from the novelty of the teaching of Jesus.

[38]The image of Christ as servant is prominent in the Phil. hymn, but does not appear in Colossians.

as created and empowered in the Lord, and the subordination of all to the Lord and to one another. The subordination it effects, however, is not a subordination of women to men, children to parents, or slaves to masters, but rather the equal subordination of all to the Lord and to one another, in the image of the one through whom God exposed false claims to domination that Christ might "be pre-eminent in all things" (1:18), and that all human beings renewed through him might be equal to one another, equally empowered, and equally subordinated in one body to the Lord who "is all things and in all" (3:11).[39]

[39]I would like to thank participants in the Scripture section of the College Theology Society for their lively and critical response to this paper. I am especially grateful to William Werpehowski for invaluable critical assistance.

AFFECTIVITY IN ETHICS: LONERGAN, RAHNER, AND OTHERS IN THE HEART TRADITION

Andrew Tallon

I propose in this exploratory paper to make a modest contribution toward locating and justifying the reasons of the heart in moral decision-making. Pascal's phrase is one Bernard Lonergan has made his own. Karl Rahner, who speaks much more of the heart than does Lonergan, does so chiefly in the context of devotion to the Sacred Heart; out of that discussion has come his main general doctrine, if we may call it that, on the meaning of heart in a metaphysical anthropology. Rahner's relevant treatment of our topic, however, comes from his development of the Ignatian idea of discernment of spirits, especially with reference to the experience of consolation without cause. Underlying both philosopher-theologians' ideas on the role of affectivity is a doctrine, older than Plato, one given high status by Aquinas and some contemporary Thomists, as well as by some non-Thomists, both implicitly and explicitly, namely, that of knowledge by affective connaturality.

I divide these reflections into three parts. First, (I) Bernard Lonergan's treatment of affectivity, then, (II) Karl Rahner's, and finally, (III) a synthesis of these two in dialogue with some other relevant contributors to the heart tradition with special attention to the work of Emmanuel Levinas, Daniel C. Maguire, and Robert Doran.

I. The Heart Tradition in Lonergan

As should be expected, my main source for Lonergan's ideas on this theme is *Method in Theology*. As he says there, he is drawing, at a certain remove, from Max Scheler's tradition, by way of Scheler's student and interpreter, Dietrich von Hildebrand, and from Manfred Frings's work on Scheler. But the resulting doctrine is imperfectly

integrated into Lonergan's own well-known and carefully worked-
out understanding of cognitional and volitional structure. This is
certainly not the place to repeat what Lonergan himself and his
students have clearly and often spelt out. Nevertheless, some bare
minimum must be presented in order to show how and where
affectivity fits into that structure.

Briefly, then, Lonergan steps beyond an older approach (namely,
faculty psychology) to identify and describe the operations performed by knowers in moving from experience to action. Along the
way from the many life experiences that make us raise questions and
require us to gather data, organize the data, and try to understand
this manifold, we construct images more or less fit for insight. Our
insights lead and allow us to form the concepts and ideas, the
theories and hypotheses, that are the expressions of our understanding, the products of our intelligence. As he and his explicators have
so often emphasized, concepts come at the end of this process,
completing the second level of cognitional consciousness. We do not
yet know, in the full sense, however, that of which we are empirically
conscious, until, after having moved from experience, through insight, into understanding, we then also go on to verify or certify our
insights by a further third step, by a second insight, at the level of
critical reason, whereby we make certain that all the conditions for
truth are fulfilled, thus allowing us to go on to judge, completing the
third level of cognitional consciousness and reaching the fullness of
knowledge in judgments, where truth and falsity first formally enter.
Decision comes fourth, at the level of responsibility, therefore,
empowered by the three steps preceding it. Without the two steps
between experience and decision, our decision, including ethical
decision-making, is perhaps not responsible but irresponsible. Then
comes action itself.

But where does feeling fit into this schema? Might it be that what
some call intuition, and others call reasons of the heart, is, in actual
practice, i.e., in terms of operations, a kind of shortcut at times
enabling the skilled and accomplished knower-agent to move rapidly if not instantly from experience to action by omitting the image-
creating and concept-forming (and sometimes, perhaps under time
pressure and/or in emergencies, even explicit decision-making)
stages? With the sureness and confidence that comes of often moving
felicitously and successfully from experience to action, one may in
time obviate the necessity of plodding through steps essential to
beginners. The traditional naming of this sort of move and its

knowledge is non-conceptual and non-discursive, and appropriately so, because, on Lonergan's explanation of when and how concepts are produced by us knowers, no concepts, and perhaps explicit judgments, would have yet been produced. Not coming at the beginning but one or two steps later in the process, they could—perhaps irresponsibly, but also perhaps responsibly—be omitted.

This hypothesis is confirmed in those places in *Method* where feeling is related to cognitional structure, and not merely where it is discussed more or less in its own right. And it is all the more appropriate to feeling's being related to cognition that the relation depend on what is the central concept in any metaphysical understanding of heart, namely that of affective intentionality and affective connaturality. Though relatively undeveloped by Lonergan this idea underlies the relation of feeling to cognition.

But I wish to do more than just argue for the integration of the relatively independent heart language into the general structure of consciousness. It seems also true to claim that the non-verbal, non-representational, non-discursive, non-conceptual move emerges not as the substitute for Lonergan's "complete" series of the stages from encounter on to decision and action, but the other way around: the way to decision that is "image-based, uses thinking in concepts, and is an explicit approach to action through judgment" is not the only way to move between experience and action and in fact becomes the substitute, and the way of the heart in affective connaturality becomes the paradigm. Such was Aquinas's understanding of how the good man knows ethics or the saintly woman knows the Holy, i.e., connaturally, in praxis and discipleship, by and through one's being, and not by possessing a Ph.D. in ethics or an S.T.D. In Lonergan this doctrine of feeling as value apprehension is put in terms of the subject's *being*, when converted, as criterion, analogous to grasping the virtually unconditioned on the third level of cognitional consciousness; that is the doctrine we must explain.

Lonergan's Use of Affectivity

So let's back up and see whether in fact a case can be made for this understanding of Lonergan's use of affectivity. We first find feeling mentioned at the level of experience, at the empirical level of consciousness.[1] Next, in the formal treatment, Lonergan, following

---

[1] See Bernard J. F. Lonergan, *Method in Theology* (New York: Herder and Herder, 1972), p. 9; hereafter cited as *Method*.

von Hildebrand, distinguishes those feelings that are intentional
from those that are merely non-intentional states (e.g., fatigue) and
teleological trends (e.g., thirst).[2] Now it is a phenomenological com-
monplace that some feelings are intentional. If we had only Sartre
and Merleau-Ponty as sources establishing this, they would be
enough, but the *apres coup* discovery, or rather rediscovery, by way
of Brentano and through him by Husserl, of the Scholastic concept
of intentionality, applied also to feelings and even to moods by
Heidegger (with a nod to Kierkegaard), and then adamantly reinforced by Ricoeur and Levinas, just to mention a few major figures,
suffices to justify without a hint of doubt the full attribution of
intentionality to the affective. It may perhaps be added that the
intentionality of affective consciousness should have already shared
fully in the benefits brought about by differentiation in cognitional
consciousness—but it hasn't: an intentionality analysis of affectivity
is one of the highest priorities on the agenda of both theoretical and
practical philosophy.

Has what this means, in its full import, has been taken seriously
by most philosophers and theologians? Affectivity[3] seems to remain
a mysterious and neglected dimension, especially for males, according to some psychologists, and perhaps even more for the males who
do most of the professional philosophizing. Feminization has caused
a broadening of horizons, however, with a concomitant need to
pursue the affective as a fundamental epistemological difference
between the masculine and feminine; Isabel Briggs Meyers, in her
Gifts Differing, has documented that the feeling function, to use a
Jungian term, is the only one that is sex-related.

Lonergan himself leaves no doubt that affectivity is irreducible to
cognition; as Matthew Lamb shows in his diagram,[4] (*see* **Diagram A,**
p. 113). There is a parallel structure of affectivity, and Lonergan
speaks of feeling developing distinct from the cognitive[5] despite the

---

[2]Lonergan, *Method*, p. 30.

[3]See Robert D. Sweeney, "The Affective 'A Priori,' " *Analecta Husserliana* III (ed.
Anna-Teresa Tymieniecka) (Dordrecht, Holland: D. Reidel, 1974), pp. 80–97.

[4]See Matthew L. Lamb, *History, Method, and Theology* (Missoula: Scholars Press,
1978), p. 368. Matt added the note with asterisk at the word feeling: "Feeling is co-
extensive with consciousness." N.B. To avoid a contradiction between Matt Lamb's
words and his diagram let's grant that the dotted line does not stop at "evaluation"
but extends into the fourth level, and would have extended into the fifth, had it been
included. (*See*, **Diagram A,** p. 113)

[5]Lonergan, *Method*, p. 30: "Distinct from operational development is the development of feeling."

intimate relation between consciousness as cognition and consciousness as feeling.

The crucial point in Lonergan's presentation of feeling, without
which his version becomes merely interesting and useful rather than
decisive, is the *development* of feeling.[6] In a very old terminology,
admittedly somewhat reminiscent of a faculty psychology but still,
of course, very much used in common practice, we might refer here
to the head's influence on the heart. The fact of *development* of
feeling, akin to what Lonergan calls moral self-transcendence[7] (i.e.,
metanoia, conversion, change of heart), is, of course, precisely what
allows him to locate the heart and its reasons—" . . . by the heart's
reasons I would understand feelings that are intentional responses
to values . . ."[8]—not any longer only "down" on the first level of
cognitional structure but on all four (and, in fact, even five). How
does this happen? Feeling goes from first to fourth, from experience
to decision, from the empirical to the existential, responsible level
where, as Lonergan says, one becomes "self-transcendent affectively,"[9] by "a process of conversion and development."

Life is a process of personal becoming, of becoming a person of a
certain quality and with a distinct character in proportion to the
values to which and to whom we respond in our feelings, from vital
feelings, through social, cultural, personal, and religious feelings.
The development of feeling consists in a differentiation and a dialectic that moves more or less continually from spontaneity, through
reinforcements or curtailments—necessitating occasional sus-
pended spontaneity or "retreats from spontaneity"[10]—and culminating in what Charles Davis calls an "achieved spontaneity,"[11] the
result being that one becomes increasingly responsible for making
oneself an authentic or inauthentic human being.[12]

Now it is impossible to repeat Lonergan's rich pages on feelings
and values, nor will I pause over the excellent pages on symbol and

---

[6]Lonergan, *Method*, pp. 32–34.

[7]Lonergan, *Method*, p. 122.

[8]Lonergan, *Method*, p. 115.

[9]Lonergan, *Method*, p. 289.

[10]I take this expression from Lonergan's, "The Ongoing Genesis of Methods," p.
353, cited in Matthew L. Lamb, *Solidarity with Victims. Toward a Theology of Social
Transformation* (New York: Crossroad, 1982), p. 135.

[11]See Charles Davis, *Body as Spirit. The Nature of Religious Feeling* (New York:
Seabury, 1976), p. 53. Chapter One, "Feeling as the Human Response to Reality," has
a lot to say about heart, connaturality, and affectivity as intentional.

[12]Lonergan, *Method*, pp. 38–41. These are powerful pages on the development of
moral feelings, especially with reference to judgments of moral value.

embodied meaning.[13] To keep this brief I turn to where Lonergan discusses "our natural orientation to the divine."[14] The pages on self-transcendence, religious experience, faith, and love[15] speak of conversion and of "God's love flooding our hearts,"[16] of grace transforming, divinizing, and connaturalizing us to God; here we find Lonergan's answer to our question about the transition of affectivity from the first to the fourth level.

Essentially that move consists in the effect of the highest affectivity we humans can reach, which Lonergan somewhat infelicitously calls "otherworldly falling in love":[17] "being in love with God is the basic fulfillment of our conscious intentionality,"[18] "conscious on the fourth level of intentional consciousness."[19] This love-consciousness has something different about it, and it is worth quoting Lonergan in order to avoid misunderstanding.

> That fulfillment is not the product of our knowledge and choice. On the contrary, it dismantles and abolishes the horizon in which our knowing and choosing went on and it sets up a new horizon in which the love of God will transvalue our values and the eyes of that love will transform our knowing.
>
> Though not the product of our knowing and choosing, it is a conscious dynamic state of love, joy, peace, that manifests itself in acts of kindness, goodness, fidelity, gentleness, and self-control (Gal. 5, 22).
>
> To say that this dynamic state is conscious is not to say that it is known. For consciousness is just experience, but knowledge is a compound of experience, understanding, and judging. Because the dynamic state is conscious without being known, it is an experience of mystery. Because it is being in love, the mystery is not merely attractive but fascinating; to it one belongs; by it one is possessed. Because it is an unmeasured love, the mystery evokes awe. Of itself, then inasmuch as it is conscious without being known, the gift of God's love is an experience of the holy, of Rudolf Otto's *mysterium fascinans et tremendum*. It is what Paul Tillich named a being grasped by ultimate concern. It corresponds to St. Ignatius Loyola's consolation that has no cause, as expounded by Karl Rahner.
>
> "It is consciousness on the fourth level of intentional consciousness.

---

[13]Lonergan, *Method*, pp. 64–78.
[14]Lonergan, *Method*, p. 103.
[15]Lonergan, *Method*, pp. 104–123, 240ff.
[16]Lonergan, *Method*, p. 115.
[17]Lonergan, *Method*, p. 240.
[18]Lonergan, *Method*, p. 105.
[19]Lonergan, *Method*, p. 106.

It is not the consciousness that accompanies acts of seeing, hearing, smelling, tasting, touching. It is not the consciousness that accompanies acts of inquiry, insight, formulating, speaking. It is not the consciousness that accompanies acts of reflecting, marshalling and weighing the evidence, making judgments of fact or possibility. It is the type of consciousness that deliberates, makes judgments of value, decides, acts responsibly and freely. But it is this consciousness as brought to a fulfillment as having undergone a conversion, as possessing a bias that may be broadened and deepened and heightened and enriched but not superseded, as ready to deliberate and judge and decide and act with the easy freedom of those that do all good because they are in love. So the gift of God's love occupies the ground and root of the fourth and highest level of man's intentional consciousness. It takes over the peak of the soul, the *apex animae*."[20]

Now this could not be possible, this overwhelming and determinative influence of love on knowledge—ultimately Lonergan's definition of faith—were there not potentiality already in us (a supernatural existential connaturalizing us, if you like) according to which affectivity can in general positively influence action. No one needs proof that emotion can cloud reason or that passion can disturb perception and judgment; but these negativities are based on the possibility of a more primordial positivity. That "love is blind" to someone's faults is grounded upon an ability to sense, recognize, and respond to more good than evil in someone.

If we keep in mind the essential condition of *development* of feeling, a life long dialectic of progress and regress, of conversion and backsliding, of sin, repentance, and rising, then we can accept at full strength what Bernard Lonergan says about the heart:

Finally, by the heart I understand the subject on the fourth, existential level of intentional consciousness and in the dynamic state of being in love. The meaning, then of Pascal's remark would be that, besides the factual knowledge reached by experiencing, understanding, and verifying, there is another kind of knowledge reached through the discernment of value and the judgment of value of a person in love.

Faith, accordingly, is such further knowledge when the love is God's love flooding our hearts.[21] . . . It used to be said, *Nihil amatum nisi praecognitum*, knowledge precedes love. The truth of this tag is the fact that ordinarily operations on the fourth level of intentional con-

---

[20]Lonergan, *Method*, pp. 106–107.
[21]Lonergan, *Method*, p. 115.

sciousness presuppose and complement corresponding operations on the other three. There is a minor exception to this rule inasmuch as people do fall in love, and that falling in love is something disproportionate to its causes, conditions, occasions, antecedents. For falling in love is a new beginning, an exercise of vertical liberty in which one's world undergoes a new organization. But the major exception to the Latin tag is God's gift of his love flooding our hearts."[22]

II. The Heart Tradition in Rahner

Unlike Lonergan's equally significant use of the heart concept, Karl Rahner's has attracted more attention.[23] Most of it, as was mentioned above, is unfortunately not germane to our discussion. For our purposes the connection between the two Thomists is epistemological and goes back to their both being fundamentally metaphysicians for whose metaphysics of knowledge the Aristotelian-Thomist doctrine of *conversio ad phantasma* is central. It is the core of Lonergan's *insight* and method and was the entire focus of Rahner's *Geist in Welt*, which was a long meditation on Thomas's *Summa Theologiae* I, q. 84, a. 7, where intellect's dependence on image holds center stage. All this is well known and by now should have been fully assimilated by a whole generation of contemporary students.

The question we are pursuing here is whether that hallowed doctrine really constitutes Aquinas's paradigm of knowledge after all—and so also Lonergan's and Rahner's—or whether it is instead actually the substitute for another kind of knowledge, namely, post-conversion knowledge, knowledge of the changed heart, knowledge by affective connaturality.

I have two suggestions to offer for integrating heart language, that of affective consciousness, into consciousness in general. The first depends on properly understanding the meaning of the *phantasma* of *conversio ad phantasma*, the image. The second, to be offered in the third section of this paper, depends on an analogy that Robert Doran recommends to us.

Now the visual bias[24] is so strong in all epistemology that we have

---

[22]Lonergan, *Method*, p. 122.

[23]Just to mention two studies, see Michael J. Walsh, *The Heart of Christ in the Writings of Karl Rahner* (Rome: Gregorian University Press, 1977), and the work by Annice Callahan (Washington: University Press of America, 1985), *Karl Rahner's Spirituality of the Pierced Heart. A Reinterpretation of Devotion to the Sacred Heart.*

[24]On this subject see my "Emmanuel Levinas's *Autrement qu'etre ou au-dela de l'essence, Man and World* 9 (1976), 451–462.

to clarify something before going on. We must clarify the meaning of image. The overwhelming tendency among most of us is to take image or phantasm to be visual. If this were true, i.e., if image meant visual representation, then we would be forced to offer an explanation of non-representational (i.e., presentational) intentionality that omitted an essential part of even the first level, the empirical level, of cognitional structure. But if image is not equated with the visual, then we can retain the complete first level of consciousness (see **Diagram A,** p. 113), while facing a different sort of decision: can image be construed broadly enough to encompass feeling, so that, as Meinong holds, in the absence of images more narrowly construed as cognitive (i.e., as derived from the senses operating in the active mode of cognitive sensing rather than in the relatively more passive mode of affective feeling), feelings can take the place of images[25] and can serve as the "matter of the cause," *materia causae*,[26] the raw material of the intellect forming concepts, judging, etc.? If not, then as an alternative we have reduced feeling to an accompaniment to the image, riding piggy-back, as it were, on the image as its color, its tonality, its timbre. This ultimately rationalist, intellectualist, idealist reduction must be rejected: true knowledge and converted feeling, as representational intentionality and affective intentionality are respectively co-equal means to the end of action. Otherwise we end up holding that the end of feeling is knowledge instead of action, and fall into the gnostic trap of salvation through gnosis instead of through love. Knowledge is for love, not vice versa; no matter how much love can benefit knowledge, love is not related to knowledge as means to end. The proper relation is to connect both love-as-feeling and as love-as-full personal-response to love-as-action, as deeds of justice and love in action, in praxis. Praxis is both foundation and goal of theory.

Presuming, then, a certain basic understanding of Rahner's metaphysics of cognition, we can plunge right into our chief question. Is conceptual knowledge the norm or paradigm, or, as Rousselot[27]

---

[25]See Alexius Meinong, *On Emotional Presentation* (Evanston: Northwestern University Press, 1972), pp. 114, 115.

[26]This phrase is, of course, from Aquinas's *Summa Theologiae* I, q. 84, a. 6.

[27]Besides consulting Pierre Rousselot's *intellectualism of St. Thomas Aquinas,* see John W. McDermott, *Love and Understanding. The Relation of Will and Intellect in Pierre Rousselot's Christological Vision* (Rome: Gregorian University Press, 1983). I found in this book strong confirmation of the two related ideas that discursive reason is a substitute for a better human knowing and that affective connaturality is the Thomist name for it. When Lonergan says that faith is knowledge born of love, he

suggests, is it really the surrogate, the substitute for a connaturality, perhaps a lost connaturality we regain to the degree we cooperate with the gifts of the spirit bearing fruit in our hearts as faith, love, and hope? In his "The Logic of Concrete Individual Knowledge in Ignatius Loyola,"[28] right at the start Rahner comes to grips with our problem, explicitly denying that knowledge is limited to the objective knowledge acquired by turning to phantasms; staying within the terminology of a traditional faculty psychology he says that beyond that "cognition of the rationally discursive and conceptually expressible kind" there is another truly "intellectual knowledge which is ultimately grounded in the simple presence to itself of the intrinsically intelligible subject . . .".[29]

Rahner is careful to exclude feeling in the sense of an instinct, such as might correspond to a moral sense theory or be restricted to Lonergan's first, empirical level of consciousness.[30] Instead he, like Lonergan, is clearly presupposing a subject (e.g., the exercitant discerning spirits during the thirty day retreat) at the level of decision, trying responsibly to learn to elect to follow God's will. One is instructed by Ignatius to ask God to stir the soul, to move the soul by interior consolation. In fact, these motions of the spirit are to be desired and preferred over thoughts and insights; they are all aimed at decision and action—at election—and then at living it out concretely; they are not aimed at vague generalities or universal concepts but at specific particulars. To go from the universal moral law to definite deeds requires an individuation.

Here Rahner, like Rousselot, allows for a certain likeness between the human spirit and those angelic spirits[31] each of which, in Aquinas's, unlike Suarez's, doctrine of individuation, is a species

---

expresses the same basic idea. Thomas Gilby's "love-knowledge" also echoes this theme (*Poetic Experience. An Introduction to a Thomist Aesthetic* [New York: Russell & Russell, 1934], pp. 39–45).

I postpone considering the question whether Lonergan's use of the category of experience is broad enough to include both of Buber's terms experience (the I-It relation) and encounter (the I-Thou relation), since prima facie it appears that Buber's challenge to any single attitude or method for both relations would be wrong because it tried to relate in the same way to things and persons. This is, again, the problem of integrating later Lonergan with the method of *Insight* and its cognitional structure.

[28]Karl Rahner, *The Dynamic Element in the Church* (Freiburg: Herder, 1964), pp. 84–170, hereafter cited as Rahner, *DEC.*

[29]Rahner, *DEC*, pp. 94–95, n. 9.

[30]That he is not excluding feeling *tout court* is very clear on p. 166, cited later.

[31]Rahner, *DEC*, p. 112.

unto itself: insofar as each of us is spirit "not wholly absorbed by its relation to matter as the principle of multiplicability, he or she must also in his or her acts share in that individuality that belongs to the spiritual. . . ."[32]

Now how exactly does this individual self-presence, specific to each person as analogously unique, and this election or life decision (vocation)—which we can consider the model for all ethical decision-making writ large, as it were—become operative and enter consciousness, become psychologically and experientially accessible? It does so as feeling, but as *differentiated* feeling, as feeling in a sense that needs careful nuance. No facile or merely verbal concordance works. There can be no equation of this feeling with undeveloped or uncritiqued feeling or unconverted, ethically irresponsible heart (= *Heart I*). To establish what he means by feeling in a precise and correct sense Rahner has recourse to thee helpful concepts: horizon,[33] consolation without cause,[34] and connaturality.[35] All three are non-conceptual experience. All three are characterized by absence of representation, either due to its impossibility or to its disappearance, and in its place a kind of spiritual feeling, not so much physical or empirical in the sense of the peripheral senses but as felt at the heart, core, and center of the spirit.

Three Rahnerian Concepts

1. By horizon Rahner means the non-objective co-known ground or field on or against which objects are known, the background consciousness—a content of consciousness that is not an object, is not objective knowledge. Lonergan's distinction between consciousness and knowledge recalls the same experience. For Rahner this experience of consciousness, a "horizon given in a non-explicit and non-conceptualizable manner . . .,"[36] is the general case of consciousness: "being consciously known and being susceptible of being known by deliberate explicit reflection are not the same thing. . . ."[37]

2. "Consolation without cause" means, in terms of an object co-

---

[32]Rahner, *DEC*, p. 113. Recall the Thomist dictum about the highest point of the lower form touching the lowest point of the higher form.
[33]Rahner, *DEC*, pp. 124 ff.
[34]Rahner, *DEC*, pp. 132–155.
[35]Rahner, *DEC*, pp. 160–166.
[36]Rahner, *DEC*, p. 125.
[37]Rahner, *DEC*, p. 126.

given with a horizon, that in this case the horizon is given without an object (a cause), the ground without a figure. "What is decisive is . . . absence of object."[38] Rahner is aware that this doctrine would not go down easily with anyone who equated intentionality with representationality and therefore devotes most of a long footnote to emphasizing the point:

> Of course, if someone identifies by definition without more ado "being the object of a concept for consciousness" and "being known" (of something in a consciousness) we get nowhere here. But to warn and preserve us from making this identification, the simple fact can serve, that there is certainly at least one awareness which is not consciousness of an object: the concomitant self-awareness in every act of the mind when it is directed to any object. This awareness is something different in kind, too, from cognition wherein one's own "I" can be conceptually made the focus of a mental act, that is, when I reflect upon the first kind of awareness and express it in concepts and propositions. The question can, therefore, only be whether there can be such a non-conceptual awareness of other realities as well as of one's own "I." If an affirmative answer can be given with regard to God, then, quite independently of the question whether such a mode of experience can exist only within mysticism or also outside it, a "non-conceptual" experience of God in being totally drawn up into his love, is a concept that is conceivable.[39]

The love of God flooding our hearts is the extreme and full instance (Lonergan's "major exception") of the effect of affectivity upon consciousness as ground and upon all its objects on that ground. It seems logical to admit other, less extreme examples (Lonergan's "minor exception")[40] throughout the range of differen-

---

[38]Rahner, *DEC*, p. 134.

[39]Rahner, *DEC*, pp. 134–135.

[40]Though this note could go elsewhere, I take my cue from Lonergan's phrase "minor exception" juxtaposed with Rahner's "absence of object" to remark that much of the obscurity associated with Levinas's ethical metaphysics is dispelled by realizing that his seemingly outrageous and extreme characterizations of the relation between oneself and the other are humanizations of Lonergan's and Rahner's statements about relation to the Transcendent Other. Consonant with Rahner's identification of love of God and of neighbor, Lonergan's two exceptions unite in an epiphany: not only God, but every person is an untotalizable horizon, an infinite who is ungraspable as an object. This is Levinas's affective obsession with the value and worth of persons. Levinas's use of the superlative, his hyperbole about being held hostage and being persecuted by the other, whose incalculable worth as a person makes any responsibility beyond measure—once I, as ethical subject am subjected to his or her value—is just his way of trying to express what Lonergan and Rahner try to express in their languages, i.e., this fundamental ethical event. In a very "Levinasian" sentence Daniel C. Maguire says "Justice is just the first assault upon egoism" (*A New American Justice* [Minneapolis: University Press, 1980], p. 58).

tiated human feeling. Not that God—or the human love—is represented[41] in consciousness, but, as Rahner suggests, is present as "pure non-conceptual light of the consolation of the whole human person who is being drawn above and beyond all that can be named into the love of God."[42]

This experience can also be called transcendence, because it is a going beyond, beyond all objects toward the ungraspable horizon. If horizon is the term of the movement, transcendence is the act, "for a mode of experience which occurs without sensible imagery or in which at all events the imagery does not correspond in the usual relation to the thought content, is itself, objectively speaking, precisely the experience of transcendence. For if we do not imagine the *species intellectualis* as yet another pictorial double of the sensible species (which would render the *conversio ad phantasma* superfluous), then what is left when sensible imagery is absent can only be the experience of transcendence as such, and this as a consequence will signify an experience which is 'without object' (non-conceptual), though not without content."[43]

Now at this point in his discussion Rahner explains at some length our human inability to distinguish by introspective reflection our natural transcendence from the supernatural elevation of that natural transcendence by grace. One can attend more to one's dynamic transcendence as activity or operation and less and less to objects[44] (perhaps in the manner of a kenotic emptying of objects from the mind or the suspension of discursive reasoning as by a Zen koan). Rahner makes love[45] a necessary condition of this movement's being positive, placing us on Lonergan's fourth (or possibly fifth) level: "this experience of transcendence . . . in no way has the character of a merely 'transcendental subject' in metaphysical abstraction. It concerns, by the very nature of the case, since freedom and love are involved, a concrete person in his or her innermost center, as unique, responsible, and free."[46] Following Ignatius, Rahner links

---

[41]Rahner, *DEC*, p. 136.

[42]Rahner, *DEC*, p. 137.

[43]Rahner, *DEC*, p. 139.

[44]Rahner, *DEC*, p. 145: "The conceptual object which in normal acts is condition of awareness of this transcendence can also become more transparent, can almost entirely disappear, remain itself unheeded, so that the dynamism itself alone becomes more and more the essential."

[45]Rahner, *DEC*, p. 146.

[46]Rahner, *DEC*, pp. 147–148. On p. 150 he adds: "All that has been said is, of course, not meant merely of an intellectual phenomenon but as freedom and love.

"absence of object,"[47] experience of ground parallel to "our soul wide open"[48] ("this experience lays hold of the soul completely"),[49] with a certain spiritual feeling, perception,[50] or sense as the way or mode of this experience.

Since my purpose here is not to attend to the mystical aspect but to the more ordinary ethical aspect of the role of affectivity, we can omit those "full strength," graced, supernatural considerations and turn finally to what is generalizable from Rahner's explanation of Ignatian discernment and is therefore applicable to the moral choice.

3. Our last Rahnerian point, then, is the notion of connaturality, that resonance of one's nature as conscious, thus as both understood through the cognitive mode (experience, insight, judgment)—the representational—and also as felt—as non-representational, and not, in the latter, as a mere accompanying glow added to the representation (such as would be merely an *undifferentiated* feeling, i.e., the "experience" of experience, the "feeling" of insight, the "sense" of judgment, or the "passion" of decision).[51] This ultimate reducibility of all intentions, even the non-representational, to representations, was an error that Levinas's calls Husserl's *refroidissement*, his going cold (or loss of nerve), for we have learned from the above analysis of Rahner not to relate this feeling to an object. Instead it is the felt rapport of the whole subject's self-presence to the whole other (as ground, as horizon). This holistic relation is whole to whole, ground to ground, not figure to figure, and suggests heart to heart more than head (or mind) to head. That this is the sense of Rahner's use of feeling as related to fundamental option,[52] to spirit and not instinct, to full situation, total attitude, and global awareness and attunement comes across clearly in the Thomist idea of affective connaturality.

He explicitly says that for decision and choice "it is not a case of

---

But conversely the 'consolation' in it is not merely an added concomitant feeling, supplementary to this experience of the free transcendence of the whole mind and spirit. This latter *is* the consolation. . . ." (Rahner's emphasis).

[47]Rahner, *DEC*, p. 153.

[48]Rahner, *DEC*, p. 152.

[49]Rahner, *DEC*, p. 153.

[50]Rahner, *DEC*, p. 154. "Unless we think of a cognitive power as a kind of peep-show or photographic plate registering indifferently anything presented to it from outside . . . we will be obliged to say that if there is a non-conceptual mode of knowing, it can only be a non-conceptual awareness of transcendence (which certainly exists), or a heightened prolongation of it." For Levinas this event is ethical, because a person is a ground or horizon infinity transcending all figure or object.

[51]See note 46.

[52]Rahner, *DEC*, p. 161.

'thinking it over' . . ., not analyzing the object of possible choice,'' but a "preliminary getting attuned to, a putting oneself into, a certain situation . . . in order to mobilize the actual real center of his or her own nature in relation to the situation, so as to bring into full awareness how the person he or she really is (which may be hidden from him or her), reacts to some possible object of choice. . . . One is trying out in a sort of . . . play-acting experiment whether one can discover in oneself in regard to the object of choice a certain global 'connaturality' . . .''[53]

For Karl Rahner this "innermost center of the person . . . is mobilized . . .;" "it is always a matter of a person's putting himself or herself into a certain situation . . .," and this Ignatian method, Rahner adds, "is not purely a discursive one."[54]

The ethical equivalent of knowing that God is the source of consolation—a condition Rahner calls radical—[55] when discerning spirits, is the affective connaturality of developed feelings, the converted heart, very like, as will be shown later, following Doran, an analogy to the criterion of grasping the virtually unconditioned. We do no violence to Rahner's intention to interpret his essay in this broader fashion; in fact such was his own intention and he takes the lead in this ethical interpretation:

> It may be said too that nearly everyone in grave decisions makes a choice more or less exactly in the way Ignatius conceives it, just as a man in the street uses logic without ever having studied it, and yet it remains useful to draw inferences by means of logic that one has studied. In such decision a person thinks things over for a long time. Consequently in every case he or she will probably make decisions through a fundamental global awareness of self actually present and making itself felt in him or her during this space of time, and through a feeling of the harmony or disharmony of the object of choice with this fundamental feeling he or she has about himself or herself. A person will not only nor ultimately make a decision by a rational analysis but by whether he or she feels that something "suits her" or "suits him" or not. And this feeling will be judged by whether the matter pleases, delights, brings peace and satisfaction. There is much significance in this use of the word peace to describe what is found in a right decision.

The difference between Ignatius's logic of concrete particulars and

---

[53]Rahner, *DEC*, p. 161, n. 43.
[54]Rahner, *DEC*, p. 161, n. 43.
[55]Rahner, *DEC*, p. 163.

that of daily life does not, then, lie in the formal structure of each, but in their application to a particular range of objects. With Ignatius it is a question of recognizing the harmony between the object of choice and person's precise individual mode of religious life. But we can also suppose that the faithful who have never heard of St. Ignatius's instruction nevertheless instinctively make their religious decision by their everyday religious logic in essentially the same way as Ignatius provides for.[56]

Rahner "authorizes" an ethical application when he says "it is not a logic of a deductive ethics of general principles. . . . It is a logic of concrete individuals which can only be attained in the actual accomplishment of concrete cognition itself. . . ."[57] And as if to conclude the matter he writes, on the last page: "ascetical theology can only be conceived as an integral part of moral theology."[58]

III. The Heart Tradition in Some Contemporaries

My purpose in this third segment is to review a few other voices in the chorus I call the heart tradition. Complete coverage is not my aim. Not everything has come to my attention.

The human paradigm in the heart tradition is not the Logos principle, in Jung's terminology, but the Eros principle, i.e., human relatedness. The feminization of ethics has called our attention forcefully to our reversed paradigm. Reason ought to be at the service of relation, not vice versa.

No one has proclaimed the need to reverse this reversal more than has Emmanuel Levinas. His otherwise very obscure and mysterious works make sense when understood as describing the pre-cognitive and pre-volitional (i.e., before head and reason) infinity of the other person in a non-representational language of affectivity. This can be expressed apropos two ideas. *First*, the present consciousness-raising being effected by feminization can best be understood in terms of affectivity (specifically, affective connaturality), because women's liberation itself can best be understood in terms of hermeneutical privilege, the latter being based on affective connaturality. *Second*, the precise role of religion today is to live (in praxis, in discipleship) the reversed paradigm—this first and foremost—and then to preach

---

[56]Rahner, *DEC*, pp. 166–167.
[57]Rahner, *DEC*, p. 169.
[58]Rahner, *DEC*, p. 170.

and prophesy that reversed paradigm, the preaching and prophesying being best done, of course, by the praxis of living, by justice as biblical coming to the cause of the poor and oppressed. This second point also relates to hermeneutical privilege grounded in affective connaturality.

The Theme of Feminization

1. First, on the theme of feminization in human self-understanding in general, and, more in particular on the theme of the relation of affectivity to ethics, I refer to the work of Daniel C. Maguire. It is correct to say in his case, as I am sure is true of others, that an initial commitment to the heart tradition, i.e., to the primacy of persons as the values of infinite worth, and of affectivity as access to their value and worth, disposed him positively toward the feminine as access to the primary human embodiment of affectivity.

Justice, as minimal love, requires a strategy, he says, a method adequate to the complexity of contemporary personal, interpersonal, and political existence. Not just in one chapter, corresponding to his "wheel of method,"[59] but in five (of thirteen) chapters, the role of feeling is seriously considered, not in a mushy way as though to cover cases reason can't settle, but as the basic first line of approach. Maguire explicitly works within the heart tradition, not only when establishing the ground of ethics in the foundational moral experience—the supreme value and worth of persons (and thus in the foundational human, personal experience)—but also as the critical difference in moral decision because recognition of the cognitive nature of the affections can afford a "higher level of moral awareness."[60] To establish this he too has recourse to the idea of affective connaturality.

It seems to me extremely important that the one thing Maguire notes as flagrantly missing from most ethical treatises is almost the sole thing that consumes Levinas's entire interest. And both gain access to that foundational moral experience through affectivity.

In Levinas's writing, meeting another person face to face is the beginningof all metaphysics, by which he means transcendence (meta) of all nature or being (physics); and that event is the ethical,

---

[59]See Daniel C. Maguire, The Moral Choice (Minneapolis: Winston Press, 1978), p. 115, for the wheel illustration. "All moral experience is grounded in affectivity, in the foundational moral experience of personal value" (p. 281).

[60]Maguire, Moral Choice, p. 281.

i.e., encounter with the "good beyond being" (Plato). When all the hyperbole, exaggeration, and superlatives, like persecution, obsession, hostage, and the like, are interpreted, we find affirmed, quite emphatically, to be sure, essentially this same foundational moral experience, the infinite value of persons. Nor is this assertion the conclusion of a logical syllogism but is the very presence (a presentational intentionality) of the other before the advent of reason and freedom. The move from experience to responsibility in Levinas omits the second and third levels of Lonergan's cognitional structure by using converted affective consciousness instead. My thesis is that Levinas's experience of personal presence and Maguire's foundational moral experience, use this same paradigm or model according to the heart tradition: only because one lacks a connaturalized, converted heart must one have recourse to cognitional structure's three successive levels. My thesis has the corrollary that not only the foundation but the method also omits the two mediating steps in someone who has progressed through what Lonergan called development of feeling, for that is the conversion, change of heart, and transformation of affectivity that constitutes a heart one can trust because connaturalized to the infinite value of persons. Consonant with Rahner's Ignatian discernment through affective connaturality, Maguire says that "the moral virtues also so attune a person to the morally good that it becomes 'connatural' to judge correctly about the good. A virtuous person judges well about the material of that virtue because it becomes connatural, or second nature to him or her to do so."[61]

Note that in all these claims about the heart and its reasons the basis of replacing the intellectual paradigm of the four step "book" knower consists in that same knower's having become connaturalized, presumably after many a year, through a great deal of living, and with perhaps no little suffering. There has been a development of feeling, a lifetime of many conversions, of continual conversion, an asymptoptical approximation of the heart paradigm, toward *Heart II*.

Now when men awaken to awareness of affectivity in their maturation as persons they do so usually through women, from mother on. So runs the common course. And yet is seems promptly forgotten and/or methodically ignored when in fact the epistemological rele-

---

[61]Daniel C. Maguire, "Ratio Practica and the Intellectualistic Fallacy," *Journal of Religious Ethics* Vol. 10, No. 1 (Spring, 1982), pp. 22–39; see p. 27.

vance of this principle is permanent. Feminization in ethics is but a belated catching up with this truth. Feminization has much to contribute not only to ethics but to philosophy, theology, religion, and all human studies. In ethics today feminization is joined by another consciousness-raising principle, that of liberation (both as theology of liberation and as philosophy of liberation), and their joining gives rise to the idea of a hermeneutical privilege. The idea of a hermeneutical privilege makes most sense within an already worked-out concept of affective connaturality.

What source is there, after all, what ground or basis, for a hermeneutical privilege if not one's affectivity, i.e., one's personal suffering, one's own, direct, irreplaceable *Jemeinigkeit*, as Heidegger puts it in *Being and Time* (paragraph 9), namely, one's individual knowledge through experience, through Rahner's Ignatian "individual knowledge"? The hermeneutical privilege of the poor, for example, furnished the victims of poverty an access to truths of existence as well as interpretations of the Scriptures unavailable to the winners and writers of history.[62]

Something like a generalizable hermeneutical privilege applies to women in matters feminine, not the least, but not the sole significant application being a woman's decision about her abortion. In his "The Feminization of God and Ethics," Daniel Maguire makes two important points relevant to the present discussion. The first is this: "The most fundamental form of otherness is male/female otherness. If this otherness is marked by opposition and disdain, it will be easier to oppose other others—be they black, Jewish, foreign, or poor."[63] The second is a four point summary of feminine advantages in moral affectivity, the generally enhanced evaluative capacities women "enjoy" because of both positive and negative aspects of biological and cultural factors. Without repeating his whole development of these two points we can say that the backbone of his position in this article is the decisive difference affectivity makes in moral decision-making. The point is brought home even more forcefully through a five point summary of "macho-masculinity." It

---

[62]I'm going to presume that I need only mention the names G. Gutierrez, L. Boff, J. Secundo, E. Tamez, J. Miranda, J. Sobrino, S. Galilea to indicate the writers I mean. One of the best introductions to the idea is forty-eight pages by Monika Hellwig, *Whose Experience Counts in Theological Reflection?* (The 1982 Pere Marquette Lecture) (Milwaukee: Marquette University Press, 1982); see esp. pp. 28, 34, 35, 39, 41, and 41, where the connection with affectivity and connaturality is clear.

[63]Daniel C. Maguire, "The Feminization of God and Ethics," *Christianity and Crisis* (March 15, 1982, pp. 59–67), p. 59.

would not be too much to say that something like an "affirmative
action" in favor of the feminine voice behooves the predominantly
male ethics academy.[64] In the last resort the sole significant challenge to all the reigning ethical systems, all ethics betraying the male
rationalistic bias or "intellectualistic fallacy," is an ethics of the
heart, not as a "single rubric ethics," but first as foundational and
then as paradigmatic methodologically, in such a way that ethics
never be done, philosophically or theologically, whether in the
working out of general theory—all of which derives from praxis—or
in the handling of cases, without hearing from those who have the
hermeneutic access most affectively, most connaturally.

The Primary of Praxis

2. At first there may seem to be at best a tenuous connection
between a plea for more affectivity in ethics and promoting a
theology of praxis. But as soon as one realizes, as Gregory Baum
points out, that the philosophy that influenced Christian theology
from its beginning was conditioned by a slave culture that looked
down on work and defined humans by reason, intellect, and happiness through contemplation, one immediately is alerted to the strong
possibility of a hermeneutical lacuna. For the Scriptures, humans
are workers, co-creators with God. "Yet the Christian theological
tradition, nourished largely by classical Greek thought, following
Plato and later Aristotle, did not pursue this approach to man as
worker. What distinguished man from the animals was reason. The
ancient Greek centers of culture were slave societies. Here labor was
assigned to the slaves. Free men did not work. Their glory was the
pursuit of the intellectual life and the governance of society. What
defined man's essence here was rationality. Women were acknowledged as rational too, even though in a subordinate way. Women
were believed to be so absorbed in giving birth and the processes of
nature that they did not manifest the full meaning of humanity. This
aristocratic tradition, which defined man as rational and assigned

---

[64]A start might be Carol Gilligan's In a Different Voice. Psychological Theory and
Women's Development (Cambridge: Harvard University Press, 1982). Also good for
the Jungian perspective are M. Esther Harding, The Way of All Women (New York:
Harper & Row, 1970) and Anthony Stevens, Archetypes. A Natural History of the Self
(New York: Quill, 1982), esp. ch. 11, "The archetypal masculine and feminine," and
ch. 13, "On being in two minds," where much of the recent work on brain hemis-
phericity is updated. Also Isabel Briggs Myers, Gifts Differing (Palo Alto: Consulting
Psychologists Press, 1980).

workers and women to a subordinated place, profoundly influenced Christian theology, even though the Scriptures honor work and workers."[65]

This is not the same problem as that called the hellenization of dogma. Rather we should catch the connection between two liberations, that of workers and that of women, for, as Baum more than broadly hints, what has been operative is a self-definition of the human exclusively by and as a *male thinker*, and one not very close to "giving birth and the processes of nature" either.

There is thus something of a common cause between these most recent signs of life in theology, the liberation theologies, and this because they are theologies of praxis more than of theory, even though this may not be clear in the practical turn when they take the form of a redefinition of the human through the feminine and through the imperative of social transformation. My thesis is that both moves are essentially ethical, and in both moves the unifying principle is release or liberation from the Logos principle, as Jung calls it, from a one-sided domination by *theoria*, not a little of which is the visual bias over the dialogal[66] (Athens over Jerusalem again),[67] to "the move to praxis," as Dermot Lane puts it.[68] The primacy of praxis becomes orthopraxis only through affective obsession with the foundational human, moral experience, the infinite worth of all persons (not, for example, through the presently reigning primacy of capital).

Now one international institution able to resist, albeit nonviolently, the current genocidal pursuit, the male game of war which is war for the sake of business, is the Church. While some signs of clerical leadership, in both pope and bishops, are promising, nevertheless much resistance still remains among other clerics, as we sadly know, on the subject of women's liberation. The failure occurs

---

[65]Gregory Baum, *The Priority of Labor. A Commentary on Laborem exercens, Encyclical Letter of Pope John Paul II* (New York: Paulist Press, 1982), p. 11.

[66]On Levinas see my "Emmanuel Levinas and the Problem of Ethical Metaphysics," *Philosophy Today* 20 (1976) 53–66. On the visual bias see my article mentioned in note 24, and on the dialogal, my "Intentionality, Intersubjectivity, and the Between: Buber and Levinas on Affectivity and the Dialogal Principle," *Thought* 53 (1978) 293–309. See also the Marquette doctoral dissertation by William Cooney, *Homo Spectans and Homo Particeps: The Non-optical Philosophy of Gabriel Marcel* (Milwaukee, 1983).

[67]See William Barrett's chapter on "Hebraism and Hellenism," ch. 4 in his *Irrational Man. A Study in Existential Philosophy* (Garden City: Anchor, 1958).

[68]See Dermot A. Lane, *Foundations for a Social Theology. Praxis, Process, and Salvation* (New York: Paulist Press, 1984), ch. 1.

because the voices that can speak from hermeneutical privilege, such as the sisters who signed the declaration on theological pluralism, are not only not invited to speak but are dealt with peremptorily and degradingly; the sexism is blatant and insulting. Unless the feminine force is released, the force of the feminine will not be released. This is not a "let the women save us" romanticization, for the feminine is not a monopoly of women nor do women monopolize affective connaturality.[69]

Now the relation between feminization and praxis theology is their common root in affective connaturality; they both manifest the heart rather than an intellectualistic monopoly of reason unassisted by affection. And they both claim the hermeneutical privilege, which derives from affective connaturality. It is connatural knowledge that grounds hermeneutical privilege. What does this privilege say after all? Not so much that its possessor knows something better than someone without it, and knows through experience,[70] i.e., through oneself as changed by life, but more that one has grounds to call into question the truth claims of others against oneself. Now it can be presupposed that everyone has some hermeneutical privilege because of his or her uniqueness of experience in something—if only in being oneself and so knowing oneself in and through one's own story, in "individual knowledge" (Ignatius) or "personal knowledge" (Polanyi). We have already noted the metaphysical basis for this as given by Rahner in *Dynamic Element in the Church* where human self-presence is a participation in the angels' being each one its own species; the conclusion is that for ethics the ultimate paradigm is hermeneutical privilege based on affective connaturality.

A corollary follows. Since action stemming from affective connaturality is the more perfect to the degree that one is connatural to the good to be done (or as disciple is connatural to master), the is/ought controversy drops out, because the imperative in general drops out (including the love command, since love "needs" to be commanded—and the love command is only felt *as* a command— precisely to the degree that one is not yet connaturalized to God who is love). In God, of course, there is love but no love command, no ought. Love may well be the primary ought (commandment,

---

[69]See Rosemary Radford Ruether, *Sexism and God-Talk. Toward a Feminist Theology* (Boston: Beacon Press, 1983), pp. 104–115.

[70]See Lee Cormie, "The Hermeneutical Privilege of the Oppressed: Liberation Theologies, Biblical Faith, & Marxist Sociology of Knowledge," *Proceedings of the Thirty-Third Annual Convention CTSA* (1978), pp. 155–181.

imperative, etc.), but only in absence of connaturality; we need imperatives and commands for what has not yet become connatural, or second nature, grace being God's connaturalizing us to Herself.[71] "Ethics is the default of aesthetics" might be the provocative way to express this, using "aesthetics" somewhat in von Balthasar's sense, but at least in the sense of doing the good because of its beauty with which we are in harmony and consonance, and failing that, because of duty instead, by default.

Thus the hermeneutical privilege claimed by and/or for liberation theology really comes down to invoking the primacy of the affective, of the heart, which is what is meant by affective connaturality. And this is clearly what is also at the basis of praxis theology, which is a theology of experience over theory. As Matt Lamb shows convincingly, that experience is not to be conceived naively but, for a theology open to the supernatural, to God as mystery of the world, that experience must be first and foremost the imperative of social transformation, coming to the aid of the oppressed in solidarity with victims.[72] What is this but the "love thy neighbor" commandment having come of age in the social age, in the political age, and thus having become the imperative of social transformation of systems and structures, of political conversion including the business world and that of economics.[73] In other words, not only at the micro level of the ethical but at the macro level of the socio-political, where hermeneutical privilege first came to consciousness at all, the primacy of the affective is at work.

Even Levinas's major theme, responsibility, as *burdensome* ought, drops out; the other is oppressing me, holding me hostage, persecuting me, by the "interpersonal curvature of space," by the way the other "bends" the space around him or her, which tension I feel as nearness and as a presence making me responsible for that neighbor; but that feeling changes as soon as and to the extent that connaturality develops (Lonergan's development of feeling) culminating in affective conversion, or in psychic conversion, to use Robert Doran's term. To flow from nature, without forcing (the *wu wei* of the *tao*),

---

[71]I have developed this point at some length in an article, forthcoming in *Anglican Theological Review*, where I use connaturality, following a lead of Raymond Brown's, to interpret 1 John's doctrine of being born of God as empowering the love for one another that, in a "virtuous" circle, reveals that one is born of God.

[72]See Lamb, *Solidarity with Victims*, ch. 1 ("Social Sin and Social Transformation"), and p. 120.

[73]See Stephen Charles Mott, *Biblical Ethics and Social Change* (New York: Oxford University Press, 1982), especially ch. 7 ("The Church as Counter-Community").

without ought, is to act without head (*wu hsin* i.e., according to the "not-mind" that is heart). The prime analogue is, as the commandment notes, self-love, and, as Alquie points out, we love ourselves without reasons, without prior justification, and without first contracting to do so out of freedom, again without the mediation of head; it is second nature (barring the aberrations of neurotic or psychotic self-hatred, a sort of affective unnaturality or contranaturality). When one is in health (including mental health), what is natural is good and what is good comes naturally. "As you love yourself" is meant to come naturally, without resistance, with resonance, for when resonance is highest then resistance is lowest, and at that point imperatives become superfluous and simply are not experienced at all (or at the least not as such but as pleasurable operation). As Abraham Maslow says somewhere in *Motivation and Personality*, a good person is loving the way a rose is sweet-smelling. It just is, by nature, by its nature connaturally. To feel an imperative is thus to give proof that one is not yet connatural to the good. And this applies to a society and its imperative for social transformation.

Finally, that the ground of praxis theology is affective connaturality is shown by a moment's reflection on the theme of discipleship. What, after all, does discipleship mean if not that the disciple comes to know the master by living as committed a life as the master, thereby experiencing what the master experienced, becoming enough like the master that self-knowledge approximates knowing the master; the knowing comes from the being. Knowledge through discipleship, like that from hermeneutical privilege, comes directly from praxis rather than from *theoria* (theory itself, one hopes, drawn also from others' praxis). This, too, is recognized as knowledge through love, a knowing in one's heart, in flesh and bone, not just in though or velleity.

Affectivity in Ethics

3. I now turn to the second suggestion, mentioned above, for integrating the language of the heart and that of the head in order to help us in ethics. We have a set of dualities in consciousness that seem to be recurrent and to cry out for integration. That synthesis of head and heart keeps escaping us for the simple reason that head and heart speak different languages. The solution cannot be to translate one language into the other, for that would be to lose the genius of both, nor would it make sense to coin an artificial third

language; there's no solution but to learn to speak both. I suggest that we follow a lead that Robert Doran offers, and call this last section a modest contribution to the ongoing attempt to learn again from Lonergan.

From Lonergan, then, let us again take the main outline of the structure of consciousness, summarized very schematically above, especially the clarification of the two insights by which we move from the first level of cognitive consciousness to the second, and then from the second to the third.

From Levinas let us take the concept and partial analysis of affective intentionality, also mentioned before: this is a concept that Doran also uses, that Bollnow has explained, and that a recent book by Quentin Smith *The Felt Meanings of the World* has explored in very rich detail. Now although some phenomenologists go beyond description to conceptualizations and judgments, phenomenology, of itself, methodically spends itself in attending to the preconceptual.[74] We are left to make the unmade moves ourselves.

---

[74]Lonergan gives what is for me the clearest statement of what phenomenology does and doesn't try to do; in reading this quotation please also use it for an insight into the analogy between a cognitive insight that grasps a possible fact or truth, content for the time being to do no more than that, and an affective apprehension of possible value (or disvalue), worth, or good, before one submits this feeling to the criterion or criteria needed to legitimate action on the basis of that affective response. See Bernard Lonergan, *Understanding and Being* (Lewiston, NY: Edwin Mellen Press, 1980), pp. 50–52: "In this connection, Aristotle, in his *Metaphysics*, Book Seven, ch. 10, distinguished between parts of the matter and parts of the form. It is the same distinction we made with respect to the image in the example of the circle. In the circle, parts of the matter are the color of the background, the color of the line, the size of the circle, the size of the dot used to represent the point, the thickness of the line used to represent the real line which has no thickness at all. These are all parts of the matter. Parts of the form are the elements that have to be there to have the insight: radii, center, perimeter, and equality.

"The Aristotelian distinction between parts of the matter and parts of the form offers, I think, a fundamental clue to what the phenomenologist is after. The phenomenologist does not want to describe absolutely everything. He gives a selective description, a description of what is significant or, as he himself says, of what is essential, of what is relevant. That description, the presentation of data that communicates to us what is essential, is a selection of the parts of the form that are in the matter. It is not discussion on the level of conception where one tries to give a general formula that covers all possible cases. The phenomenologist presents us with a concrete situation, and in that concrete situation he picks out the parts of the form from the viewpoint of certain insights. . . . one does not settle any epistemological or metaphysical questions by phenomenology. What I have said is consistent with this. Epistemological and metaphysical questions arise on a level that we have not dealt with yet, while phenomenology is not even talking of the level of conception. . . . There is, then, a considerable movement at the present time with respect to describing the concrete by selecting the parts of the form that are in it from the viewpoint of

Further, from Robert N. Bellah and his four co-authors of *Habits of the Heart* let us take the idea of the language of the heart as a second language, as they call it, in American culture, recommended as a much needed complement to the dominant head language of individualism.

Now it seems obvious that ethical decisions, though formally occurring, as decisions, on the fourth level of consciousness, involve the levels of consciousness that are co-extensive with feeling, which is *all* of them, because as feelings, as apprehensions of values, they are essential to the realm of moral values (as well as of all values). But how do we talk about facts and values in the same schema of consciousness when the main event seems to be the cognitional and volitional sequence, with feeling relegated to a dotted line running up the side? What does they say about feelings? Feelings are obviously not without enormous complexity and differentiation of their own, and so the dotted line must be taken as shorthand for the levels of differentiation of affective consciousness, the kind of consciousness given in feelings all the way up to and beyond evaluations (the other end of the dotted line). Clearly we have the right and duty to ask whether the language of affective consciousness, that of being touched, moved, at peace, anxious, jealous, etc., is correctly diagrammed until the differentiation of feelings as apprehensions of values is integrated into the rest of consciousness.

Let us therefore try to make the connection between the language of the heart and ethics by taking a lead from Robert Doran, which, when integrated into Matthew Lamb's diagram (*see* **Diagram A**, p. 113), results in the expanded diagram (*see* **Diagram B**, p. 114): open to suggestions for revision, I hasten to add!).

According to Lonergan, then, we have two reasons, two knowledges, the head's, i.e., the first three levels of cognition, and the fourth and fifth, i.e., the heart's. But this manner of speaking leads to confusion because the fourth level of consciousness is formally volitional rather than cognitional: it is conscious, of course, but the operations of the fourth level concern volition (based on the prior three levels of cognitional consciousness); so we really shouldn't speak of the fourth level as a second reason or knowledge as Lonergan does, nor should we, *a fortiori*, extend this manner of speaking

---

certain insights. Phenomenologists are communicating insight through the concrete, and not through the general conception that selects what is essential and is found in every case. Phenomenology is talking to the Athenians the way the Athenians could understand, not in the way Socrates did and for which he was put to death."

Diagram A[1]
The Basic Levels and Structures of Consciousness

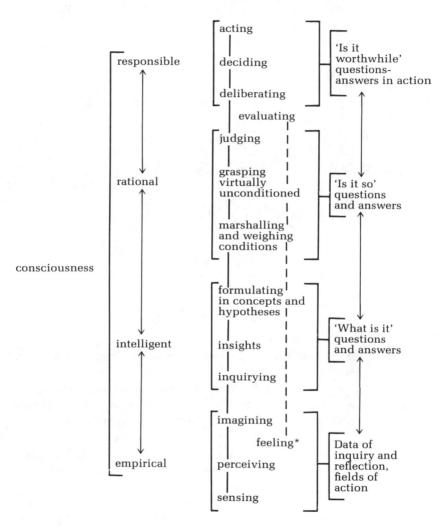

* Feeling is co-extensive with consciousness.
1. Matthew L. Lamb, *History, Method and Theology.* (Missoula: Scholars Press, 1978), p. 368.

Diagram B
Differentiation of Affective Consciousness as Partial Extension of
Matthew Lamb's Diagram According to Robert Doran's Analogies

```
----- evaluating
    : A
    : F                    ⎧   affective response = real value
    : F  C                 ⎪
    : E  O                 ⎨   affective apprehension II
    : C  N                 ⎪
    : T  S                 ⎪   affective conversion
    : I  C                 ⎩
    : V  I
    : E  O                 ⎧   affective response = possible value
    :    U                 ⎪
    :    S                 ⎨   affective apprehension I
    :    N                 ⎪
    :    E                 ⎪   inner affective condition
    :    S                 ⎩
    :    S
----- feeling
```

into the fifth level, that of being in faith, love, trust, and hope, as
again Lonergan does, insofar as he speaks of the heart's reasons as
consciousness on the fifth level.

What this means is that clearly we have the task of integrating
several levels of highly differentiated consciousness, and—paradoxical as it may seem—the only correct way to integrate them is first to
differentiate them even more, for the problem precisely is the undif-
ferentiation of *affective* consciousness; cognitional consciousness
and colitional consciousness have received relatively adequate attention in comparison with the affective dimension. Another way to
put this is to say that chapter 4 of *Method* has to be integrated both
with the three sections on "Feelings," "The Notion of Value," and
"Judgments of Value" in chapter 2 of *Method*, which have to do with
how we apprehend and judge *value*, and with the teaching in *Insight*
on how we apprehend and judge *truth*, for Doran's clue is that there
is a fruitful analogy between our cognitive and affective consciousness.

The texts from *Method in Theology* clearly constitute a considerable advance over the doctrine of *Insight* where the word feeling occurs ex professo once and is dealt with in an entirely pejorative fashion. Clearly also in *Method* there seems to be much more going on in consciousness than that feeling be just a dotted line running up the side of the cognitional and volitional operations, riding piggyback, as it were, on the only four "Basic Levels and Structures of Consciousness" that are recognized there.

What of affective consciousness, then, as a distinct kind of consciousness, with a distinct kind of intentionality, namely, affective intentionality, with its distinctive apprehension of values, analogous to the cognitive operation called understanding through insight, and of its distinct way of doing something analogous to grasping (though the word is wrong, since it is more grasped than grasping) the virtually unconditioned and making true value judgments possible?

Doran's Proposals

To respond to these questions I turn to Robert Doran. As is well known he has been working for years on related questions. His first two books are important contributions to the whole realm of affective or psychic conversion, which is the key to the justiciation of differentiated and developed (converted) feeling as operative on the level analogous to the third level of cognitional structure. His studies constitute very significant complements to Lonergan's own still imperfectly argued and integrated opening of the structure of consciousness to include the affective. I am grateful to him for letting me see a chapter from his third book, in progress. What I offer here is obviously indebted to him; I have simply worked out something of a philosophical justification and expanded on his suggestion by integrating what he proposes with *Insight*.[75]

The analogy he proposes is that feeling (what I call *Heart I*, i.e., still unconverted heart) is to *possible* or potential value or good what insight is to possible or potential truth. So feeling, i.e., apprehension of value, is analogous to understanding through insight.

---

[75]I am omitting Doran's very helpful comparison of the apprehension of possible and actual values with two of the three "times" (or inner conditions) of the person making an election during the Spiritual Exercised according to Ignatius's "Rules for the Discernment of Spirits." Suffice it to say that there is a remarkable coming together of the formal and material insights of Lonergan and Rahner, respectively, on the relevance of Ignatius's extraordinary perception of the role of feeling in matters ethical and theological.

And as insights are a dime a dozen, so also are feeling at this second level. (The word apprehension, by the way, is not the best, but neither is it good to describe insight, as I will say in a minute.)

The second analogy is with the second insight, the one that grasps the virtually unconditioned and lets us move from possible or potential truth to real or actual truth, and so to judgment. Doran suggests that there is something analogous in our becoming sure that our values are real goods. In *Method* we read that value judgments are objective insofar as they come from a self-transcendent subject, i.e., in their being those of a subject whose being is authentic: authenticity is the criterion. This is what I have called *Heart II*, the converted heart, i.e., the subject of psychic conversion, in Doran's terms. In a very helpful text Lonergan talks about the very criterion we are looking for, namely, something analogous to the grasp of the virtually unconditioned, and says explicitly that that criterion is the *being* of the subject (he does not say it is the *knowledge* of the subject, and thus we are immediately put in mind of the doctrine of knowledge by affective connaturality). Here we touch the difference between representational and non-representational (= affective) intentionality: from feeling, at the low end of the dotted line, at the empirical level, where all intentionalities, including the cognitive, are presentational (Lonergan speaks of the activities of the first level of consciousness, in *Insight, Understanding and Being*, and *Method*, as presentations, not representations), all the way, through its differentiations (and let us not forget these differentiations), to evaluation (the other end of the dotted line). Feelings, as affective intentions, remain non-representational, however, and do not terminate in images, concepts, judgments. They are felt: we are touched. In emotion we are moved. In passion we are gripped. But they *are* intentions, which means that with all this apparent subjectivity they also have objective content; the obvious point of that difference with affective intentionality is that the authenticity of the subject who is making the value judgments makes all the difference, and this is precisely what Lonergan says:

> Such judgments are objective or merely subjective inasmuch as they proceed or do not proceed from a self-transcending subject. Their truth or falsity, accordingly, has its criterion in the authenticity or the lack of authenticity of the subject's *being*. . . .
>
> Judgments of value differ in content but not in structure from judgments of fact. . . . In both, the criterion is the self-transcendence of the

subject, which, however, is only cognitive in judgments of fact but is heading towards moral self-transcendence in judgments of value. . . .

The judgment of value, then, is itself a reality in the moral order. By it the subject moves beyond pure and simple knowing. By it the subject is constituting himself as proximately capable of moral self-transcendence, of benevolence and beneficence, of true loving.

Intermediate between judgments of fact and judgments in value lie apprehensions of value. Such apprehensions are given of feelings. . . . Apprehensions of value occur in a further category of intentional response which greets either the ontic value of a person or the qualitative value of beauty, of understanding, of truth, of noble deeds, of virtuous acts, of great achievements. For we are so endowed that we not only ask questions leading to self-transcendence, not only can recognize correct answers constitutive of intentional self-transcendence, but also respond with the *stirring of our very being* when we glimpse the possibility or the actuality of moral self-transcendence. . . .

Finally, the development of knowledge and the development of moral feelings head to the existential discovery, the discovery of oneself as a moral being, the realization that one not only chooses between courses of action but also thereby makes oneself an authentic human being or an unauthentic one. With that discovery, there emerges in consciousness the significance of personal value and the meaning of personal responsibility.[76]

Let us pursue Doran's suggestion of an analogy between the two insights of cognitional consciousness and two kinds of apprehension

---

[76]Lonergan, *Method*, pp. 37–38 (emphases added). Beverly Wildung Harrison, *Our Right to Choose. Toward a New Ethic of Abortion* (Boston: Beacon Press, 1983), recognizes the need for something like conversion or moral self-transcendence as condition for self as criterion in moral judgments. See pp. 265–266: "By moral intuitions, I mean those deeply felt reactions—empathy or revulsion—which catapult us into ethical reflection. I affirm the importance of intuition as a ground for moral reasoning, but I am not an intuitionist when it comes to moral theory. Often our moral intuitions function well in registering things morally amiss in a given situation. Sensitive people with a well-developed conscience are deeply attuned to their moral intuitions and do well to trust them. Our intuitions per se, however, are not infallible. Moral reasoning serves to test our intuitions, provided of course that conditions of openness and mutual respect prevail. In political debate, however, the necessary condition of genuine openness is rare. Given this rarity, it is understandable that many women are drawn to moral intuitionism. Certain in the knowledge that their feelings are a good moral guide, they are reluctant to trust, and some even mistrust, their power of reason-giving. To a great extent, their embrace of intuitionism is a defense against the abstract character of much moral theory. I believe we are right when we value feeling as the point of departure for our reasoning, but unwise when we endorse complete reliance on it as a full and sufficient theory."

of value (two, at least, differentiations of feeling). To verify whether his idea is acceptable let us go back to *Insight* (pp. 3–4). We find that the event of insight is characterized on the second level of cognitional structure by five notes; "insight

(1) comes as a release to the tension of inquiry,
(2) comes suddenly and unexpectedly,
(3) is a function not of outer circumstances but inner conditions,
(4) pivots between the concrete and the abstract, and
(5) passes into the habitual texture of one's mind."

Account taken for the differences between affective (presentational, non-representational) intentionality and cognitional (representational) intentionality, these five points also describe the way feelings intend their objects. Despite their being two kinds of consciousness, they are both consciousnesses, i.e., ways of intending, and as such are alike enough to make analogy possible. The differences between them are sufficient, however, to make analogy necessary. If one advert to these five points about how insight happens and then compare the advent of insight to the advent of the kinds of feelings that happen to us with a remarkably similar spontaneity on the second level of affective consciousness, the parallel should not be missed.

And then look at the way the second insight is described (*Insight*, p. 280): "a virtually unconditioned involves three elements, namely:

(1) a conditioned,
(2) a link between the conditioned and its conditions, and
(3) the fulfilment of the conditions."

This is the *formal* structure of the second insight. It would not be unreasonable to ask: "Is that all?" And yet Lonergan repeatedly characterizes the link in the same cautious terms, as though adamantly refusing it any specific content. That content is, then, able to be (and should be) considered a repetition and (or "in") sublation (*Aufhebung*) of the content that mediated the first insight that occurred on the second level, with the content, of course, brought into relation with new conditions; it may take a lot of thoughtful work to set up those conditions, a lot of headwork, but again the act of insight comes in the same way the first insight did, fulfilling the same five conditions; the difference lies in our bringing the content of first insight into contact with a new requirement without which the possible truth remains merely possible and not actual, disallowing our affirming it in judgment.

But in both occasions of insights as in both occasions of feelings, the remarkable similarity seems too obvious to be missed—once it has been pointed out. Doran has called our attention to this similarity in the form of the analogy suggested: "feelings are to possible goods what insights are to possible truths." The analogy succeeds because insights, like feelings, are operations that as much happen to us as they are performed by us. Indeed we do work hard to prepare the terrain for correct insights and appropriate feelings, especially by trying to bring to consciousness the appropriate images, whether to prepare for insights that result in cognitive understanding—they certainly come infinitely more frequently and reliably when mediated by good examples, appropriate images, and suitable illustrations—or to prepare for mediating the desired affective consciousness evoked by symbols, which are feeling-charged images, into good actions, as Lonergan points out in the rich section on symbols in chapter 3 of *Method*.

When insights and feelings come they both occur to us and are performed by us. We are given them; we receive them, and all our activity in view of reception. Trying to give them to ourselves really means making ourselves possible and apt recipients of them. And notice the relevance of interior conditions for both. (Recall also Dietrich von Hildebrand's discussion, in his *Ethics*, of "being able to respond.")

Notice again the move from the second level of consciousness to the third (grasping the virtually unconditioned by a kind of second insight). Here we do seem to be more active, more operational, but how? Granted there may be a lot more headwork in setting up the exact experiment needed to verify what came relatively spontaneously (although usually after years of study). But here too, truth is not reached by forcing the possible truth to fit the evidence or vice versa, but again by accepting what is the case: in a sense insights at both levels are undergone, suffered in a way analogous to the way feelings are. There is a harmony, a fit, a consonance, as we realize that the claim or thesis fits the data; this connaturality is not unlike the Thomist affective connaturality whereby the feel of a deed fits (= is befitting) the nature of the doer, or not, by either jarring or harmonizing with his or her nature. This too happens—though it is a highly prepared happening—and no forcing is possible without falsifying the whole process.

My point is that in both cases what we do is to become and thus be the kind of persons who can be given insight and given the analogue of insight in affective consciousness that feeling is: we can neither force insight nor feeling. A kind of cunning is needed, as the later Scheler might put it, in order to negotiate both, because of the inherent weakness and radical finitude of the human spirit which manifests itself in its dependence on its material embodiment.

When insights don't come we have to work all the harder to get better data and ask better questions. The same thing happens when we want to change our hearts and respond to higher values (goods), namely, we must bring into consciousness the power of transforming symbols: better images are to desired insights what better symbols are to desired feelings. As Bernard Lonergan puts it: "This need is for internal communication. Organic and psychic vitality have to reveal themselves to intentional consciousness and, inversely, intentional consciousness has to secure the collaboration of organism and psyche. Again, our apprehensions of values occur in intentional responses, in feelings; here too it is necessary for feelings to reveal their objects and inversely, for objects to awaken feelings. It is through symbols that mind and body, mind and heart, heart and body communicate" (*Method*, pp. 66–67). There's no mistaking the parallel with insight into phantasm, the *conversio ad phantasmata*.

This parallels our need, when moving from the second to the third level, cognitively to marshall and weigh conditions; the equivalent in the realm of feeling is, for Doran, and of course for Lonergan ultimately also, being someone who has undergone a psychic or affective conversion. This is an important clue. It reveals both the similarity with other conscious operations and the difference between cognitive and affective consciousness, namely that both are intentional (i.e., have objective content) but that affectivity means, unlike cognition, that the "grasp" is not a grasp but a feeling; i.e., its "word" is not "I judge . . ." or "It is so" but a feeling or mood (*Mut*, as in *Gemut*, heart), a being in peace or fear or joy (harmony, dissonance, concord, discord). Through affective conversion one has to become the kind of person who responds rightly to true values, to real goods, not only to apparent or merely pleasurable goods. The parallel is remarkable. Both insights and feelings are undergone; in both we are as much patients as agents, receivers as givers (recall the classical language of agent and possible intellects).

Conclusion

To conclude I refer to "A Technical Note" with which Lonergan ends Chapter 4 of *Method*. He says that his transcendence of faculty psychology means that the notions of pure intellect or pure reason as well as of pure will both vanish, and do so because of his differentiation of consciousness into its four levels, the fourth being the *Aufhebung* of the three below. Then he adds, remarkably, the fifth level. How does he do this? What insight or its equivalent in affective consciousness allows, or, I should say, draws consciousness past the fourth level? Recall that one could not without such justifications move from the first to second and from the second to the third, under pain of experiencing and using concepts without understanding and of judging without having grasped the virtually unconditioned, which is to judge rashly. The move to the fourth level required its own justification, namely, the mediation of value. So how do we now get to level five?

Lonergan answers that love floods our hearts and that that love affects consciousness in such a way that what I would have to call yet a third insight occurs, this time going by the name faith, a "knowledge born of love," as Lonergan calls it, an apprehension of value, of transcendent value this time, an apprehension that consists in fulfilment of the whole person in the mystery of God. So faith is an apprehension of value (*Method*, p. 116). But values are apprehended in feelings. Is faith then a feeling? Yes it is, as also are love and hope, which is another reason to forsake forever the inaccurate model of consciousness that stops short of the kind of differentiation of affectivity as *affective consciousness*. Differentiation of affective consciousness makes it a full partner of our human life. Just as consciousness changes in its cognitional and volitional quality as it moves from empirical through intelligent into rational and responsible, so also does affective consciousness. Feeling means something at the empirical level, something else at the intelligent level, with the apprehension of possible values, something else still at the rational level, with the apprehension of real values, and even something more at the fourth level as we move into volitional consciousness, and feeling takes on yet a fifth meaning when the will is transcended and faith, love, and hope, coming from not just the converted heart but the heart transformed by God's gracious gift of Self in love. The head and the heart really are distinct kinds of consciousness, and, both continually undergoing demythologizing and critique, have to be recognized as full partners on all levels, ethical and religious included.

The common thread to be found in the several sources cited in this paper concur in calling attention to the affective in ethics, in both philosophy and theology, and in both personal and social ethics. The paradigm in ethical judgment is the person whose heart or feelings have both differentiated and developed through life's experience and across all levels of consciousness. "To know God means to do justice to the poor."[77] "We know Jesus only to the extent that we try to follow him";[78] ". . . to be a disciple is to follow him.[79] The face of the Lord is revealed to us in the experience of discipleship.[80] My neighbor is that one to whom I am committed."[81] When Leonardo Boff asks "How Can We Know Christ? The Hermeneutic Problem" he answers in terms of an "existential hermeneutics,"[82] of "the primacy of orthopraxis over orthodoxy:[83] The following of Jesus means translating utopia into practice. We must try to change the world on the personal, social, and cosmic level."[84] "Only in and through the process of conversion and practical change do we have access to the God of Jesus Christ. Abstract reflection (theory) does not provide us with that access."[85]

---

[77]Elsa Tamez, *Bible of the Oppressed* (Maryknoll: Orbis Books, 1982), p. 77.
[78]Segundo Galilea, *Following Jesus* (Maryknoll: Orbis Books, 1981), p. 14.
[79]Galilea, *Following*, p. 1.
[80]Galilea, *Following*, p. 14.
[81]Galilea, *Following*, p. 28.
[82]Leonardo Boff, *Jesus Christ Liberator. A Critical Christology for Our Time* (Maryknoll: Orbis Books, 1978), p. 38.
[83]Boff, *Liberator*, p. 46.
[84]Boff, *Liberator*, pp. 291–292.
[85]Boff, *Liberator*, p. 279, his emphasis and parenthesis.

KARL RAHNER AND POPE JOHN PAUL II: ANTHROPOLOGICAL IMPLICATIONS FOR ECONOMICS AND THE SOCIAL ORDER

Ronald Modras

The theology of Pope John Paul II, no less than that of Karl Rahner, can be aptly described as an "anthropological turn." For both of them, the anthropocentrism of modern thought is not inimical to Christianity, so long as one's understanding of human nature is not unduly reduced. In opposition to a neo-scholasticism that took the cosmos for its perspective on both the human and divine, Rahner accepted Immanuel Kant's "turn to the subject" as his point of departure, reading virtually all of Catholic doctrine as a "theological anthropology." Similarly, Pope John Paul II, from the time of his inaugural encyclical, has made the human person and human dignity his principal appeal for accepting the Christian message. A seasoned opponent of Marxist humanism, he now evangelizes both the industrialized and the developing nations with the same claim that he raised in Communist-dominated Poland: that, more than any capitalistic-liberal or Marxist-socialist ideologies, the gospel of Jesus Christ and Christianity altogether provide a unique basis for "authentic humanism."[1]

That there are similarities between the anthropologies of these two thinkers comes as no surprise, given not only their Catholicism but backgrounds in Thomism and phenomenology. It is not the etiology of their thinking that I intend to consider here, however, let alone attempt an exhaustive comparison of their respective anthropologies in all their detail. My more modest aim is to survey their anthropologies for the sake of drawing out the implications of each with respect to current questions on economics and the social order. No one could ever accuse Karl Rahner of being an ivory-tower

---

[1]*Redemptor hominis*, #10. (Washington: National Catholic News Service, 1979.)

theologian nor Pope John Paul II of being a prisoner of the Vatican. The pressing issues of social and economic justice could not help but command their attention and theological consideration.

I. KARL RAHNER

In an early essay on human dignity, Rahner described human nature as characterized by spirituality, freedom, spatio-temporal incarnality, community-building, and individuality, all determining one another mutually.[2] Read superficially, Rahner does not appear to have developed sociality to an extent comparable to the other "existentials" or characteristics of human existence, thus opening himself to the allegation of harboring an individualistic bias. Rahner's principal treatment of sociality has been in terms of freedom and the self-forgetting love which he described as not merely a "regional" happening in our lives as persons but the whole of ourselves in which we possess ourselves.[3] But here too Rahner was criticized by no less than his student and friend, J. B. Metz, for neglecting the political dimensions of human existence in favor of a privatized, I-Thou sociality.[4] Prodded perhaps by Metz's own political theology, Rahner did give more attention to socio-economic concerns toward the end of his career than was his wont earlier, but not only under the rubric of sociality. The other dimensions of human existence in Rahner's anthropology bear upon questions of economics and the social order as well. Rahner's approach to these questions was virtually always ecclesiological, however, never abstract; his anthropology was ever theological and his questions regarding social ethics were framed in terms of the responsibility of the church.

1. Transcendent Freedom

Freedom lies at the heart of Rahner's anthropology, another name for spirituality or transcendence.[5] In his analysis of knowing and

---

[2]"The Dignity and Freedom of Man," Theological Investigations, henceforth TI (20 vols. London: Darton, Longman, and Todd, 1961–76; New York: Seabury, 1974–81) 2, 239.

[3]"Theology of Freedom," TI 6, 187.

[4]Johann Baptist Metz, Faith in History and Society: Toward a Practical Fundamental Theology, transl. by David Smith. (New York: Seabury, 1980) 230.

[5]William V. Dych, S.J., "The Achievement of Karl Rahner," Theology Digest 31 (1984) 325–33.

choosing, Rahner perceived the same dynamism of "reaching out" (Vorgriff) toward being in its totality, always asking questions and striving for fulfillment. This perpetual restlessness, this infinite openness, is what renders us human and, aware of it or not, "reaching out" toward the incomprehensible mystery that is God. If we were to cease questioning about God, we would cease being human.[6]

In our experience of ourselves as reaching out, we experience ourselves too as responsible and free. Freedom, for Rahner, is "the power to decide about oneself and to actualize oneself," for, just as knowing another involves simultaneously knowing oneself, so too in choosing another, we choose ourselves and create our identity.[7] Thus freedom is an a priori condition for love, the one basic moral act in which we decide about ourselves by disposing of ourselves. The whole incalculable mystery of the human person is contained and exercized in the act of loving another human being. From both his analysis of experience and the biblical doctrine, Rahner concluded that the love of God and the love of neighbor are but two names for the same reality; the one does not exist without the other.

The socio-economic implications of transcendent freedom were drawn out by Rahner himself in reaction to what he described as "pure horizontalism." Writing in the mid-1970's, Rahner perceived, among both Catholic and Protestants in both Western Europe and Latin America, attempts to reshape the substance of Christian faith and use it as a tool for "solely" secular, social aims. "Radical horizontalism" reduces God to a mere cipher, an old-fashioned and replaceable symbol for humankind, its dignity and future. It views Jesus as simply the most fruitful example of commitment to one's neighbor and a better society, and the true task of the church as being "responsibility for the world." Rahner absolved serious exponents of political theology of this kind of horizontalism, and he was willing to assume that it was far from frequent. But he did perceive, in some measure at least, an attempt to view the church as an "exclusively horizontally directed utopian power for worldly and secular changes in society."[8]

In reaction to this "radical" or "exclusive" horizontalism, Rahner did not suggest that Christianity imposes the vertical dimension as

---

[6]*Foundations of Christian Faith: An Introduction to the Idea of Christianity*, transl. by W. Dych, S.J. (New York: Seabury, 1978) 48.

[7]*Ibid.*, 38.

[8]"Opposition in the Church," *TI* 17, 133. See also "The Church's Commission to Bring Salvation and Humanization," *TI* 14, 295–96.

something supplementary to the horizontal. God is not a particular
factor alongside other factors, and our relationship to God is mediated through our relationship to our social environment as a relationship of unreserved trust, self-commitment, and love. It is precisely in speaking about God, however, that Christianity lays bare
the ultimate radicality, dignity, and mysterious depth of our horizontal relationships.[9]

This does not mean that a "certain priority" cannot be given at
times to the horizontal over the vertical. The situation of the church
is no different from that of an individual Christian who has to miss
church on Sunday in order to put out the fire in his burning house.
Faced with the danger of a general conflagration in our world, the
church may well emphasize the duty of our loving one another more
radically than it did in the past. But even a Christianity aware of its
responsibility for the world still needs to pray, reflect theologically,
thank and praise God.[10] No horizontal dimension is whole and
complete in itself without the vertical, whereby we are set free to
open ourselves unreservedly to our neighbor, protected from being
enslaved by our social material environment.

If God and the world may not simply be identified, it follows not
only that the absolute may not be exhausted in the world, but neither
may the world be regarded as absolute. Human transcendence thus
provides the basis for the protest against all idolatry. Our transcendent reaching out to God relativizes all our theories, tasks, and
utopias. When we refuse to acknowledge God, the temptation arises
to construct absolutes out of partial realities, to create ideologies
that justify our social systems, and demonize those who disagree
with us. Transcendence disallows our attaching absolute importance
to any particular social theory or political-economic system, and
protests the fanaticism and intolerance which follow upon such
secular idolatries.[11] With their eschatological hope that human transcendence will be fulfilled, Christians should be the last to cling
desperately to conserve the present or the past.

A further corollary of human transcendence is the realization that
personal happiness and fulfillment or a freer, better world cannot be
the ultimate values which govern our actions. To seek happiness and

---

[9]"The Church's Commission," *TI* 14, 306. See also "The Theological Dimension of
the Question about Man," *TI* 17, 60.

[10]"The Church's Commission," *TI*, 14, 310.

[11]"The Inexhaustible Transcendence of God and our Concern for the Future," *TI*
20, 185.

will one's own self-development are legitimate enterprises, but, in the end, only the love of God can save us. Christianity disabuses us of the illusion that complete freedom and fulfillment can be attained within history. As individuals and as a human race, we approach the consummation symbolized by the Kingdom of God, but it is attained only at the end of history. Such "Christian realism," as Rahner called it, permits us to treat the here and now as relative. It gives us the courage to take risks, to give of ourselves and thereby give up experiences and enjoyment of the here and now for the sake of a better future. This Rahner regarded as one of Christianity's most important contributions to society. "The Church's gospel of Christian realism is and remains the primary service that Christianity performs for the freedom of the individual and society."[12] The illusion that perfect freedom can be attained here and now leads only to disillusion and the temptation to abandon the struggle for greater freedom altogether; the same is true for justice.

In giving up utopian dreams of social perfection or personal fulfillment, we are thereby free to forget ourselves in a love that alone allows us to discover our true nature. Self-forgetfulness is necessary if we are to avoid turning the love of God or others into a mere instrument for self-fullment. The only way to find stability is by not seeking to avoid a fall. Love creates happiness only if it does not seek its own happiness. The paradoxical truth of Christianity is that we find ourselves only by forgetting ourselves. Such love is no mere affection or private inter-communion, but (and here one detects the influence of J. B. Metz) the sober service of "political love."[13]

2. Spiritual Materiality

In opposition to the platonizing tendencies which still distort much popular Christianity, Rahner insisted on the unity and materiality of the human person. The "soul" is not something which can exist apart from materiality but rather a way of speaking about the essence of the human person, an essence that includes bodiliness. Our loftiest concepts and most sublime moral decisions are rooted in the earth. The human spirit is not alien to the material universe but seeks and finds its perfection in and through the universe, not escaping the world but penetrating into it. That basically Thomistic

---

[12]"The Church's Responsibility for the Freedom of the Individual," *TI* 20, 56.
[13]"Christian Humanism," *TI* 9, 188.

stance led Rahner to protest against both pseudo-realists and idealists.

In one of the last articles to be published before his death, Rahner
discussed the Christian structuring of life and the world as lying
between claim and reality.[14] There is an abiding and fundamental
duality to human existence which is signified by the words reality
and utopia: we are not simply identical with ourselves but measure
reality on the basis or standards that are different from reality.

There are two false ways of dealing with this fundamental duality
to human existence. *Idealists* escape into the consolation and com-
forts of their ideals by rejecting public life and refusing to get their
hands dirty. They do not find their ideals present even in germ in
the social reality around them, only shabbiness and pitifulness, and
so they avoid it, creating quiet kingdoms for themselves far away
from the madding crowds. *Realists* are moral Darwinists, for whom
life is a struggle in which only the fittest survive thanks to their clear
heads and cold blood. If they think of God at all, it is in terms of
blessing the social order which they staunchly defend for the privileged situation it affords them.

In contrast to these false forms of idealism and realism, Christianity views life as existing in unremitting tension between utopia and
reality. Rahner is not concerned here with particular goals to be
achieved or particular formulas as the means to achieve them. The
issue is that of human existence as it is encompassed by the mystery
of God. Utopia implies more than goals for which we strive even
though they are difficult to attain. Economic security, justice, personal self-fulfillment, an ideal form of social order—all are utopian
precisely because they overtax our capacities and factually remain
ever unfulfilled. Christianity responds to this situation with the
conviction of faith that what appears as utopian is ultimately what
is real and what goes by the name of reality is what must be seen as
relative and provisional.

This radical reversal of standards is possible only with a courage
born of hope. Christian faith declares that we are moving in the
direction of the incomprehensible mystery that is God, and that we
are responsible to this God for our world and for the apparently
banal details of our inner-worldly tasks. Provisional and relative
though it is, we do not leave our world behind but take it with us in

---

[14]"Ütopie and Realität: Christliche Lebens- und Weltgestaltung zwischen Anspruch
und Wirklichkeit," *Geist und Leben* 56 (1983) 422–32.

this hope-filled movement toward God. We do what time and daily life demand of us, without even the right to hope for inner-worldly success, for it is not we who choose our own time of salvation.

We live, Rahner believed, in a wintery time for society and the church, and we should not think that with just a little more courage and a little more good will we can change our situation. The more we know about nature and ourselves through science, the more impenetrable our situation becomes for making decisions. At one time nature pre-programmed most of our decisions for us as a destiny, limited as we were by our natural environment. But now, thanks to modern technology, we can change our environment and thereby ourselves, so that we find ourselves, both as individuals and communities, groping forward half-blind. "Individually or collectively, only the simple and the stupid know exactly what we have to do."[15] We all have the responsibility before God to answer whether we have fulfilled our political obligations and loved our neighbors by making more freedom and justice possible in our world. But we should not have recourse to ideological sweeteners to spare ourselves the bitter thought that failure and decline are real possibilities for us. We have reason to demand more from ourselves than we can achieve, but to expect inner-worldly success is a sign that we are trusting in ourselves more than in God.

3. Historicity

Historicity is not one aspect alongside others in Rahner's anthropology. Every aspect of human existence is immersed in history. Every human cognition, every metaphysical concept and moral principle, involves our turning to something that is essentially historical. Moreover, to an extent that is startlingly new, we have become agents of change. Scientific research and technology allow us today to transform our physical earthly environment, our history and ourselves.

The implications of historicity for social as well as personal ethics are obvious. If historicity is central to human nature, it must be central as well to any theory of natural law. When we speak of authority, sexuality, money, and the like, we cannot help but use concepts that are historically conditioned and therefore not eternally valid. We argue falsely when we appeal to an historical and cultural

---

[15]*Ibid.*, 430.

situation that is now past or soon will be. A good number of the controversies in ethics result from the fact that the disputants, though calendar contemporaries, are living culturally in different eras.[16]

Poverty and riches are among the concepts that Rahner recognized explicitly as historically conditioned. Wealth at one time connoted great resources for one's enjoyment. In our own modern mass-consumer society, however, the poor have opportunities for enjoyment not substantially different from the rich; there are biological limits to enjoyment after all, and the rich, as often as not, are characterized by an ascetical work ethic. In our society, the rich are those who have the instruments of work at their disposal and thereby enjoy power over others. So too with poverty, which used to mean being exposed to a certain elemental insecurity in one's existence. The really poor in our industrialized northern hemisphere constitute a relatively small portion of the society.

This cannot help but have implications for religious life and for the church in our society. A member of a religious order who is dependent upon a community that is rich cannot be seriously called poor; dependency and poverty are not the same thing. A rich order cannot have poor members. The same is true for the church. When Jesus called his disciples to poverty, it was not in order to inaugurate a social program. His was not a radical rejection of possessions or an idea of a universal economic or social transformation. His call was to an act of faith in the definitive fulfillment of human existence that comes from outside our human situation as a grace. Amid the abundance of our consumer-oriented society, religious poverty means at most being satisfied with a relatively modest way of life. Similarly, Christian discipleship today means that the church is now called to provide an example of consumer ascesis in non-conformity with modern mass consumption.[17]

Christian discipleship has always meant helping the poor, but it means more today than merely giving alms. An explosive tenion exists between the northern and southern hemispheres, which Rahner did not hesitate to describe as a "global revolutionary situation" requiring a "theology of revolution."[18] According to Pope Pius XI

---

[16]"Über schlechte Argumentation in der Moraltheologie," Schriften zur Theologie, (16 vols. Einsiedeln: Benziger, 1954–84) 13, 102–06.

[17]"The Theology of Poverty," TI 8, 168–214. See also "Reflections on the Theology of Renunciation," TI 3, 47–57.

[18]"On the Theology of Revolution," TI 14, 314–30.

(Firmissimam constantiam), a social situation can be so unjust and contrary to basic human rights that it is legitimate to use force against it. In *Populorum progressio*, Pope Paul VI recognized a right to revolution when grave corruption exists in a state. It is a matter for secular social science and practical reason, however, not for theologians or the church to decide if a situation justifying revolution exists. Neither, Rahner points out, is it the task of theology to justify a revolution once it is carried out.

A revolution should not be defined primarily in terms of force. A process is revolutionary insofar as it aims at greater scope for freedom and an increase of justice and social harmony. Described negatively, a revolution attempts to eliminate social conditions which are represssive or unjust. Simply attempting to change an unjust social situation, however, without new effective alternatives for a freer, more just society, cannot be called a revolution.

The church cannot be the agent of a revolution, but it can provide a Christian motivation for a revolutionary movement and, indeed, sometimes must do so. The biblical exhortation should still conduce us to giving alms, but also to "producing changes either of an evolutionary or revolutionary kind in social structures."[19] The church has the task of arousing its members to take part in a global revolution in an appropriate way. Those who are striving to bring about a fairer balance between the two hemispheres are really outsiders and not part of the systems in power; their efforts deserve to be called revolutionary. When merely appealing to good will and principles already accepted in a society will achieve nothing, even a peaceful revolution is still a revolution.

The Christian message of eschatological hope can provide the motivation for necessary changes in society, provided that the church itself takes its message seriously. If the church sees itself merely as a conservative force, it will render its eschatological hope unworthy of belief. Being a church of the poor in today's revolutionary situation means self-criticism by the church regarding its own past and present, acknowledging its historical guilt. It means learning from contemporary history and secular society what concrete consequences follow from human rights. It means, above all, if the church is to have any credibility, making these rights real in the church's own sphere of influence and authority, giving an example of how human rights today are to be practiced and safeguarded. It

---

[19]"The Unreadiness of the Church's Members to Accept Poverty," *TI* 14, 272.

means loosening the bonds of mutual protection which exist between church authority structures and those of secular oligarchies.

4. Guilt

The freedom we exercise in history results in our being "threatened radically by guilt."[20] As individuals and as a church, we
experience a difference between what we are and what we ought to
be. Just as we know ourselves to be free and accountable, we know
ourselves too as coming into conflict with ourselves, with our self-
actualization, and thereby with God. Guilt is a permanent possibility
for individuals and societies which, in Rahner's sober view, disallows any easy, inner-worldly optimism about the future.

Rahner's sobriety regarding human nature led him to draw what
he himself described as "terrible conclusions" about the global
socio-economic situation and the "unreadiness" of the church's
members to respond to its challenge.[21] The structures of wealth and
power in our global economy are such that the industrialized northern hemisphere is accorded privileges while the undeveloped
nations of the South, like Lazarus at the gate, are left unable to help
themselves. We in the North are not only rich, we are rich "because"
the poor are poor. To will seriously the elimination of poverty for
others requires renouncing goods for oneself, and "no one among us
likes to pay enough for a banana to ensure that the banana picker
can be given a really just reward for his labor."[22]

The world is failing to do what is necessary to overcome the
economic inequities between North and South. The church's message about the need to relieve poverty is largely ineffectual. The
reason it is ineffectual is not only the fact that the clergy share too
much in the high standard of living of our modern consumer society;
they merely share in the deafness that is universal. Individuals,
clergy and laity alike, need to work together to mobilize the rest of
the church, but must realize that, even though the church has a duty
to lead the struggle against poverty, it will not do so. "The Church
will not, in any adequate sense, succeed in mobilizing the Church.
There is an unreadiness to accept poverty."[23]

The New Testament links poverty voluntarily embraced with alle-

---

[20]*Foundations*, 91–104.
[21]"Unreadiness," *TI* 14, 270–79.
[22]*Ibid.*, 278.
[23]*Ibid.*, 274.

viating the poverty of others. The coat one foregoes is intended to warm another. But the church is "a great mass of average individuals," a church of sinners. The church has failed in major historical situations in the past (e.g., its confrontation with the cultures of Asia, its inability to cope with the Enlightenment, its loss of the European working class). It is "not impossible" that the church will fail in this crisis. Indeed, all the signs point to failure. Preaching high ideals substitutes for real deeds. Obligation is divided up among everyone in such a way that no one is held responsible for discharging it. We praise evolution in preference to revolution, say we cannot when we mean we will not. We appeal to the doctrine of original sin or the saying about the poor being always with us to excuse ourselves from taking the course of action prescribed by the situation.

Inside and outside the church, both in our public and private lives, we are sinners. Rahner harbored no illusions. The church will act more or less exactly the same as secular situation, perhaps "very slightly better," but "by and large just the same." Despite all the discussion about the church ranging itself with the poor, despite heroic efforts on the part of individuals both inside and outside the church, the prospects are that we will execute half-hearted measures which will serve only to evade the problems instead of overcoming them in any genuine sense. Our unreadiness to exercise self-renunciation remains. The process needed to change basic attitudes is too slow; the creative imagination is not there. The church is influenced not only by the gospel but by the general historical and social milieu.

Just as we do not expect "heroic virtue" from individuals, we have no reason to expect it from groups or societies made up of very average individuals. The great mass of humankind is seldom ready for heroic deed, even when such are necessary. There have always been heroic individuals, but this does not mean that there has ever been a heroic church. In this instance, it will be much if the church does not form a rearguard action as it has done in many ways since the Enlightenment and French Revolution.[24]

Although Rahner was not optimistic, to expect failure is far from excusing failure. His "terrible conclusions" were not meant to enervate or destroy all will to embrace the poverty necessary to alleviate poverty. Going along with the crowd is no sure defence before the judgment seat of God. We must all struggle even when we foresee

---

[24]*Ibid.*, 277.

that we will be defeated. God may yet spare this present generation, if a few just inhabitants are found. The question each of us must ask ourselves is, are we "too rich really to help the poor."[25]

5. Individuality

Both Rahner's participation in Marxist-Christian dialogue and his studies as a Jesuit of Ignatian spirituality contributed to his thinking on the individual uniqueness of the human person. Contrary to Marxism, the Christian belief that every human person has an eternal destiny means that an individual may not be satisfied for the sake of a future humanity. Christian anthropology rejects as well the pessimism which holds that in the end it is of no consequence what any individual does. Each human person is unique. It is this affirmation of the dignity and value of every concrete human being that allows Christianity to be called a "humanism."[26]

Furthermore, a tacit presupposition behind St. Ignatius' doctrine on the discernment of spirits is the conviction that God's will can be discovered for an individual in a concrete situation above and beyond general norms. There is, Rahner concluded, an "inexpressibly individual" element in the concrete instance, bringing with it individual obligations. Individuals, whether persons or collectivities, are confronted by historical tasks which do not allow us to be guided by universal norms alone. Once it was the choice of a spouse or a profession that eluded application of general norms. Today even when recognizing the usefulness and binding nature of universal norms, we often find ourselves at a loss when confronted by questions of politics, economics, disarmament, environmental pollution, and the like. In questions such as these, individuals require the maturity to take responsibility for decisions which cannot be legitimated by universal norms alone.[27]

Morally and otherwise, the situation for Christians today is much more complex than in earlier generations. In questions of social justice as of sexual ethics, where it is not a matter of absolutely binding definitions of faith, the church's magisterium can propound teachings that are insufficient, too little nuanced, perhaps in a certain sense "simply wrong." In many areas of individual and

---

[25]Ibid., 279.

[26]"Christian Humanism," TI 9, 187–204.

[27]"Der mündiger Christ," Schriften 15, 119–32. For a digest in English, see "Reflections on the Adult Christian," Theology Digest 31 (1984) 123–26.

social life, the church can offer us guidelines toward solutions but not the concrete solutions themselves. It belongs to the church's magisterium not only to propose binding doctrines but also to allow Christians to make their ultimate decisions alone.

The church's teaching authorities have the right and responsibility to enunciate moral principles which follow from our essential nature and dignity as human persons. But besides these general principles, the magisterium also has a right to counsel and advise. Rahner perceived in papal encyclicals such as *Mater et magistra* and *Pacem in terris* and, above all, the pastoral constitution of Vatican II, *Gaudium et spes*, a new mode of expression in church teaching: not permanently valid dogmatic pronouncements nor binding canonical regulations but prophetic appeals, pastoral instructions (*Weisungen*). The distinction is of obvious significance in weighing the authority of the pastoral letters of the U.S. bishops on nuclear arms and economics. Following not simply from revelation or human nature but also from encounter with specific situations, such "pastoral instructions" are unable to impose obligations, yet they impart more than just an opinion. They are a legitimate exercise of the church's right to criticize society.[28]

The mission of the church is to mediate salvation not only for individuals in their interior, private lives but for all dimensions of human existence, including the social. Jesus was not a social revolutionary, Rahner contended, but his death was a "political event," and the church's mission, if it will be true to Jesus, must necessarily embrace the secular and social spheres as well as the cultic. Furthermore, it is precisely the fact that it has a theological understanding of its nature, a dogmatic structure, that allows the church to judge what is on the basis of what should be and thereby function as a critic of society.[29]

The church cannot deprive secular society or its institutions of the right to make autonomous political decisions. The church should not guide, manipulate, or control in any direct sense matters of culture, society, economics, or the state. But opposition, criticism, and protest belong to the very nature of a pilgrim church that respects human dignity and preaches justice. The church cannot supply concrete formulas for specific new social realities. It cannot

---

[28]"On the Theological Problems Entailed in a 'Pastoral Constitution,' " *TI* 10, 293–317. See also "The Problem of Secularization," *TI* 10, 330–36.

[29]"The Function of the Church as a Critic of Society," *TI* 12, 229–49.

impose political decisions. But the church can and does offer a transcendent perspective that recognizes concrete social realities as relative and thus open to alteration. The church can criticize what already exists so that practical changes may be more easily introduced.

One of the conditions, indeed a primary condition for the church to function as a social critic, is the separation of church and state. Even though tensions arise at times between the church and the secular state, the secularization of society is something which derives historically from the very spiritual intention of Christianity. The separation of church and state is a legitimate outgrowth of Christianity and allows the church to exercise its function of social criticism, primarily through the laity, whose responsibility it is to apply the gospel to the social and economic orders.

6. *Sociality*

In Rahner's conceptualization of the human person, human freedom, materiality, historicity, and even individuality are all interrelated to human sociality. As the foregoing makes evident, we discover ourselves and find fulfillment as human beings only by reaching out to others, not only to individuals but to communities. As Christians we find salvation mediated in and by the ecclesial community, so that the implications of human sociality are found throughout Rahner's anthropology and his theology of church. One of those implications constitutes a positive contribution which the church can make to contemporary society.[30]

Both in secular society today and in the church, there is a need and a searching for new forms of social structure, Rahner maintained, for both in secular society and in the church there is a gap between the people and their leadership. Whether in the democratic, capitalist West or in the socialist countries of the East, the problem is the same: a distance between the masses of people and controlling elites. Parliamentary government is often a facade behind which forces and agencies exercise untrammeled power over other people's lives. For both democratic and socialist societies, the challenge is one of closer contact between the enormous masses of people with the indispensable machinery of leadership so that decisions from below by the people themselves become a real possibility.[31] New

---

[30]"Modern Piety and the Experience of Retreats," *TI* 16, 135–55.
[31]"The Church's Responsibility for Freedom," *TI* 20, 59–63.

social structures are needed which can reconcile the dignity and value of the individual with human sociality while at the same time facing the social and material demands for human survival. And here, Rahner suggested, is where the church can make a contribution to an emerging historical epoch and social order.

Instead of following belatedly the social forms developed by secular society, the church in our day has an opportunity to develop within itself new models of social structure. As Vatican II made clear, the church is not just the hierarchy but a pilgrim people in which each member is called to active participation. There is a need in the church as well as in society to search for new "democratic structures" which are not mere appendages to modern democracy but embodiments of the higher forms of socialization needed today. To discover these new forms of social structure, we have to concentrate less on the universal church and more in a creative and imaginative way on the local church. The grass-roots or base communities, for example, "represent new types of genuine community life which correspond to the new groupings in society for which mankind is searching today."[32]

Instead of one individual making decisions for a group, decisions affecting a group should be made by the group itself. This requires a communal decision-making process, a collective discernment of spirits comparable to the Ignatian discernment of spirits practiced by an individual in the *Spiritual Exercises*. St. Ignatius and his companions knew and practiced this sort of *"deliberatio communitaria."* The group, as a subject, faces God and seeks to know God's will for it beyond the guidance offered by general norms and within the situation of an existential choice. Making collective decisions in such a manner, a religious order or secular institute would be doing more than merely answering a demand raised by modern social awareness. No less than decisions made by individuals, by bishops or a pope, such collective decisions are in the strictest sense self-expressions of the church. Just as when it gathers for the Eucharist or prayer, a community of Christians gathered together in a collective decision-making process makes the church to be a reality.[33]

The church, like any social body, is subject to the process of institutionalization, guilty of not adapting swiftly enough to changes in the historical situation and tempted to become an end in itself or

---

[32]"Modern Piety," *TI* 16, 147. See also "Basic Communities," *TI* 19, 159–65.
[33]*Ibid.*, 151.

merely conservative force. If the church is *semper reformanda* as
Vatican II taught, then so too are its institutions. Self-criticism and
reform is a prior condition to criticizing or positively contributing
to society. It follows, Rahner reasoned, that the church must consider the relationship between its central authority and the legitimate autonomy of local communities. The abiding structure that is
a *jus divinum* does not preclude the introduction of democratic
structures in the church.[34] A church that defends the dignity of the
individual must be on guard not to appear as a form of clerical
totalitarianism. Besides its official structures, there is need for a
charismatic and prophetic church, in which there is freedom for
research in theology and freedom of association for individual
Christians. In this post-modern age the church can contribute to
society by living according to its own principles and providing an
example of freedom, sociality, and genuine collective decision-
making from below.

Pope John Paul II

Even though Rahner wrote relatively little on social ethics, the
implications which he himself drew from his anthropology for
economics and the social order are both rich in insight and suggestive of further development. They belie any earlier accusations of
individualistic bias and neglect of the political dimensions of human existence. No one, on the other hand, accuses Pope John Paul II
of being apolitical. His reputation is precisely that of a champion for
human rights and social justice. He speaks out constantly on the
dignity of the human person and the rights which derive from it.
Thus, when his "Apostolic Exhortation on Reconciliation and Penance" appeared in 1984 with its emphasis on personal over social
sin, his approach to social issues was thought to be a "paradox."[35]

That Pope John Paul II would warn against emphasizing social sin
may appear inconsistent with his popular image, but it is not at all
inconsistent with his earlier writing, both before and after his
election to the papacy. Perhaps more than any other pope in history,
Karol Wojtyla has written and spoken on anthropological issues and
drawn from them explicit ethical implications. Even a summary

---

[34]"The Church as Critic," *TI* 12, 231.
[35]Kathleen Healy, R.S.M., "To Sin Socially is More Human," *National Catholic
Reporter* (March 8, 1985) 11.

review of the more important of those teachings demonstrates that the Pope is anything but inconsistent.

1. Early Writings

a. From almost the very beginning of his academic career, Karol Wojtyla has written in the areas of anthropology and ethics. His philosophical dissertation qualifying him to teach at a university (habilitation) investigated the possibility of constructing a Christian ethics on the principles of the system of phenomenologist Max Scheler.[36] His concluding theses were that phenomenological analysis of consciousness was not enough to obtain objective moral norms and that metaphysics was necessary for Christian ethics. A year later, in a 1960 article comparing Scheler to Thomas Aquinas, he described Thomism as the "one and only example" of theological ethics which, because of its metaphysical categories, adequately interprets "revealed" Christian moral teaching philosophically. He admits in The Acting Person that his "acceptation" of the personalism of Kant and Scheler is only "partial." For the sake of discussion with contemporary philosophy and, as he apparently believes, wider acceptance, Wojtyla has resorted to the methods of phenomenology and the language of personalism to translate Thomism into what he describes as "Thomistic personalism."[37]

b. In a 1961 article under that title,[38] Wojtyla assembled and analyzed what he regarded as personalist elements from St. Thomas' writings, especially his ethics. He describes personhood as the "highest perfection" in the created order and morality as its foremost characteristic. In his analysis of the human person as a rational compositeand creator of culture, one is struck by his emphasis upon the will and the concept of domination. "It is through the will that man is lord of his actions, and self-consciousness reflects that domination in a particular way." Love is described as truly human when "sensual energy and appetites are subordinated to a thorough understanding of the true value" of the one loved. Personalism is described as explaining the meaning and means of obtaining self-discipline.

---

[36]Ocena możliwości zbudowania etyki chrześcijańskiej przy założeniach systemu Maksa Schelera, (Lublin: KUL, 1959).

[37]See R. Modras, "The Thomistic Personalism of Pope John Paul II," The Modern Schoolman 59 (1982) 117–27.

[38]"Personalism Tomistyczny," Znak 13 (1961) 664–76.

Within this context Wojtyla examines the relationship of the individual to society. He adopts the Thomistic position that the good of the individual must be "subordinated" to the common good but not so as to disvalue the individual or to cancel out individual human rights. He cites here as an example the right to freedom of conscience. Social morality is concerned with finding the fullest correlation between the "true" good of the individual and the common good of society. To put one's individual welfare above the common good constitutes "the error of individualism, from which liberalism has developed in recent times and, in economics, capitalism." The "error of totalism" on the other hand subordinates the individual to society "for the supposed common good," while in actuality canceling out the "true good of the person." Society must guarantee rights such as freedom of conscience, invariably violated by totalism. But, Wojtyla insists, the individual must be "subordinated" in all that is indispensable for the common good, even if it means "heavy sacrifices."

c. In 1969, Wojtyla's most extended work on anthropology appeared, The Acting Person.[39] In it he insists on the priority of the conception of the person and of action as the basis for any interpretation of community and interpersonal relations. With both phenomenological description and metaphysical reasoning, he attempts to demonstrate the spirituality and transcendence of the human person in action. Whereas Rahner identifies spirituality and transcendence as the essential nature of being human, Wojtyla distinguishes between the two. In our experience of ourselves as acting persons, we intuit a transcendence, defined by Wojtyla as self-determination or self-governance which in turn depends upon self-possession. There is a duality or bi-polarity to this intuition, however. We experience ourselves not only as governing and possessing ourselves but as governed and possessed. Spirituality or immateriality, unlike transcendence, is not experienced but inferred as a commensurate cause of our transcendence or self-determination, and with it of our experience of freedom, responsibility, and obligation. It is our spiritual nature which allows us to experience ourselves as a unity amid our complexity. The soul is the principle of integrity whereby we possess and govern our bodies, employing them as a "compliant tool."

Wojtyla admits to strata in his conceptualization of the human

---

[39]Transl. by A. Potocki and A.-T. Tymieniecka (ed.). (Dordrecht, Holland/Boston: D. Reidel Co., 1979).

person: midway between the somatic and spiritual is the psychic or emotional sphere. Authentic spiritual power consists in the intellect and will subordinating the physical and emotive spheres, if need be in an "absolute" manner (315, n. 72). Integrity consists of controlling that which is "lower" in us by that which is "higher." Such self-control allows for the fullest exercise of self-determination, which is "probably the most fundamental manifestation of the *worth* of the person himself" (264).

After analyzing the experience of ourselves as conscious, acting, self-determined individuals, Wojtyla devotes a final chapter to "intersubjectivity by participation." We exist and act together with others not only usually but universally, so that participation is a "specific constituent" of the human person. We realize ourselves as persons by fulfillment of our obligations (169). An action is moral or immoral inasmuch as it fulfills or does not fulfill the person. Participation allows for personal fulfillment, and fulfillment in action is both a human right and obligation.

Even when discussing sociality, Wojtyla accents the individual. Actions are performed by individuals not groups, and the common good of a community consists of the good of the individuals who comprise it. The authentic attitudes which individuals should have acting within a community are solidarity and opposition. *Solidarity* consists in individuals accepting their share of duties and obligations in a group. It recognizes that sometimes the common good requires assuming the obligations of others. It allows us to find fulfillment in complementing others. *Opposition* aims at more adequate means for attaining the common good. It does not withdraw from participation, though it may make cooperation more difficult. Both these attitudes contrast with conformism, a merely superficial participation that evades opposition, and non-involvement, which withdraws altogether. Participation is a fundamental good both for individuals and for the community. If members see withdrawal as the only solution for their personal problems, the functioning and life of the community must be defective (285–91).

d. In 1971, further light was thrown on Wojtyla's anthropology with what he called "Notations on the Margin of the Constitution 'Gaudium et Spes.' "[40] His comments pertained to the Council's positive valuation of the world as the theater of human history,

---

[40]"Natatki na Marginesie Konstytucji 'Gaudium et Spes,' " *Atheneum Kapłańskie* 74 (1970) 3–6.

created and sustained by God's love, fallen yet emancipated. Wojtyla was concerned that the opposition between God and the world not be glossed over or "artificially eradicated." He reminded his readers of the three-fold concupiscence and that love for God is not in those who love the world (1 Jn. 2:15–17). God is the basis for all good in the world, the guarantee of the whole "hierarchy of value." Real love is self-disinterested and seeks to enrich the world. Concupiscence is the opposite to real love, impoverishes the world, destroys human dignity, and does not permit real value and beauty to be perceived. To speak about salvation or of Jesus as "Savior of the world" is to speak about "conquering concupiscence."

e. Karol Wojtyla's concept of the human person, as the foregoing indicates, is highly individualistic, his concept of human dignity and liberation intimately connected with discipline and self-control. This explains his unrelenting interest in sexual ethics. Birth control is not a peripheral matter of secondary importance for him. In a 1978 article on "The Anthropology of the Encyclical 'Humanae Vitae,' " he described marital ethics as possessing "such powerful anthropological implications" that it has become the field for a "struggle concerning the dignity and meaning of humanity itself."[41]

f. Somewhat earlier, in a 1976 article, he described the struggle as being one between Christian philosophy and materialism.[42] Community, he writes there, is not a gift or a given but a task to be fulfilled by individuals who find their self-fulfillment in community. One cannot help but notice but that here too the accent falls on the individual and self-possession. For Karol Wojtyla, only those who possess themselves can give themselves freely as persons conscious of their dignity. There is no freedom, no dignity, no self-giving or self-fullment without self-control.

2. Pontifical Pronouncements

a. Shortly before issuing his first inaugural encyclical, *Redemptor hominis*, Pope John Paul II announced that there would be found in it thoughts which "had been maturing in me during the years of my

---

[41]"Anthropologia Encykliki 'Humanae Vitae,' " *Analecta Cracoviensia* 10 (1978) 13. See R. Modras, "Birth Control, Personalism, and the Pope," *Currents in Theology and Mission* 8 (1981) 283–90.

[42]"Osoba: Podmiot i Wspólnota," *Roczniki Filozoficzne* 24 (1976) 5–39. ET of excerpts to be found in A. Bloch and G. T. Czuczka (eds.), *Toward a Philosophy of Praxis* (New York: Crossroad, 1981).

priestly and then episcopal service." He expressed the conviction that Providence had brought him to the chair of St. Peter to disseminate his ideas to the church and world at large.[43] Obviously, the Pope does not believe that he has been called to the papacy to change his mind.

Apparent as the background to the central message of his inaugural encyclical is the Pope's struggle in Poland with official Marxist atheism: with its gospel of human worth and dignity, Christianity constitutes an "authentic humanism" (#10). The church must evangelize and compete with secular humanisms by making human dignity part of the very content of its proclamation (#12). In the name of human dignity and rights, the Pope criticizes the consumerism of the West and the uncontrolled technology that does not take human needs and the environment into its planning. He calls for "daring and creative resolves" in confronting inflation, unemployment, and the unequal distribution of the world's good. He describes as "economic imperialism" the situation whereby "privileged social classes" and "rich, highly developed societies" are able to "dominate others beyond the limit of one's legitimate rights and merits" (#15–16). He calls into question the "financial, monetary, production, and commercial mechanisms that, resting on various political pressures, support the world economy" (#16).

Compared to his explicit criticisms of the capitalist West, the Pope's criticism of the communist East is more oblique. He makes reference to the totalitarianism of the Nazis in which the "good of the state" was identified with the good "of a certain party." He calls for actualization of the spirit and not only ratification of the letter of the United Nations Declaration of Human Rights. A state fails in this respect if power is exercised only "by a certain group" so that citizens are not allowed their rightful share in political life of the community. The "fundamental duty of power is solicitude for the common good of society," which is realized only when all the citizens are sure of their rights. But the only rights the Pope expressly mentions in this context are "the right to religious freedom together with the right to freedom of conscience." He calls upon political leaders to "respect the rights of religion and of the church's activity," for the actuation of these rights is "one of the fundamental tests" of authentic human progress (#17).

In the final chapter of the Pope's inaugural encyclical, devoted to

---

[43]*Redemptor hominis*, reprinted in *Origins* (1979) 627.

the church, one is struck by the sudden shift from language about human rights to multiple references to truth, loyalty, and the church as mother. Theology's pluralism of methodology may not depart from the "fundamental unity" of the church's teaching (#19). Individual confession is highlighted over the "community aspect of penance" (#20). The fidelity of priests to celibacy is linked to the fidelity of spouses to their marriage vows (#18–21).

b. In his second encyclical, *Salvifici doloris*, on the Christian meaning of human suffering, the Pope describes suffering as a "mystery."[44] Though it is an experience of evil, it is also valued by the church as the basis for our salvation, clearing the way for grace and generating works of love. What is remarkable about the encyclical is its emphasis upon the individual aspects of suffering and its alleviation to the virtual neglect of dealing with its social causes.

c. No one, not even a pope, can say everything at one time, however, and it is in his third encyclical on human work, *Laborem exercens*, that we find the most developed expression of the Pope's social thinking.[45] Here we perceive the influence not only of Thomas Aquinas (who alone is quoted alongside the Bible and magisterium) but also of Hegel, Marx, and the community of intellectuals who helped to inspire Poland's Solidarity Movement.[46] Foundational here too is the ethical personalism of Immanuel Kant, not cited here but whose second moral imperative Wojtyla quoted in *The Acting Person* and credited for his appreciation of the personal nature of human freedom: "So act as to treat the humanity in your person and in the person of every other human being always at the same time as an end and never merely as a means."[47] Kant's personalist principle obviously lies at the basis of the Pope's insistence that workers are the purpose of labor and never merely the means of production.

The encyclical recognizes some of the most pressing socio-economic problems facing us today: automation, rises in the cost of energy, and above all the unequal distribution of wealth, now no longer just a "class" question but a "world" question. But the Pope places "at the very center" the issue of work, whose proper valuation he regards as the key, "probably the essential key," to our social problems (#1–3). Work, in all its forms, not only manual labor, must

---

[44]"On the Christian Meaning of Human Suffering," (Washington, D.C.: USCC, 1984).
[45]"On Human Work," (Washington, D.C.: USCC, 1981).
[46]See Jósef Tischner, *The Spirit of Solidarity,* transl. by M. B. Zaleski and B. Fiore, S.J. (San Francisco: Harper & Row, 1984).
[47]*The Acting Person,* 120–23, 302, n. 8.

serve to help us realize our humanity, for part of our dignity as human beings in the image of God is the universal call to co-create and humanize the earth.

Work has an ethical value by the fact it is performed by persons. The basis for its dignity is not the kind of work being done or the goods produced but the human subject performing it. The reversal of this proper order, treating labor as merely the means of production and capital as the efficient factor and purpose of production, is the error of capitalism, a form of materialism not limited to the West. Marxist as well as Western capitalist materialism reverses ends and means when it views human beings as the "resultant" of economic systems or instruments of production.

The priority of persons over goods produced means that persons have a priority over capital, that is, over the means of production which are themselves the products of human labor. The Pope emphasizes the fact that the right to private property, traditionally upheld by Catholic social teaching, has never been regarded as an absolute right. The only legitimate title to possession, whether private ownership or collective, is that ownership serve labor and make possible the universal or common use of wealth produced (#14). Private ownership of the means of production may not be seen as an "unassailable dogma" of economic life, but neither should taking the means of production out of private hands be regarded as an authentic solution. "Satisfactory socialization" is not achieved when the means of production merely passes from the hands of the owners to the control of a group of managers. It is achieved, the Pope writes, only when workers are entitled to consider themselves part owners of the workbench and know that they are working for themselves (#14–15).

The priority of the individual in the Pope's anthropology leads him to criticize the view of laborers as an impersonal "work force" (#7). It leads him too to warn against excessive bureaucratic centralization which makes workers feel like cogs "in a huge machine moved from above" (#15). One way of letting workers know they are working for themselves and of preserving the priority of labor over capital is to associate labor with the ownership of capital as closely as possible. This can be done, he suggests, by establishing "a wide range of intermediate bodies with economic, social, and cultural purposes . . . enjoying real autonomy with regard to the public powers, . . . living communities both in form and substance . . ." (#14).

With a warning once again against "one-sided centralization by the public authorities," the Pope concludes the encyclical by discussing the rights of workers, among them the right to suitable employment by all who can work and the right to "just remuneration for work done" (#18–19). He reaffirms the rights of workers to form unions but warns against the notion of class struggle or group egoism. The struggle of organized labor should not be "against" owners or managers so as to destroy an opponent, but "for" social justice and the building up of community. "It is the characteristic of work that it first and foremost unites people" (#20).

d. The anthropological principles enunciated in the Pope's encyclicals and earlier writings appear time and again in his addresses and homilies. There are far too many references in them to social and economic issues to present them in any detail, nor is there any need to, since they constitute more of a recurrent theme than a development. Speaking in Geneva, for example, at the International Labor Organization (June 15, 1982), he repeated the teaching of *Laborem exercens*, emphasizing the primacy of the person over the demands of production as the criterion for economic planning. The implications for unemployment caused by automation are obvious enough. The Pope repeated the teaching of Pope Paul VI that unemployment is a global problem requiring international solutions. He expressly stated his refusal to believe that we are incapable of finding those solutions. Our "prodigious" scientific and technical achievements convince him that we are able to find just and effective solutions to the problem of global unemployment if only we would look to "the worldwide common good" and sense of "fresh solidarity without frontiers."[48]

In Spain too (November 7, 1982), the Pope spoke to the need of making new jobs a priority over productivity and efficiency.[49] He specifically addressed the industrialists, administrators, business experts, and investors to put their entrepreneurial skills to work at creating jobs. In Canada (September 13–17, 1984), the Pope emphasized that it is the specific task of the laity to renew the temporal order by infusing the spirit of the gospel into its laws and structures.[50] There too he stressed the need to subordinate technological development to human issues and not allow it to become an auton-

[48]*Origins* 12 (July 1, 1982) 105–10.
[49]*Origins* 12 (November 25, 1982) 374–76.
[50]*Origins* 14 (October 4, 1984) 244–56.

omous force. The needs of the poor must take priority over the desires of the rich, the rights of workers over maximization of profits, the preservation of the environment over uncontrolled industrial expansion.

In speaking to bishops, however, the Pope's message often takes on a quite different tone. To the bishops of Canada, for example, it is not social justice but secularization, sexual morality, and a "generalized tendency to hedonism" that are singled out. It is not the rights of the poor that are emphasized but the rights of the church. "We are sensitive to injustice, to the unequal distribution of material good," he stated, but then went on to ask if we are "sufficiently sensitive to the fundamental freedom of the practice of one's faith," an "essential" right which is "abused every day in vast regions." In this and other concerns the Pope invited the bishops' continual collaboration "cum Petro et sub Petro."

e. Clearly, from the foregoing, Pope John Paul II was not being inconsistent when he emphasized personal over social sin in his 1984 "Apostolic Exhortation on Reconciliation and Penance."[51] All sins are social, he writes, inasmuch as we affect one another as social beings, but particularly those sins against our neighbor, against justice, the common good, freedom, and "especially against the supreme freedom" of religious worship. Analogically, the relationships between communities can be called sinful, such as class struggle, but the individuals who lead or justify it are still responsible. The Pope explicitly rejects, however, the tendency to attach blame "on some vague entity or anonymous collectivity such as the situation, the system, society, structures, or institutions." This concept of social sin "can readily be seen to derive from non-Christian ideologies and systems," he writes, with obvious reference to Marxism. Situationns of sin are the "result of the accumulation and concentration of many personal sins. . . . The real responsibility, then, lies with individuals. A situation—or likewise an institution, a structure, society itself—is not in itself the subject of moral acts. Hence a situation cannot in itself be good or bad" (#16).

III. Common and Contrasting Concerns

1. Their Christian, Catholic, and Thomistic principles provide numerous *similarities* between the anthropologies of Karl Rahner

---

[51]*Origins* 14 (December 20, 1984) 441–42.

and Pope John Paul II, though the practical implications they draw
from these principles often differ significantly with respect to economics and the social order.

• Both share a common concern that too exclusive a concern for
socio-economic issues may lead to secularism, a loss of a sense of
the radical, vertical, or depth dimensions of human existence. Rahner, however, is willing to see this vertical dimension within the
horizontal and not added to it.

• Both share an eschatological faith that relativizes the here and
now. Such a faith for Rahner, though, implies that the Church should
be more open to the future, less wed to the past, more critical of the
present and encouraging of social change. Rahner's thought is not
only compatible but amenable to a theology of revolution, at least of
peaceful revolution.

• For both Rahner and the Pope, we are creators of culture and
thereby, to some extent at least, of ourselves. The Pope conceives
this impact in terms of morality. Rahner viewed it as part of a
broader category of historicity, a characteristic almost foreign to the
Pope's anthropology. Karol Wojtyla's philosophical career has been
largely dedicated to achieving an ethics of absolute norms above the
contingencies of history, in contrast to Rahner who saw all metaphysical concepts and moral principles as affected by our concrete,
conditioned, historical experience.

• Both Rahner and the Pope are conscious of the similarities
between the capitalist West and communist East, their materialism
and ruling elites. Both expressed grave concern about the massive
inequities between the industrial North and developing South. Un-
derstandably, given his office, the Pope appears more sanguine about
our capacity to make a difference with regard to those inequalities
in wealth and consumption. A keen awareness of human weakness
led Rahner to be less optimistic about the North accepting any
serious reduction in its standard of living for the sake of greater
equity.

• For both Rahner and Wojtyla, Christianity deserves to be described as a "humanism," because of its belief in human dignity and
rights. Both highlight freedom of conscience, though for the Pope,
coming from the communist East, the accent lies on the rights of the
church and freedom of worship. Rahner, a Westerner who has taken
seriously the challenge of the Enlightenment, focused on the rights
of individuals to make autonomous decisions, since the church

cannot provide let alone impose concrete solutions to specific social, economic, or political problems.

• Both Rahner and the Pope recognize the social nature of personhood and the benefits that would accrue to creating what the Pope described as "intermediate bodies" which enjoy "real autonomy" and allow people real participation in determining their lives. One is struck, though, by the fact that Rahner stressed sociality more than the Pope, at least with respect to the opportunities and responsibilities of the church to contribute to "new types of genuine community life." Rahner calls the church to practice what it preaches and to give the world an example of self-criticism, self-reform, and more than verbal respect for human rights.

2. Focusing on human beings as acting and therefore working persons, the Pope develops his doctrine on the priority of labor over production and lifts Catholic social teaching to what is rightly described as a "new height," impressed, Gregory Baum believes, "by certain Marxist insights."[52] One might well wonder if the Pope would accept the inference, especially when he so flatly rejects as an intrusion of "non-Christian ideologies" the description of situations, institutions, or structures as constituting "social sin." The Pope prefers to draw his thought from Christian sources.[53] Moreover, he has an almost nominalist bias toward viewing sin as discrete acts and hence concentrates on the private aspects of penance. Apparently, he is either not aware of or else not convinced by recent efforts to come to a deeper understanding of the doctrine of original sin in terms of the inescapable universality of what is called the "sin of the world" (Schoonenberg). There is no need to attribute to a foreign ideology the idea that an historically inherited state, situation or social structure can be truly, even if analogously, called sinful.

3. If, as Plato indicates, one's anthropology provides a model for one's politics, then the primary difficulty we as Westerners might well have with the Pope's anthropology and its implications for church and society is its stratified, unabashedly hierarchic view of the person. For Rahner, all the dimensions of human existence are interrelated and interpenetrate each other mutually. The Pope's anthropology, however, despite its use of personalist categories, is

---

[52]Gregory Baum, *The Priority of Labor* (Ramsey, N.J.: Paulist, 1982) 3–4.

[53]See John Hellman, "John Paul II and the Personalist Movement." *Cross Currents* 30 (Winter, 1980–81) 409–19.

still substantially marked by a Thomist philosophy of nature with its "lower" and "higher" orders. This explains the Pope's concern about sexual ethics and frequent references to "subordination," as he uses phenomenology to evangelize the world with his Thomist principles, intuiting and describing his own personal consciousness and experiences. It is his own remarkable personality that gives rise to his high valuation of self-control and his concept of human worth and transcendence as a matter of being self-determining and determined.

For all their similarities, the differences between the theological anthropologies of Karl Rahner and Karol Wojtyla are even more pronounced. Both anthropologies are thoroughly Christian and centrally situated in the pluralism that is Catholic theology today. However, with regard to their respective implications for economics and the social order the question is: Are they equally adequate in assisting the church to be true to its mission and therefore credible?

ECONOMIC SYSTEMS AND THE SACRAMENTAL IMAGINATION

Joseph A. La Barge

The recently published first draft of the U.S. Catholic bishops' pastoral letter on the American economy takes as its point of departure two questions: "What does the economy do *for* people? What does it do *to* people?[1] The bishops attempt to answer these questions by evaluating the U.S. economy in light of their understanding of the Christian vision of economic life and the ethical norms which grow out of that vision.

Theologically, the bishops root their vision of economic life in biblical motifs of creation, covenant and community which achieve moral expression in the primacy of justice informed by love. While I find myself in agreement with the bishops on the foundational importance of these biblical themes and moral norms, I am somewhat less comfortable or sure about the way in which the bishops fit these themes and norms together with economic systems. With the hope of clarifying some of these issues I would like to address the following questions:

1. What, actually, is an economy and what role does it play in the life of a people?
2. What are the origins or roots of our present economic crisis?
3. What are the functional or root metaphors out of which western culture (including the American economy) draws its strength?
4. What theological resources might be employed for renewing the social order?

The Nature of an Economy

The bishops look at the American economy and ask what "it" does "*for* people" and "*to* people?" While these are perfectly reason-

---

[1]"Catholic Social Teaching and the U.S. Economy," *Origins* 14, 22/23 (Nov. 15, 1984), 341.

able questions to ask, they do seem to portray the economy as *some thing* extrinsic to people, affecting them from the outside.[2] In contrast to this rather deductive approach, I would argue for viewing the economy (and other social systems) as people—expressing themselves, their values, their social relationships, their visions and dreams, and embodying them in economic processes and social patterns. More specifically, an economy embodies those strategies and structures a society devises for producing, distributing, exchanging and consuming goods and services. There are several points to note here. First, social systems such as economies don't just "happen"; they are the result of decisions people make. Secondly, once created, an economy becomes part of the world people "inherit." Thus, an economy is both process and product.

The creation of social systems such as an economy is described by Peter Berger and Thomas Luckmann as three dialectically related "moments" of world-building involving acts of externalization, objectivation and internalization.[3] Through *externalization* persons or groups of persons project their own meanings onto their world and sustain these meanings through institutions and social structures. This meaning-shaped world is then experienced (particularly by succeeding generations) as having a certain factual or *objective character*. *Internalization* is the reappropriation into human consciousness of that objective world through education, value formation and role modeling. In this way the humanly fabricated structures of the world are able to exert a formative influence on consciousness itself.[4]

---

[2]Cf. Joe Holland, "Economic Pastoral ... Should Put Work Over Economy," *National Catholic Reporter* (Feb. 22, 1985), 18. Holland further observes: "This has been the dominant tendency of modern liberal mechanistic thought, namely to see the economy as a machine outside of people. The bishops accept this frame of reference but call for a humanized machine. Mostly, they ask that the fruits of the machine, including access to decision-making and employment be distributed justly. But they do not foundationally challenge the objectified mechanistic vision that lies at the root of the modern liberal or capitalist economy" (*ibid.*).

[3]Cf. Peter Berger and Thomas Luckmann, *The Social Construction of Reality* (New York: Doubleday, Anchor Books, 1967); also: Peter L. Berger, *The Sacred Canopy: Elements of a Sociological Theory of Religion* (New York: Doubleday, Anchor Books, 1969), 3-28. As Berger and Luckmann note: "These moments are *not* to be thought of as occurring in a temporal sequence. Rather society and each part of it are simultaneously characterized by these three moments, so that any analysis in the terms of only one or two of them falls short. The same is true of the individual member of society, who simultaneously externalizes his own being into the social world and internalizes it as an objective reality. In other words, to be in society is to participate in its dialectic" (Berger and Luckmann, *op. cit.*, 129).

[4]Lest an overly-mechanistic impression be given of this process Berger and Luck-

When the fabricated nature of the economic order is lost sight of, the status quo is most often perceived as normative. At that point an economy becomes an ideology (with sacral overtones), legitimating the existing order by glossing over or de-emphasizing the contradictions and inequities generated by the system. When this happens, as Gregory Baum observes,

> people begin to feel that it is disloyal to doubt the values and institutions approved by society. They learn not to ask certain questions. Even when the present order makes them suffer—for instance, through unemployment, job insecurity and destitution—they shy away from challenging the existing economic system. Public ideology is so powerful that people easily put the blame on innocent groups, or they accuse themselves for being failures and feel guilty.[5]

Yet because people do more than produce, exchange and consume goods and services, a society is more than just its economy. Political institutions (affecting the distribution of power) and cultural structures (including ethnic and racial heritages, religious beliefs, value systems, etc.) are also essential to a society, interfacing with economic systems in ways that are as important as they are complex. Consider, for example, the feminization of poverty, or who makes the corporate decisions which direct the economic and political energies of a nation. Clearly, gender, wealth, race, and power often fit together in frequently predictable ways. Unfortunately, this makes it difficult to talk simply about an economy and its effects, since an economy is but one of the many social systems that people create and, in turn, are created by.

It strikes me that analyzing an economy as a dynamic social system might be fruitful for a number of reasons. It would provide a fuller and more accurate picture of the ways in which such a system

---

mann caution: "No individual internalizes the totality of what is objectivated as reality in his society, not even if the society and its world are relatively simple ones. On the other hand, there are always elements of subjective reality that have not originated in socialization, such as the awareness of one's own body prior to and apart from any socially learned apprehension of it. Subjective biography is not fully social. The individual apprehends himself as being both inside *and* outside society. This implies that the symmetry between objective and subjective reality is never a static, once-for-all state of affairs. It must always be produced and reproduced *in actu*. In other words, the relationship between the individual and the objective world is like an ongoing balancing act" (Berger and Luckmann, *op. cit.*, 134).

[5]Gregory Baum and Duncan Cameron, *Ethics and Economics: Canada's Catholic Bishops on the Economic Crisis* (Toronto: James Lorimer, 1984), 64.

is a partial embodiment of a people's public life, interlocked with
political structures and institutional alliances, and steered by a set
of national priorities. Secondly, it would serve to illuminate the
cultural matrix of a society containing the dreams, myths, symbols
and root metaphors which are the driving force of any social group.
Finally, such an approach would be theologically significant because, as a human creation, an economy takes on the sinful and
graceful characteristics of its creators.[6] Such an analysis will succeed, however, only to the extent that it is possible to capture the
dynamic interaction, over time, between economic, political and
cultural forces. It is to the past then, that we must now turn to trace
the roots of our present crisis. (Because of the attention devoted to
the problems of economics and world order, the analysis presented
here draws, in many ways, on that of Pope John Paul II in his
encyclical *Laborem Exercens.*[7])

Origins of the Present Economic Crisis

In his encyclical on the importance of labor, Pope John Paul
identifies two phases of industrial capitalism which have already
appeared and mightly affected the world; he then points to a third
phase which has only recently begun. The first stage, which spanned
much of the nineteenth century, John Paul calls "rigid capitalism,"
because it staunchly resisted the efforts of political forces to affect
the economic market.[8] Based largely on enterprising, family-owned
companies, this phase of capitalism was characterized by risky
business ventures, low wages, and few consumer goods. The prevailing societal response to this first phase was largely one of freedom:
political freedom from government intrusion into business; cultural
freedom to be enterprising in any way that was profitable and
productive. The result was that even if many such ventures failed,
those that were successful frequently gained much. And while
poverty was widespread among working people, there was always
the hope that conditions would improve.

---

[6] Cf. Thomas E. Clark, *Above Every Name: The Lordship of Christ and Social Systems*
(New York: Paulist Press, 1980), 4–5.

[7] Cf. Pope John Paul II, *Laborem Exercens*, in appendix, Gregory Baum, *The Priority
of Labor* (New York: Paulist Press, 1981); cf. also: Joe Holland and Peter Henriot,
Social Analysis: Linking Faith and Justice, rev. and enlarged ed. (Maryknoll: Orbis,
1984), a work inspired in large part by *Laborem Exercens.*

[8] John Paul II, *Laborem Exercens*, #8.

Around the turn of this century, due in large part to the emerging labor movement and the support it received from socially sympathetic governments, John Paul suggests that industrial capitalism entered its second phase of development. He calls this phase "neo-liberal" or "neo-capitalist" because market forces became more affected by political, social and cultural factors.[9] During this period (lasting perhaps to the mid-1960's), improved technology made more goods available, family-owned businesses gave way to larger corporations and social welfare legislation flourished. All this combined to make prosperity more widespread, though not universal. Politically, the emergence of federal agencies to regulate commerce, banking, and many industrial transactions, meant more restrictions on the so-called "free market." Culturally, the improved lot of some fed the desire for even more freedom for many, with the freedom movement reaching perhaps its finest rhetorical expression in this country in the "dream" of Dr. Martin Luther King, Jr.

Yet, John Paul continues, this more benevolent form of capitalism seems to have ended. With the transnationalization of capital and the emergence of new computer-based technologies, a new era seems to have arrived. While the pope doesn't give this period a name, two social analysts, Joe Holland and Peter Henriot, drawing on the insights of John Paul, call this phase "national security industrial capitalism."[10]

Some suggest this period is different in many important ways from anything seen before. Now that technology has made industry more capital-intensive and more mobile (greater emphasis on automation and less need for common laborers), when the cost of raw materials, taxes and wages rise, industry often finds it easiest to pull up and move to where the conditions are more favorable. The social consequences of such changes are not hard to detect: frequent local unemployment and a global industrial marketplace. Politically, as Holland and Henriot note, "this development places authoritarian states that repress their workers and provide few social services at a competitive advantage in the world market. Hence the flourishing of dictatorships and the crisis of democracy worldwide."[11]

The name of the game is now geopolitics and geoeconomics. As Holland Henriot again observe: "The state has [now] become to the

---

[9]Ibid.
[10]Holland and Henriot, op. cit., 77–83.
[11]Ibid., 78.

world market what the corporation once was to the national market, and before that, the family firm to the local market. The state is now charged, not only with moderate economic regulation within the boundaries of the national economy, but with streamlining the whole national system for efficient transnational competition."[12] With commerce now on a global scale, many industrially advanced nations find themselves forced to emphasize greater fiscal austerity, lower wages, fewer social services, more law and order and, above all, more for defense. Hence, national security industrial capitalism.

The way in which the industrialized world has developed economically, politically and culturally is of concern to the Pope (and to the American bishops) for two reasons: the crisis in human hardship that has accompanied these developments, the moral insensitivity that has contributed to and perpetuates much of this suffering, and what all this says about the culture which an economy both reflects and shapes. The symptoms are all too well known: widespread unemployment; frequent disregard of basic human rights in the pursuit of economic and political goals; the priority of profits over people; an economy geared largely to satisfy the wants of the rich over the needs of the poor; the growing emphasis on militarization as a means to protect what people have or to obtain what they consider necessary; the marginalization of increasingly larger numbers of people who, through poverty, unemployment and discrimination, find themselves without power to change the system and improve their condition. Yet, John Paul insists, the roots of the problem lie deeper than just economics. As he noted in his earlier (1979) letter, *Redemptor Hominis*:

> Man cannot relinquish himself or the place in the visible world that belongs to him; he cannot become the slave of production, the slave of his own products. . . . The present solicitude for man has as its root this problem. It is not a matter here merely of giving an abstract answer to the question: Who is man? It is a matter of the whole of the dynamism of life and civilization. It is a matter of the meaningfulness of the various initiatives of everyday life and also of the premises for many civilization programmes, political programmes, economic ones, social ones, state ones, and many others.[13]

Or, as another author has put it: "living only to labor and to cling to the products of our labor, we recreate ourselves in the image and

---

[12]*Ibid.*, 81.
[13]John Paul II, *Redemptor Hominis (Redeemer of Man)*, (Washington, D.C.: United States Catholic Conference, 1979), #52.

likeness of our products."[14] When the ethos of a culture, expressed in its economy, so defines and controls a people that it becomes an unchallenged, objective reality against which they judge themselves, evaluate their worth, seek their fulfillment and find their meaning and purpose, the economy (and the culture it expresses) becomes a salvific religious myth turned ideology within which all else is seen and interpreted. Such, I believe, is the thrust of John Paul's criticism.

A crisis with implications so profound requires equally profound questions—questions that search for and probe those root metaphors with which people begin to interpret the nature of the world and the way they will shape it through the social systems they create.

Root Metaphors and the Crisis of Culture

As meaning-seeking creatures, persons dwell in a world by gathering and sustaining that world into coherent patterns and fields through a symbolic interpretation of their lived experience. Those interpretations which confront life in its most elemental form are root metaphors, which Gibson Winter suggests are "guesses or discerning intuitions of the character of the totality of life and cosmos."[15] Such encompassing "guesses" are important for understanding a culture or civilization, Winter maintains, because they give people

> clues to the symbolized world enacted in lived interpretations. From day to day people treat things, other persons, and the meanings that guide their actions according to some such clue as to how things fit together and which things take priority. In reflective interpretations, guesses may also function as paradigms or social theories, guiding inquiries and selecting particular kinds of data as appropriate. Ideologies, in this sense, unfold societal or political guesses in myths.[16]

To understand the symbolic roots of our present crisis it is helpful to review briefly the major shifts in our symbolic interpretations of

---

[14]John Francis Kavanaugh, *Following Christ in a Consumer Society: The Spirituality of Cultural Resistance* (Maryknoll: Orbis, 1982), 11.

[15]Gibson Winter, *Liberating Creation: Foundations of Religious Social Ethics* (New York: Crossroad, 1981), 82.

[16]*Ibid.*

the world, pointing out the social and religious implications of these developments.[17]

Society as organism. The root metaphor which nourished premodern societies, especially in the Christian west was the human body, in which members obeyed the head, and the pope and emperor vied with each other for control of the body. In a society so conceived, order and harmony through obedience were the chief social virtues, and holiness consisted in transcending the ebb and flow of history to contemplate God as the supreme, transcendent Being. As Holland notes, within this model,

> the social structure and its aristocratic authorities are the protectors of the Gospel and instruments for bringing it to society. Individual authorities may be corrupt and need to be chastized, but the office itself and the structure behind it have a clear and unchallenged place in the divine plan. The Gospel thus proceeds from elite to base and from center to periphery (e.g., from rich to poor, from powerful to powerless, from man to woman, and from the white West to other cultures).[18]

Society as machine. Under pressure from the Enlightenment, reforms (e.g., the Protestant revolt) and revolutions (e.g., French, American, Industrial), the medieval organic/authoritarian model of society eventually gave way to a modern mechanistic/managerial understanding of society whose watchword was freedom: freedom from the past, from religious authority, from political autocracy and from economic restraints. With less and less emphasis on commonly shared goods and goals, harmony and order remained ideal social attributes, attained, not through obedience, but through the perfection and balance of society's individual parts. Thus, "the ideal of a well-balanced society in nineteenth and twentieth-century Europe and North America was a 'market' environment within which unrelated individual parts interacted competitively through 'free enterprise' (economics), liberal democracy (politics) and 'free thought' (culture.)"[19]

Key to maintaining this balance among a society's many compet-

---

[17]Cf. Winter, *op. cit.*, 1–28; also: Joe Holland, "Linking Social Analysis and Theological Reflection: The Place of Root Metaphors in Social and Religious Experience," in James E. Hug (ed.), *Tracing the Spirit: Communities, Social Action and Theological Reflection* (New York: Paulist Press, 1983), 170–91; also Holland and Henriot, *op. cit.*, 31–45.

[18]Holland, "Linking Social Analysis . . . ," 180.

[19]Holland and Henriot, *op. cit.*, 36.

ing factions was (and continues to be) the manager, perceptively described by Robert Bellah:

> The manager, in accordance with his utilitarian orientation, is a specialist in effective means, and does not feel called upon to speak of common ends. . . . The manager does not claim to know anything about the good in itself. He exercises power through his claim to understand the technical constraints of external reality and his ability to provide means to cope with those constraints. He exercises power not through some vision of a shared life together but because he claims to know the right decisions to make in the face of scarce resources, the laws of the market, and perhaps the number of missiles the Russians have. He claims only to provide the resources and protections which will allow individuals in their 'private' lives to pursue their multifarious private ends.[20]

In a society with minimal restraints on freedom institutions have been able to dramatically increase their size and power, the result being the proliferation of transnational and multinational corporations, mergers and takeovers. Yet the underside of this unprecedented expansion of power by the few has been a pervasive feeling of powerlessness by the many. In a very real sense, Holland observes,

> the modern world comes full circle. Born of the desire to liberate humanity from classical domination, it produces a technological domination which makes the classical form pale by contrast. Born of the desire to liberate humanity from its technological limitations, it now produces a militarized technological system stealing resources from the poor and threatening to destroy all the earth. Born of the desire to liberate humanity from the constraints of religion, it now discovers its own god, autonomous technology, destroying foundational values, human community, and the ecological matrix.[21]

Because many now perceive the modern project of a radically individualist, market-driven and increasingly militaristic society to

---

[20]Robert N. Bellah, "The Return of Religion: The Second Noble Lecture," *Religion and Intellectual Life* 1, 2 (1984), 41–42. Bellah extends his analysis to another figure, prominent in contemporary society, the "therapist," who, like the manager, "disavows any knowledge of the good in itself. He, often she, supplies only the technical assistance to the patient, more recently, the client, to discover and pursue his or her own ends. The manager organizes work, the therapist emotions and, since emotions are central parts of the work process, managers are themselves more and more in part therapists" (*ibid.*, 42).

[21]Holland, "Linking Social Analysis . . . ," 180.

be turning against the bulk of humanity, the challenge is one of summoning the imaginative powers of a culture to stem the erosion of public life by fashioning new foundational symbols capable of creating and sustaining a more humane world. Given the depth of the social crisis, religious sensibilities seem indispensable. "At stake," Holland notes, "are the basic perceptions of the nature of society, its source, its redemption, and its end."[22] With this agenda before us, it is important to locate the religious resources that can guide this process.

Theological Resources for Renewing the Social Order

Over the past twenty-five years people have drawn on a variety of theological insights as they have awakened ever so slowly to the present crisis. Among the means employed must be numbered the strategies of liberation theology, papal teaching (especially since John XXIII) dealing specifically with social issues, a renewed emphasis on justice, faith and prayer as leading to personal and social transformation, and an understanding of ministry broadened to include the transformation of society in ways that promote equity and respect human dignity.

Yet, in scanning these developments, it strikes me that relatively little has been said, at least explicitly, about an aspect of life that lies at the heart of the Catholic tradition: I refer here to the sacramental dimension, or what some recent writers have come to call the "sacramental imagination."[23]

It is worth noting that I am not pointing to any lack of emphasis on "the sacraments," narrowly construed in Catholic theology as the ecclesial, ritual expression of seven liturgical symbols. References to these abound in nearly every church document, including the pastoral on the economy. Curiously, they appear there, as they do most often, in the closing paragraphs, where the bishops call on all Christians "to seek that integral form of holiness to which the Gospel beckons, a holiness in which work and worship, economic life and Christian vision interpenetrate and constantly interact."[24] What is unclear, however, is the grounds on which that interpenetration and

---

[22]Holland, "Linking Social Analysis . . . ," 186.

[23]Cf. David Hollenbach, "A Prophetic Church and the Catholic Sacramental Imagination," in John C. Haughey (ed.), *The Faith That Does Justice* (New York: Paulist Press, 1977), 234–63; also: Clarke, *op. cit.*

[24]"Catholic Social Teaching and the U.S. Economy," #331, p. 377.

interaction take place. And, lacking a convincing rationale for integrating work and worship, the spiritual and the temporal, the economy appears (along with the world of work which it symbolizes) as extrinsic to the religious world of prayer and worship.

In the final portion of this essay I wish to suggest a possible basis for linking the world of economics with the world of religious faith by: (1) exploring briefly a broader understanding of sacramentality within the Catholic tradition; (2) examining the relationship between a sacramental emphasis and the root metaphors prevailing in a given society; and (3) in light of the above, suggest ways of integrating the motifs of creation, covenant, community and justice with economic systems.

Sacramentality in the Catholic Tradition. Generally speaking, to affirm the centrality of the "sacramental dimension" in Catholic theology is, as Richard McBrien suggests, to recognize Catholic belief in "the 'mysterious' dimension of all reality: the cosmos, nature, history, events, persons, objects, rituals, words. Everything is, in principle, capable of embodying and communicating the divine."[25] Joined to this belief are two convictions: (1) if God communicates to humankind it will (necessarily) be symbolically, i.e., in and through the finite medium of the created order; and (2) human beings can only experience God in and through the finite medium of the world in which they live.[26] In light of this, Dermot Lane concludes: "all knowledge and understanding including knowledge and understanding of God, is derived from man's experience of the world in which he lives."[27] These insights have, accordingly, led some theologians to identify the world as the first or original divinely expressive symbol or sacrament: the primordial embodiment of the divine in human terms.[28]

Coupled with these convictions is the anthropoligical insight which sees the human person as an ascending self-transcending being. Particularly through the work of Karl Rahner and Bernard Lonergan, many have come to understand the essence of personhood as self-transcendence—unbounded openness and capacity for the

[25]Richard P. McBrien, *Catholicism* (Minneapolis: Winston, 1980), II, 731.

[26]Cf. Thomas Aquinas, *Summa Theologiae* I, q. 12, a. 11, where Thomas argues that the kind of knowledge one has follows from the nature of the knowing subject.

[27]Dermot Lane, *The Reality of Jesus: An Essay in Christology* (New York: Paulist Press, 1975, 1975), 118.

[28]Cf. Theodore Runyon, "The World as Original Sacrament," *Worship* 54, 6 (1980), 495–571.

infinite, revealed in the relentless drive of an unrestricted desire to know and the unending quest, in freedom and knowledge, for the supernatural.[29]

When God is seen as a descending self-communicating being and persons are viewed as ascending self-transcending beings, then the person of Jesus becomes, for Christians, the point of symbolic or sacramental encounter between God's self-communication and man's self transcendence.[30] Continuing in this same vein, many see the Incarnation of Jesus, not as a secondary intention of God, made necessary by sin, but as something intrinsic to the very plan of creation itself. As Lane puts it:

> The Incarnation is the supreme exemplification in a uniquely human way of a divine pattern which is already given in creation itself. The Incarnation therefore is not an isolated exception but rather the definitive culmination of a process already set in motion through the gift of creation. To this extent creation is the basis of Incarnation and Incarnation is the fullness of creation.[31]

And just as God cannot be known outside of history, so Jesus as the Christ cannot be known except through his humanity.

Recent developments in Catholic sacramental theology have tended to stress the centrality of this broader sacramental understanding over the Tridentine emphasis on seven discrete sacramental rituals. This is particularly apparent in two areas: the church and, more recently, the social order.

The sacramental principle is applied to the church in this way. Just as Jesus Christ is the symbolic yet real expression and embodiment of God, so the Church, is the continuation of Christ in space and time. In the words of Vatican II, the church is "the universal sacrament of salvation, simultaneously manifesting and exercising the mystery of God's love for man."[32]

The sacramental principle is extended to social systems by reflect-

---

[29]Cf. Bernard Lonergan, *Insight: A Study in Human Understanding* (New York: Philosophical Library, 1958), 634–86; also: Karl Rahner, *Hearers of the Word*, trans. by Michael Richards (New York: Herder and Herder, 1969).

[30]Hence the title of Edward Schillebeeckx's seminal work, *Christ and the Sacrament of the Encounter with God* (New York: Sheed and Ward, 1963).

[31]Lane, *op. cit.*, 135.

[32]Second Vatican Council, "Constitution on the Church in the Modern World, #45, in *The Teachings of the Second Vatican Council* (Westminster, MD: Newman Press, 1966), 492.

ing on the insight discussed earlier, namely, that such systems are an expressive embodiment of a people's ethos and ethics.[33] The deeper theological significance of this insight lies in seeing it in continuity with the earlier comments on creation, christology and ecclesiology. Thomas Clarke writes:

> As the human body is symbolic of spirit, so the extension of the body in social systems manifests the human which it embodies. To the degree that the manifestation is humanizing rather than dehumanizing, it reflects the presence of God and his Christ in human society, and so takes on a certain sacramental character, as the world created by humans becomes 'charged with the grandeur of God'.[34]

This is the genius of the sacramental vision in Catholic theology: the insistence on integrating what are usually separated: God and world, sacred and secular, grace and history, Christ and humanity, Christian faith and everyday life. It is not a question of collapsing one into the other, but of seeing each in light of the other.

Yet, when theologians attempt to apply a sacramental perspective to the current cultural crisis they face the same challenge as that confronting thinkers in other disciplines: overcoming the excesses of organicist and mechanistic thinking. The symptoms of such excesses in Catholic life and thought are well known to anyone familiar with the history of that tradition, especially since medieval times: e.g., a spirituality that isolates and compartmentalizes religious energies; a privatization of religious symbols and a quantification of spiritual realities; a one-sided emphasis on the necessary efficacy of divinely instituted sacramental symbols; a preoccupation with matters of personal morality, often to the neglect of social and structural evils; an attitude of suspicion and hostility by those in authority to ideas which challenge the traditional wisdom and order of the day.[35]

To recognize the extent to which such thinking has dominated the "religious" as well as the "secular" lives of people is simply to acknowledge the cultural matrix within which every religious group always exists. It is to confess, with David Hollenbach that

> neither the human mind nor the human heart is a *tabula rasa*, whimsically poised to move in any and every direction without preference.

---

[33]Cf. also: Otto Hentz, "Symbol and System: Embodying Love," in Clarke, *op. cit.*, 136.

[34]*Ibid.*, 5.

[35]Hollenbach, *art. cit.*, 249.

Human experience is shaped by the history of the person who experiences, and by the symbols or 'root metaphors' that provide identity
and a means of communication within the community to which the
person belongs.[36]

Yet to acknowledge the extremes of the past is not to abrogate the
entirety of the past. What is needed is a way of combining the
continuity and participatory roots of organicist thinking with the
technical ingenuity and creative capacities of mechanistic thinking,
but in a new root metaphor which can imaginatively reinterpret the
meaning of human existence by transforming the symbolic horizon
within which that meaning takes shape.

The root metaphor which some writers, especially Winter, have
identified as central to this task is that of artistic creativity.[37] In the
final portion of this essay I would like to discuss this root metaphor
briefly, assess its implications for informing a renewed sacramental
vision and suggest ways in which such a sacramental vision might
provide a constructively critical perspective on the economy as a
social system.

Root metaphors and the sacramental imagination. The process of
artistic creativity is proposed as a more adequate model of life in the
modern world because of its greater explanatory power to account
for how people actually live, and for its ability to suggest new
insights into the nature of life and new possibilities for human
existence.

The artist is one who draws on the elemental ingredients of life
and attempts to disclose, in various creative, symbolic forms, the
meaning of being for each new generation of hearers, readers or
viewers. Because art represents a coming together of humanity and
nature, a bonding of bios and cosmos, the artist speaks of the world
and from the world. Those who look upon art as mere decoration or

---

[36]Informative historical insights regarding many of these matters, especially the
church, may be found in Avery Dulles, *Models of the Church* (New York: Doubleday,
1974); *idem, Models of Revelation* (New York: Doubleday, 1983); cf. also: Thomas F.
O'Meara, "Philosophical Models in Ecclesiology," *Theological Studies* 31, 1 (1981),
3–21. Among the more important studies on ministry, cf. Edward Schillebeeckx,
Ministry: Leadership in the Community of Jesus Christ (New York: Crossroad, 1981);
also: Bernard Cooke, *Ministry to Word and Sacraments* (Philadelphia: Fortress Press,
1976). A good overview of sacramental practice, with particular emphasis on the
Eucharist can be found in Joseph Powers, *Eucharistic Theology* (New York: Herder
and Herder, 1967).

[37]Cf. Winter, *op. cit.,*; Holland and Henriot, *op. cit.*; Holland, "Linking Social
Analysis. . . ."

embellishment might instinctively reject the artistic process as the way people live. Yet, as John Dixon persuasively argues, "art is not an ornament to an existing world, it is the primary means of forming the world.[38] The making of a work of art, Dixon insists, is a delving into the secret life of things, "to find the bonds between them."[39]

Because artistic expression is always symbolic (revealing yet also concealing), it is at best only relatively adequate as representation. As a result it is necessary to speak of the artistic *process*—occurring in time, but always pointing beyond itself to possibilities not yet realized. In the language of hermeneutics, the relationship between the artist and the world is one of ongoing dialogue in which the symbolic expression—insofar as it contains that "surplus of meaning" of which Ricoeur so often speaks—suggests the direction in which the conversation is to be continued.

Standing at the boundary between the actual and the possible, the already and the not yet, the artist, suggests Arthur Koestler, "is on a tightrope between the practical world and the world of imagination: in that tension becomes the creative impulse."[40] Relieve the tension and the artistic process collapses. Each element in the process is necessary: the practical world, the imagination which interprets that world, and the symbols which mediate that interpretation. Forsake the world and there is nothing to question. Surrender one's imaginative powers and no creative questions can be asked. Abandon the symbols through which the world is encountered and insight is expressed and there are neither questions nor answers.

Yet, once again, to argue for the advantages of artistic creativity over organicist and mechanistic thinking as a more suitable description of human living is not to argue for the abolition of the latter. It is rather a question of balance, of proportion. The organic linkage and interaction among parts is essential to a work of art just as mechanistic impulses move toward dynamism and movement. What is decried is an organicism that allows for development but not change; a mechanicism that is merely repetitive.

Given the sacramental emphasis in Catholic theology outlined above and granting also the ways in which organicist and mechanistic images have tended to dominate sacramental thinking until very

---

[38]John Dixon, *Art and the Theological Imagination* (New York: Seabury, 1978), 12.
[39]*Ibid.*
[40]Arthur Koestler, quoted in Karen Laub-Novak, "The Art of Deception," in Diane Apostolos Cappadona (ed.), *Art, Creativity and the Sacred: An Anthology in Religion and Art* (New York: Crossroads, 1984), 14.

recently, how might the root metaphor of artistic process enhance the Catholic sacramental emphasis and even help it become more faithful to its basic dynamism? In several ways, I would propose. First, by restoring to sacramental theology an emphasis on movement, dynamics, change, creativity. Once again, it is not a question of either total stasis or protean permutation, but rather an honest recognition that just as there is nothing quite so deadly to art as mere repetition, so the interpretation of sacramental symbols must arise out of the ongoing dialogue between the forms of the past and the needs of the present. A lucid illustration of this would be the recent efforts to include the problems of world hunger in an adequate interpretation of the symbolically shared meal of the Eucharist.[41]

Second, the artistic metaphor would give greater emphasis to the centrality of the imagination as that which makes creative change possible. For what imagination designates is the potential of human freedom and creativity to rearrange the elements of experience in ways that project new possibilities for human existence. In this regard, Karen Laub-Novak has observed:

> The creative imagination gathers all types of impressions and sees the similarities even between dissimilar things. It is the creative imagination that plays with veiling and unveiling, creates illusions, shocks the eye. Creative imagination simplifies, eliminates details or adds them, gives emphasis or distorts.[42]

Many see as one of the great failures of modern religion the claim that there is no connection between the world of economics or politics and the concerns of religion. Such blindness could be described as a failure of the imagination to inform a people's moral vision.[43]

Third, the artistic model would restore a healthy recognition of the inherent ambiguity and incompleteness of all symbols, including sacramental symbols. As Langdon Gilkey has observed: The great temptation of Catholicism as a sacramental religion has been the tendency "to absolutize the relative and sanctify the ambiguous."[44]

---

[41]Cf. Monika Hellwig, *The Eucharist and the Hunger of the World* (New York: Paulist Press, 1976).

[42]Laub-Novak, *art. cit.*, 17.

[43]Cf. Hollenbach, *art. cit.*; cf. also: William V. Dych, "Theology and Imagination," *Thought* 57, 224 (1982), 118ff.

[44]Langdon Gilkey, *Catholicism Confronts Modernity: A Protestant View* (New York: Seabury, 1975), 196–97.

While dogmatic statements have long been regarded by many as unalterable and fixed, more recent theological reflection has stressed the necessarily limited (because symbolic) nature of all such declarations.[45]

Symbols are ambiguous in part because of the complexity and mystery of that which they embody, in part because of the finite nature of the symbol, in part because of the discursive nature of our intelligence. Because of this ambiguity and because the interpretation of symbols is the key to all meaning, the manipulation and control of symbols is the preoccupation of those in power as well as those yearning for power. Thus the drive toward and resistance to the ordination of women in the Catholic community is primarily a question of the real-because-symbolic nature of power and authority.

But how can even a renewed sacramental vision, with its emphasis on creativity, imagination and incompleteness, constructively address the economic and cultural crisis we face? First, by continuing to confront people with the claim that they are not simply the passive victims of an impersonal economic system foisted upon them from the outside, but rather, that all social systems are the necessary embodiments by which people express and render effectively present the relationships through which they live with one another in their common history.[46]

But what kinds of relationships are these systems to embody? And how are they to be formed? What vision and values are they to express? The answer of industrial capitalism seems to be: those which promote the greatest economic growth: viz., hard work, corporate expansion, increased production consumption—virtues frequently seen as fulfillment of the biblical motifs of creation, covenant, community and justice. Thus, creation exists for the sake of the self (individual or corporate); the challenge is to subdue the world and "have dominion . . . over every living thing" (Gen. 1:28). The covenant is with the "chosen people"—elected by God to subdue the earth and pursue their dreams in competition with others through inventiveness and hard work. Community comprises the sum total of individuals pursuing their dreams. Justice is what

---

[45]E.g., cf. Powers, op. cit., 111–79, for a discussion of the adequacy of transubstantiation as an explanation of the divine Eucharistic presence. For an application to Christology, cf.: Paul Knitter, No Other Name? A Critical Survey of Christian Attitudes Toward the World Religions (Maryknoll: Orbis, 1985), 169–231.

[46]Cf. Otto Hentz, "Symbol and System: Embodying Love," in Clarke, Above Every Name, . . ., 136.

people are entitled to on the basis of what they have produced or contributed to the system.

While this interpretation of the biblical vision is, no doubt, something of a caricature, I would argue that it does contain enough truth to dramatize the mythic power of capitalism as an encompassing social paradigm.

Some might respond: "So, what's wrong with that?" The answer is, what it has produced historically: the seemingly inevitable domination of the poor by the rich, the weak by the strong; the survival of the fittest, by cunning if possible, by subversion and force if necessary.

What perspectives could a sacramental imagination, informed by an emphasis on artistic creativity, bring to bear on the same biblical motifs? While there could undoubtedly be many variations on these themes, I would suggest the following.

Creation is seen as a divine-human work in which the world serves as the chosen medium for the self-expression of the divine, and that world, so imaging in its human form (male *and* female) the freedom and self-consciousness of its creator, collaborates with its creator by expressing and embodying in time and space that source of life from whence it has arisen. In this sense, the world does not exist for the self, nor does the self exist for the world. Rather self and world co-exist in a common life, a community of being. (By extending creation through collaboration or partnership with human agents, there is always the risk of a "takeover," a self-serving pursuit of power. Such vulnerability seem inherent in any truly reciprocal relationship.)

With the covenant comes election, not as favoritism, but as responsibility, obligation, vocation—a vocation which, Hollenbach notes, "has the weight of a moral imperative, but which also enters human experience as grace—as a gift which makes response to the imperative possible."[47] The obligation or the call is to full personhood through membership in a community whose *raison d'etre* is extending to all of humanity, especially the oppressed and the poor, the good news and saving activity of a God who is liberator and savior. The covenant has as its focus justice or righteousness as fidelity to the demands of a relationship—with God as well as neighbor, for the two are inextricably intertwined. Because such relationships are intended as one of support and care, justice is more the floor beneath

---

[47]Hollenbach, *art. cit.*, 259.

which one may not sink rather than the ceiling above which one need not rise. As John Donahue has observed: "Luther wrestled with the late medieval problem of a just God and sinful creation and translated the God of justice into a God of love. The task of our age may well be the reverse—to translate the love of God into the doing of justice."[48]

A renewed sacramental vision could also constructively address the economic and cultural crisis by sustaining the ongoing dialectical relationship between a people struggling to bring their values and vision into closer harmony with the originating symbols out of which their particular religious tradition has arisen, and the social structures which are the imaginatively interpreted expression and embodiment of those symbols in space and time.

Here, I would suggest, is where the ecclesial sacraments play a special role. For, in line with the emphasis outlined above, each of the seven sacraments is the expression and embodiment of the fundamental sacramentality of creation, celebrated by various communities in light of their specific needs, for the purpose of rededicating themselves to a life of covenant solidarity with the entire world.

For such Christians, these celebrations revolve around those symbols which, when interpreted through the prism of the Christ-event, give life a palpable Christian texture: birth, maturation, the sustenance of a shared meal, marriage, leadership in the religious community, sickness and death. These symbols, I would argue, should not be construed as an exhaustive enumeration of moments in a graced existence, any more than the only sacramental meal identifiable with Jesus was the Last Supper. Rather, all the meals of Jesus were "sacramental" in the sense of communicating through the sharing of food the salvation that comes from God. The function of the ecclesial, Eucharistic meal is not "to make Christ present" but to intensify that presence through a different modality by situating it in a broader historical and symbolic context which transforms the "significance" of the elements essential to the ritual.

The point is not to take the form of these symbolic rituals and impose it as a template on the larger world. This, Hollenbach warns, would be to impose a historically conditioned ritual structure on secular life in an "imperialistic and alienating way."[49] Rather it is

---

[48]John R. Donahue, "Biblical Perspectives on Justice," in Haughey, op. cit., 69.
[49]Hollenbach, art. cit., 256.

for a people to allow their imaginative sensibilities to be shaped by the movement between sacramental symbol and the practical world in such a way that they can extend to the larger, pluralistic world that same dynamic impetus to express and embody, in ways appropriate to different contexts, the goodness of creation, the primacy of persons, responsibility for the shape of society and the course of history.

Conclusion

If, as the American bishops contend, the injustices which have accompanied the emergence of national security industrial capitalism are morally unacceptable, then changes must be made, not only in specific economic strategies and programs, but more importantly (in the long run) in that deeper symbolic understanding of the values and vision of society that an economy embodies and expresses. It is this set of deeper issues that these reflections have tried to probe through an emphasis on the historic and dynamic character of persons as symbol-making creatures and the embodiment of this symbolic insight in institutions and social systems.

Root metaphors are crucial because they begin to define the horizon which functions as an encompassing interpretative framework for life itself. I have tried to argue that industrial capitalism has achieved a kind of mythic hegemony over the imaginative lives of American people, and that one of the more important functions of religious communities today is to provide a critique of that ideology by disclosing the symbolic horizons and mechanistic root metaphor which undergird it. In this sense a critique of economic systems is an exercise in hermeneutics.

The problem that arises here, of course, is one of competing ideologies, since the religious vision has no "Archimedean" standpoint from which to judge all others. Yet, by becoming more aware (through an appropriation of insights from the social sciences) of the ideological traits in one's own vision, and by grounding one's vision in a root metaphor that encourages criticism and is open to the future, there might be the prospect of ongoing genuine conversion.

The root metaphor of artistic creativity has the potential for revitalizing a sacramental emphasis in people's lives as well as inspiring a new understanding of the economy as a social system. For both sacraments and social systems are the ongoing expression and embodiment of a people's deepest understanding of life together in the world. The promise of artistic creativity is one of revisioning the meaning of creation, covenant, community and justice in ways that support the search for social systems and a moral foundation that better express and sustain the dignity of persons in their common history. Given the precariousness of the present world order, anything less seems woefully inadequate. For, as Winter has warned, "the resymbolization of the present age will inform and empower a creative praxis or it will perish along with the many species of life that are now being driven from the earth by rampant mechanism."[50]

Today, more than ever, an authentically religious life is one which recognizes the importance of limits, but also affirms an horizon open to the future, limited only by the finitude of the world, the imaginative vision of a people, and their willingness to embody that vision in economic and political systems that promote true justice and peace.

---

[50]Winter, op. cit., 115.

Part Three

HISTORICAL STUDIES

ADAM MÜLLER AND ADAM SMITH: A ROMANTIC-CATHOLIC RESPONSE TO MODERN ECONOMIC THOUGHT

Paul Misner

When one traces the history of Catholic reflections on the economic life back behind the papal teachings that commenced in 1891 with Leo XIII's *Rerum novarum*, one comes eventually to a deep gulf between the eighteenth and the nineteenth centuries, or between the largely agrarian world of the *ancien régime* and world of the urban industrialists and proletarians. The nineteenth century came to be preoccupied with "the social question," namely the lot of the industrial worker and all other laborers in relation to the dominant industrialized sector of European economies. Bishop Wilhelm Emmanuel Ketteler in Mainz and Cardinal Henry Edward Manning in England were leading examples of this concern in prominent places, as, in the United States, was Cardinal James Gibbons. Frédéric Ozanam and Albert de Mun, among others, showed initiative in the same arena as lay people.

In the eighteenth century, however, Catholic activities and statements on public affairs, such as they were, were preoccupied with political questions. In the economic realm, the traditional duties of the rich and the poor in respect to each other continued to be inculcated. Concessions and accommodations had been made to the necessities of commercial life, but in Catholicism they took place without the kind of basic "new conscience" on these matters that Benjamin Nelson, among others, sees as having taken place in the Protestant world.[1] The guidance theology offered on business and

---

[1] Bernhard Groethuysen, *The Bourgeois. Catholicism vs. Capitalism in Eighteenth Century France*, introd. by Benjamin Nelson (New York: Rinehart and Winston, 1968; Benjamin Nelson, *The Idea of Usury: From Tribal Brotherhood to Universal Otherhood*. 2d enlarged ed. University of Chicago Press, 1969 (originally 1949).

commercial matters dated back to time of Molina, Lessius and de Lugo, and maintained a substantial continuity with still earlier thinking on just contracts.

The clergy as a whole had quietly abandoned the struggle against usury by 1745 (when Pope Benedict XIV's encyclical, *Vix pervenit*, upholding the accepted views, appeared), even if a voice would still be raised now and then decrying the taking of any payment for a loan beyond the principal and costs. Despite substantial gradual economic advances in production and commerce throughout Europe, the capitalism of the eighteenth and early nineteenth centuries occasioned no new departures among moralists or social commentators in Catholic countries.[2] That would wait until the onset on the continent of steam-power industrialization in large textile mills and other factories in the 1830s and 1840s.

This apparent lull and lag in facing the new problems of an industrial capitalism would be rather what one would expect. And yet as it happened, when European Catholics began struggling with the problems of industrialization, they were not thrown back totally on early modern or medieval resources. There were at least three writers, Adam Müller (1779–1829), Félicité de Lamennais (1782–1854) and Franz von Baader (1765–1841), who, in the intervening Romantic period of cultural creativity, had engaged in pioneering social analysis in dialogue with the early nineteenth-century economic realities.

Of these three, Adam Müller was the earliest to turn his thoughts to economics (the other two wrote on the subject only after the Restoration of 1814/15 or even after the revolution of 1830); he also produced much the more comprehensive work, *The Elements of Statecraft*.[3] It is divided into six books, of which the fourth and fifth

---

[2]Cf. John T. Noonan, *The Scholastic Analysis of Usury* (Cambridge: Harvard University Press, 1957), pp. 357–360 and 373–382; cf. also Oskar Köhler in *History of the Church* (ed. Hubert Jedin and John Dolan; New York, Crossroad, 1981), 9:190–208, as well as Rudolf Lill, *ibid.* 7:216–227 and 8:114.

[3]Adam Heinrich Müller, *Die Elemente der Staatskunst*, 3 vols. (Berlin: Haude & Spener, 1968). Here, however, I will cite, with the abbreviation *ESK*, by lecture and page numbers, from the two-volume edition by Jakob Baxa (Jena: Gustav Fischer, 1922); all translations are mine unless otherwise noted.

On Müller, cf. H. H. Hofmann in the *Biographisches Wörterbuch zur deutschen Geschichte* 2:1950–52; for archival materials, *Adam Müllers Lebenszeugnisse*, 2 vols., edited by Jakob Baxa (Paderborn: F. Schöningh, 1966), which will be cited as *LZ* with volume and page numbers; also Jakob Baxa, *Adam Müller: Ein Lebensbild aus den Befreiungskriegen und aus der deutschen Restauration* (Jena: G. Fischer, 1930);

deal directly with national economy. It is on this work that I shall focus here. One of the earlier Romantic converts to Catholicism, Müller was the first and foremost to take classical economic theory seriously, in the form of Adam Smith's great *Wealth of Nations* (1776). Thus, for weal or woe, he presented a newly articulated view of society worked out in response to the leading representative of modern secular economics.

Müller's *Elements of Statecraft* (1809) is either the first chapter of Catholic social thought in the age of industrial capitalism, or at least a signal event in the immediate prehistory of that phenomenon. Many commentators, largely for reasons having to do with the problems of German Catholicism in the 1920s and 1930s, have been unwilling to admit the Catholic character of Adam Müller's work.[4] I do not claim that Adam Müller's work foreshadowed in all respects the best of the subsequent development, much less that it predetermined it. Its influence, however, was considerable (e.g., by way of Karl von Vogelsang, 1818–1890, Franz Hitze, 1851–1921, and Heinrich Pesch, 1854–1926), as recent research has indicated.[5] This in itself would make it necessary to take a look into this unique work, an essay on political economy from a Christian Romantic's perspective.

Approaching the topic through two preliminary steps, I discuss first the pan-European backdrop of the setting in which Adam Müller wrote and delivered his lectures, then the outlook of German Romanticism in which Müller lived and moved, and finally the economic and social theory of his principal work, *The Elements of Statecraft*.

Albrecht Langner, "Adam Müller (1779–1829)" in *Zeitgeschichte in Lebensbildern: Aus dem deutschen Katholizismus des 19. und 20. Jahrhunderts*, edited by Jürgen Aretz, Rudolf Morsey und Anton Rauscher (Mainz: Grünewald, 1980), 4:9–21 and 267; and Benedikt Koehler, *Aesthetik der Politik: Adam Müller und die politische Romantik* (Stuttgart: Klett-Cotta, 1980).

[4]This stems largely from the ill repute that Adam Müller has had among social scientists at least since Carl Schmitt's *Politische Romantik* (Munich, 1919; 2d ed. 1925), a reputation largely undeserved, according to Langner and Koehler. Carl Schmitt's perspective is itself questionable (cf. Joseph W. Bendersky, *Carl Schmitt: Theorist for the Reich* [Princeton University Press, 1983]), but his interpretation made a lasting impression; for present purposes, his interpretation was largely accepted by Edgar Alexander, who (although hostile to Carl Schmitt) incorporated it in the most detailed account of German Catholic social thought available in English, in: *Church and Society*, edited by Joseph N. Moody (New York: Arts, Inc., 1953), pp. 325–583. See also Franz H. Mueller, *The Church and the Social Question* (Washington, D.C.: American Enterprise Institute), 1984.

[5]Langner, "Adam Müller," p. 18.

I. Revolution in France and War in Europe 1789–1809

The setting in which Adam Müller gave his lectures and published them must be noted. *Aufklärung*—Enlightenment thinking—though unsettled by the French Revolution, the Terror and the Napoleonic conquests, still seemed the wave of the future, for all the vogue that its Romantic critics were enjoying in certain circles. Adam Smith in particular seemed to have uncovered the laws of a successful political economy, a matter that all rulers and patriots had to be concerned about. But after the French Revolution and the European warfare that had continued for the intervening two decades, another Briton, Edmund Burke, supplied a needed corrective to Adam Smith's optimistic outlook. A somewhat older friend of Müller's, Friedrich Gentz, translated Burke's *Reflections on the Revolution in France* (1790) into German when Müller was still only fourteen years old. By the winter of 1808–1809, when Adam Müller gave his more than faintly subversive set of lectures on the political economic, Napoleon had a firm grip on the whole of whole of continental Europe. The greater part of the diplomatic corps of Dresden responded to the invitation to attend. Almost to a man, they were representing powers officially in league with Napoleonic France.

Adam Smith's credentials as an enlightened moral philosopher were fully in order. He was a friend of David Hume. His *Wealth of Nations*[6] was published by the same publisher and in the same season as the celebrated first volume of Edward Gibbon's *Decline and Fall of the Roman Empire* (1776). Smith's book quickly became justly celebrated, at least in part for the same qualities as Gibbon's: it contained a great deal of "philosophical history," with a view to unearthing the laws of human economic progress akin to Newton's physical laws. What could be more characteristic of the Enlightenment!

The Wealth of Nations, however, is more than just a product of the Enlightenment, destined to be laid to rest when intellectual fashions changed (even if they were to change more drastically than in fact they did). It is a work of genius that stated the case for capitalism, marshalling the evidence in favor of a political economy untrammeled by attempts to defeat or control the workings of the market.

---

[6]Adam Smith, *An Inquiry into the Nature and Causes of the Wealth of Nations*, cited here as Smith, *WN*, by Book, chapter and subsections (and also by page numbers) according to the edition of R. H. Campbell and A. S. Skinner, 2 vols. (Oxford: Clarendon Press, 1976).

The discipline of market prices and costs of production would create the incentives to increase productive efficiency by the more and more advanced division of labor in larger and larger markets.

Adam Smith displayed a moderation, historical judgment and humane sense that many "Smithians," the proponents of his views in the struggle for economic modernization in Europe, lacked. Since he died in 1790, he had no occasion to comment on the events of 1789 in France (although he had pointed out how its tax system could have been reformed and improved so as to avoid the crisis).[7] It was left to another admirer of his, Edmund Burke (1729–1797), to mount the conservative attack on the principles of the French Revolution in November, 1790. Protesting that any parallels with the Glorious Revolution of 1688 in England or other English constitutional precedents was entirely out of place in the writings of propagandists for this disastrous (and, as he thought, unnecessary) revolution, Burke became the prototype of the conservative (not reactionary) stream of Western thought.

Adam Müller, for his part, became acquainted with Burke's *Reflections* very early on, probably before leaving Berlin for university studies at Göttingen in 1798.[8] Burke's rhetoric and arguments, in the skillful German translation of Friedrich Gentz, became second nature to Adam Müller and fired his enthusiasm (widely shared in his milieu in Göttingen, by the way) for all things English. *The Elements of Statecraft*, only ten years later, drew heavily on Burke for arguments in favor of respecting traditions, building on the achievements of the past rather than tearing them down and avoiding doctrinaire new departures such as some Smithians were advocating. What many critics and defenders of Adam Müller over the years have not noticed sufficiently is the abhorrence he shared with Burke of totalitarianism or absolutism from any quarter. (There are reasons why this element can be overlooked in Adam Müller, as we shall see).

Among the refrains from Burke that Adam Müller would pick up was the insistence on falling back in crises on "the ancient organized [e]states," and not on "the *moleculae* of a disbanded people."[9] Also

---

[7]Smith, *The Wealth of Nations*, V.ii.k (pp. 900–932).

[8]Edmund Burke, *Reflections on the French Revolution*, cited according to the Everyman's Library edition, London: J. M. Dent and New York: E. P. Dutton, 1910; for the German translation by Friedrich Gentz, first published in 1793, cf. *Betrachtungen über die Französischen Revolution*, ed. Lore Iser with an introduction by Dieter Henrich (Frankfurt: Suhrkamp, 1967).

[9]Burke, *Reflections*, pp. 18–20, 76 and *passim*; cf. Gentz's translation, pp. 52–54 and 135.

spoken to the Romantic's heart was the notion of societal harmony that arises from a dialectic of forces in reciprocity, a sort of harmony arising from ordered conflicts. This is what the Englishman's respect for tradition counsels, in contrast to the precipitate action of the revolution, running roughshod over custom and also over people's actual historical rights in the name of some newly excogitated "Rights of man." The "Rights of man" were a mere philosophical construct, "paltry blurred shreds of paper" (*Reflections*, p. 83), disconnected from a humane if imperfect world of multifarious and differently articulated interrelationships.

The established church and the nobility might not be the most economical institutions, but keeping them in place and modifying them slowly, by negotiations, was preferable to radical change. "Instead of casting away all our prejudices, we (Englishmen) cherish them" (*Reflections*, p. 84); instead of contenting themselves with their individual "stock of reason," they availed themselves of "the general bank and capital of nations and ages." Müller, it will be remembered, read (or devoured) Burke before going on to his fellow Briton, Adam Smith. And he appealed to what might be called Burke's economic metaphors to justify his own "esthetic" interpretation of economic issues.[10]

The leading phalanx of Romantics were already of university age during the first heady days of the French Revolution. Most of them went through at least a phase of excited enthusiasm for the events in France—not so Adam Müller. Müller's relative youth and his early acquaintance with Friedrich Gentz in Berlin made him a conservative of Burkean inspiration from the outset. (Gentz was a writer who later became what would be called today the "top aide" of Metternich; he opened the way for Adam Müller also to enter Austrian service.) Müller also followed Burke in linking the Revolution with the baleful influence of the *philosophes*. This did not prevent him from soon making the acquaintance of Adam Smith's great book. Indeed, before October 1800 he wrote or spoke to Gentz of a plan he was developing to refashion Smith's *Wealth of Nations* in the light of German circumstances and culture. This is the first glimmer of what would be the dominant concern of his creative life: to combine,

---

[10]Müller, *ESK*, Lecture 24 (1:457), quoting Burke, *Reflections*, p. 33 (tr. Gentz, p. 72): "You began ill, because you began by despising everything that belonged to you. You set up your trade without a capital."

in the spirit of Romanticism, the thought-worlds of esthetics and of political economy![11]

It is a disconcerting to find an esthete writing on economics and celebrating the necessary role of *war* in the political economy for good measure. This feature of Adam Müller's German patriotism also appears in a different light when one considers the setting.[12] The British had taken up the struggle against Napoleonic France once more in 1803; Austria joined the Third Coalition in 1805 and once again suffered the brunt of Napoleon's warfare. Then Prussia entered the war against France and went down to defeat at Jena and Auerstädt in 1806.

Saxony, like most of the smaller German states, was not in the least ashamed to play Napoleon's game and accept his rewards. In 1806 Saxony's reward was to become a kingdom, whereas in the recently defunct Holy Roman Empire it had been an electoral duchy. Adam Müller, not having found a way into a university career, was in Saxon Dresden as tutor of a young prince of the newly royal house, who was to go on to lead troops in several of Napoleon's later engagements, Saxony being one of his most loyal allies. Müller, however, was a Berliner, a Prussian subject, and one of that new breed of German patriots like J. G. Fichte who were not content with the apathetic resistance or lack of it characteristic of the old Empire's several territories.

Müller's lectures took place from November 1808 to March 1809 in the presence of his prince in tutelage and the rest of Dresden society, with the ostentatious exception of the French ambassador. They took place, that is, shortly after Napoleon had imposed the Continental System, a trade embargo against Britian affecting all of Europe. Müller conceived and delivered his addresses while the

---

[11]LZ 1:16; cf. Baxa, *Adam Müller* (1930), p. 23, and Koehler, *Aesthetik der Politik*, p. 20.

[12]Müller, *ESK*, Lecture 1 (1:10) and Lecture 4 as a whole; cf. Koehler, *Aesthetik der Politik*, pp. 100–109. Koehler has worked out the historical context of Müller's works particularly well, along with Albrecht Langner, "Zur konservativen Position in der politisch-ökonomischen Entwicklung Deutschlands vor 1848," in *Katholizismus, konservative Kapitalismuskritik und Frühsozialismus bis 1850*, edited by Langner (Paderborn: F. Schöningh, 1975), pp. 11–73 and 210–212. Cf. also Jacques Droz, *Le romantisme allemand et l'Etat: résistance et collaboration dans l'Allemagne napoléonienne* (Paris: Payot, 1966).

On the German conservative background of Adam Müller's thought, cf. Klaus Epstein, *The Genesis of German Conservatism* (Princeton University Press, 1966), and Karl Mannheim, "Conservative Thought," in *Essays on Sociology and Social Psychology* (New York: Oxford University Press, 1953), pp. 74–164.

irregular but ultimately effective uprisings against the French occupation in Spain and Portugal were taking place. Gentz and Metternich were also engaged in scheming for an uprising in the Tirol
against the French ally, Bavaria, which had complacently taken the
Tirol as its spoils from the War of the Third Coalition. This was the
sign of things to come for Napoleon's fortunes, even though he was
able to bring the Habsburgs down to defeat one more time.

When Müller spoke of war, therefore, what he had in mind was a
people's war of liberation, supported in a groundswell of revulsion
against foreign domination by the populace as a whole. In the
circumstances, it was neither necessary nor civilly possible to state
this explicitly. The fact that he later played an energetic journalistic
role in a second, successful Tirolean war of liberation in 1813,
merely illustrates the constellation of forces and patriotic desires in
which he crafted his plaidoyer for war.

In fact, throughout his lectures, Müller speaks of any vigorous
state of civil life as warfare (of interests, of classes etc.), but not
warfare to the death. One wonders to what extent this may have been
a ploy to frustrate censorship. Perhaps he could "get away with"
stirring up warlike emotions against France by referring also to all
other kinds of healthy rivalry as "warfare." Another factor certainly
disposed him to speak this way, however—his theory of The Opposite (see next section). At any rate, what to common sense and to
Adam Smith appeared as the fruits of peace, Adam Müller attributed
equally and dialectically to "war." What he was opposed to was not
peace, but apathy, the kind of apathy which had been so notable on
the part of the Prussian population when Napoleon's armies
marched through in 1806. When he called for a warlike civil constitution in peacetime, he was not thinking primarily of a militaristic
state but of a highly participatory one, where every class of inhabitants were actively engaged in promoting their interests and hence
the interests of the state. Naturally, such paradoxical play with
exaggerated Romantic dialectics quickly lessened the value of his
lectures as treatises in political economics after the particular situation of Napoleonic domination changed.

As is well known to posterity, but of course not to Müller at the
time, the European states took on a quite different complexion with
the fall of Napoleon six years later. The Restoration, the Holy
Alliance, and the principle of legitimacy set in with a vengeance
and created a renewed aversion to popular movements of any kind,
especially on Metternich's part. Adam Müller and Friedrich Schlegel

were to be employed by Count Metternich for the conservative Austrian cause during the Restoration's initial period, and Franz von Baader seemed for a while to be a welcome collaborator with reforming elements in the Tsar's government. But the statesmen who were calling the shots (like Metternich) or influencing tactics (like Gentz) were no Romantics, although the Romantics' sense of tradition made them useful in counteracting liberal political theories.

Once the turn to repression of liberal ideas became dominant under Metternich's leadership, it was clear that no Romantic ideas disruptive of the status quo would be tolerated either. The politics of the Restoration casts a shadow across the later activities of Adam Müller. I propose, for once, to discuss his *Elements of Statecraft* in its own "setting in life" only, leaving the further developments in Müller's social thought that can best be called "restorationist" for another occasion.[13]

II. The Outlook of Romanticism

Adam Müller had substantial contact with Romantic thinkers such as Novalis, Friedrich Schlegel and Franz von Baader (as well as with Goethe). He was himself a Romanticist critic and writer of acknowledged standing, but he did not belong to the first blossoming of talent in one of the early "circles" at Jena or in his native city of Berlin. In Dresden, however, he played a prominent Romanticist role; he was the one who "discovered" Heinrich von Kleist and got his first plays published. He carried his reputation with him back to Berlin (1809-1812) and to Vienna, where he attempted to found an academy for young gentry with Clement Maria Hofbauer (a project foiled by the Josephist Viennese authorities). The peculiar character of Müller's discourse, filled with *sic et non* and yet driving towards universal validity, modern and yet looking to the past, indulging in intriguing intellectual speculation and yet in full tilt against Enlightenment rationalism, opposed to absolutism and yet favoring archconservatism, can only be understood against this background.

---

[13]The later life of Adam Müller, as in the case of his political patrons, Metternich and Gentz, naturally overshadows his earlier aspirations in the judgment of posterity. Thus Müller passes for a Romantic reactionary, even though his major work, *ESK*, only justifies the first epithet, cf. e.g. Lill in *History of the Church*, 7:219. For Müller's later attitudes, cf. especially Ralph-Rainer Wuthenow, "Romantik als Restauration bei Adam H. Müller," in *Katholizismus, konservative Kapitalismuskritik und Frühsozialismus bis 1850*, ed. A. Langner, pp. 75–97.

From the time that the Enlightenment critique of authority and tradition arose and became a force in the republic of letters, there were always counter-Enlightenment currents. To be critical of the reign of reason proclaimed by the *philosophes* is a fairly constant feature of Romantics, to be sure, but it alone does not suffice to make one a Romantic. For that, one must also see the Enlightenment account of human nature as inadequate mainly because of its fixation on the mathematical or logical paradigm of reason, to the exclusion of the poetical or emotional dimensions of life. For some Romantics, as for Schleiermacher, Novalis and Müller, the esthetic or emotional realm, quite distinct from reason and will but equally fundamental, comes to be seen as related especially to religious experience.

In its most specific sense, moreover, Romanticism flourished only in the space of a generation or two: in England during the time of Sanuel Taylor Coleridge and William Wadsworth, in Germany during the lifetime of Goethe (who died in 1830, but who weighted the balance of the classic and the romantic more to the classic side).[14] It was in this relatively short period that the achievements of the age of reason were resoundingly called into question and subjected to a series of profound criticisms and even denunciations.

Of course the calamities of the French Revolution cast a peculiar light on the teachings of that "half-Romantic," J. J. Rousseau, but also on all the philanthropic views of celebrated eighteenth-century authors. Associated with this were catalogs of objections from all branches of letters and thought, however. Adam Müller himself is in many ways a typical example. In his view, every science and all departments of learning had suffered from the one-eyed logic of Enlightenment thinking, in every case leaving out of consideration the mysterious or seemingly incommensurable dimensions of a subject and thus throwing away the key to understanding its whole reality. In his *Theory of the Opposite*,[15] an early and obscure pro-

---

[14]Cf. Hans Georg Schenk, *The Mind of the European Romantics: an Essay in Cultural History* (London: Constable, 1966 and Garden City, NY: Doubleday, 1969); Peter Berglar, "Der romantische Aufstand. Zur Psycho-Historie des Zeitgeistes," *Saeculum* 27 (1976):197–210. For an appreciation of Müller's contribution to Romanticist literary criticism, cf. René Wellek, *History of Modern Criticism 1750–1950* (New Haven: Yale University Press, 1955), 2:291–97.

[15]Adam Müller, *Die Lehre vom Gegensatze* (1804), now in his *Kritische, ästhetische und philosophische Schriften*, edited by Walter Schroeder and Werner Siebert (2 vols.; Neuwied: Luchterhand, 1967), 2:193–248; cf. Koehler, *Aesthetik und Politik*, pp. 19–20.

grammatic essay in Romantic-Idealist philosophy, proto-Hegelian in its attempted dialectic, he sketched his ambition to do complete justice to both discursive reason and vital drives, both individual freedoms and social bonds, both conflict and harmony, both change and permanency, the beautiful as well as the possible, all in mutual opposition and relation to one another.

As Koehler argues persuasively, it was as a direct result of this approach that Müller combined politics (the state) and esthetics (art, *Kunst*) in the title of his major work, *Die Elemente der Staatskunst*. The failure of the absolutist *ancien régime* throughout Europe was, to him and to like-minded conservatives, enough to show the insufficiency of proceeding along strictly scientific lines in trying to understand and master the art of politics.

Among the images conjured up to illustrate the contrast between the Enlightenment and Romanticism are many that Adam Müller himself used already in the first decade of the nineteenth century. Despite his predilection for things English, however, I have not found my personal favorite, the contrast between the formal garden after the manner of Versailles and the English style of park (the popular park along the Isar in Munich, laid out in the new style at this time, is called *der Englische Garten*).

From the first pages of *Elements of Statecraft* he made his standpoint clear by contrasting the static "concepts" found in the pages of the enlightened academics of his time with the living and dynamic "idea" of the state, as being always in movement through time *ad intra* and *ad extra*, just like a living organism of the higher kinds. He also pointed out the contrast between mechanical and organic models of reality, aware of the tendency of his predecessors to see the universe, or the state, as a complex mechanism, like clockwork, and of his Romantic contemporaries' equally pronounced preference for a still more complex but less artificial model, the human organism (*ESK*, Lecture 2 [1:38]). In effect, Adam Müller applied F. W. J. Schelling's organic philosophy of nature to the realm of political life and conceived a new type of social philosophy.

This being so, it has come as a surprise and even as a reason for dismissing Müller's thought as hopelessly wrongheaded, that he rejected the notion of "natural law" with vehemence and scorn. But "natural law" was a typical rationalistic concept in the usage of his day. The myth of a pre-societal "natural condition" made natural law theory highly individualistic in perspective. Working with such a construct, the theorists of "natural law" considered all social arrangements as such to be a posteriori contractual agreements.

In the eighteenth century, only individual liberties and private property were held to be truly "natural" in the sense of being original givens, the "social contract" needing to be called into existence deliberately, much as one would construct a machine. As the reflex of such anthropological atomism, the organized state then appeared necessarily repressive. At best one would look for a regime of enlightened absolutistic rule. Karl-Heinz Ilting maintains that this understanding of natural law went back to Hobbes and was dominant at the time of Adam Müller's lectures in 1809, but did not survive the Restoration period. Although Ilting does not mention Adam Müller, he ascribes the demise of the rational natural law theory in philosophy and jurisprudence to the "historical school" of legal philosophy founded by F. C. von Savigny and carried on by F. J. Stahl, both in Müller's sphere of influence.[16]

III. Adam Müller's Response to Smith's Wealth of Nations

With the foregoing, the stage has been set to understand the economic views of Adam Müller's Elements of Statecraft. One sees Adam Müller trying to deal with the phenomenon of the all-encompassing market: its benefits as Adam Smith had described them, and its one-sidedness and incompleteness as seen by the romantic economist. The Smithians' recommendation to commercialize immobile as well as all mobile property was a challenge particularly to the time-honored roles of rural landowners and agriculture. Adam Müller is led to propose a basically anti-liberal frame of society, modernizing but carrying on in analogical forms the ordered society of estates which the reformers of the age were busy dismantling.

The Market and the State. Adam Smith regarded as a law of human nature "the propensity to truck, barter, and exchange one thing for another" (WN I.ii.1, p. 25). Since human labor is the cause of any and all increase in usable goods over and above what nature may lay spontaneously at our feet, then the key to increasing affluence for larger numbers of people is more highly productive work. The key to increased productivity in turn is the division of labor, aided by inventions, for by specializing lines of work and exchanging the

---

[16]Karl-Heinz Ilting, Naturrecht und Sittlichkeit, Begriffsgeschichtliche Studien (Stuttgart: Klett-Cotta, 1983), p. 109–113; Langner, "Adam Müller," p. 20.

products, everyone can have more and better goods than if each tried to be altogether self-sufficient. Luckily, therefore, the disposition to "truck, barter and exchange" favored the division of labor; and the larger the pool of possible exchanges (that is, the market) grew, the further the division of labor could proceed, with never-ending benefits for all frugal and active participants.

Adam Müller, for his part, was far from turning this whole description of economic reality around or denying its validity in root and branch. In fact, he incorporated or presupposed most of what Adam Smith had described and only objected that it labored under certain very serious limitations, accentuated by the Enlightenment's overemphasis on logic and calculating reason. Just as, taught by Burke, he considered the Rights of Man to be a poor substitute for the organic connections making up a state, similarly in the economic realm, he thought that the "natural law" of property and exchange was an extremely abstract, individualistic and hence incomplete account of the matter. The reality of economics was more complex and broad than Adam Smith was able to convey, judging by his "chorus of modish economic devotees in Germany" (ESK, Lecture 26 [2:38]).

Adam Müller spoke of commerce, markets, money and profits with never a hint of morally disqualifying them in principle; he even devoted parts of several lectures (nos. 20, 24, 25, 27 and especially 30) to the interest that accrues on loaned capital, with never an allusion to usury or a protest that this was not as it should be. If he was acquainted with the medieval horror of taking payment for a loan, he paid it no heed. (Ten years later he will have changed his tone in regard to the de facto role of money in modern capitalism; but that was after the Restoration, when developments that he wished to forestall were taking place.)

What then was his grievance? Why has Adam Müller gone down in history as, among other things, the first German critic of Smithian economics and a forerunner of the "historical school" of economics?[17] On the surface, it was most probably because he challenged Smith's policy recommendations for untrammeled free trade. Deeper down, he objected to the curt dismissal of the traditional corporations and guilds in the Wealth of Nations and to Adam Smith's paradigm of science after the manner of Isaac Newton's physical

---

[17]Howard R. Bowen, "Müller, Adam," International Encyclopedia of the Social Sciences (1968), 10:522–23.

laws of mechanics. Still, he respected Smith's immense achievement and ambitioned only to correct its relative one-sidedness by connecting economics more consistently with the rest of human reality.

His direct opponents were those Smithians in Germany who seized upon the skeleton of Smith's argument and on his policy proposals (abolition of privileged corporations such as guilds and of all barriers to free movement of labor and goods) and had no interest either for or against his broader social outlook in the form of a "philosophical history." Such theories were behind the post-1806 reforms of Hardenberg and Stein in Prussia.[18]

Adam Müller too had his view of history, which comes out principally in Lectures 11 to 17, the last part of his political philosophy—he was immodest enough to put it forward as replacing Montesquieu's *Spirit of Laws* (1748)! The philosophy of right (Lectures 6–17) and the economic philosophy (Lectures 18–32) form the two main interrelated parts of the *Elements of Statecraft*, which was thus intended to supercede both Montesquieu and Adam Smith. He would take the leads provided by Edmund Burke and "romanticize" them; in his context that would mean, attempt to ground them speculatively and point them more explicitly toward the ideal of the Christian state. What Montesquieu and Smith called out for, in Adam Müller's view, was completion and reintegration with each other and with the wisdom of medieval Christendom. What would result would be something more advanced than medieval Christendom and much more humane than anything that the Enlightenment approach had brought about.

As far as a market economy was concerned, then, Adam Müller saw this as the great step forward of the early modern or Reformation period. The famous inventions of printing, gunpowder and compass, the discovery of the passage to India and of the New World (and, he added, "of ancient Greek and Rome from the dust that covered them," *ESK*, Lecture 26, [2:37]), how could they not fail to dislodge Christendom out of its previous limits and carry it away in ever-increasing commercial ventures?

All this resulted in the paramount importance in the early modern world of the merchandising enterprise. Even if Adam Smith placed the accent on the productivity of agriculture and manufacturing (in

---

[18]Melchior Palyi, "The Introduction of Adam Smith on the Continent," in J. M. Clark et al., *Adam Smith, 1776–1926* (University of Chicago Press, 1928), pp. 180–233, particularly 221–23; cp. Müller, *ESK*, Lectures 1 and 19 (1:14 and 374).

an early phase of its development, not as yet much affected by the exploitation of power-producing machines and engines), still the great modern economic development which led to the passing of the Middle Ages, as Adam Müller saw it, was the growth of commerce and the dominance of money and credit. Where was the explanation for the conditions of the possibility of such an unprecedented economic development? Surely, so Müller, not in the division of labor and the propensity to exchange alone.

> Hence the one-sided economics of production comes up against an absolute boundary which it cannot master. Everyone acknowledges the economic role of civil servants, if not of the nobility or the clergy; and yet Adam Smith must rigorously exclude them from the ranks of productive workers, because they produce nothing which can be sold on the market according to the ordinary laws of trade.
>
> The great man, as high and far as his soul might aim, is confined within the iron bands of a lifeless concept; culture remains outside the pale of the economy, no matter how directly and indispensably and positively it affects production; the intercourse of minds remains outside the theory of the wealth of nations. He clings to the literal sense of the expression "value in exchange" as if mesmerized. Thus we are shown right at the beginning of his work, as he feels obliged to present something of a principle of all human commerce, a "certain propensity to barter and trade," such as one can see in children, as the basic source of the glorious phenomenon of a prosperous nation.[19]

Müller thus set out to complete the picture only partially filled in by Adam Smith, or in his terms, to combine the lifeless *concepts* of Enlightenment thinkers with their opposites in the manner of his Romantic esthetics and thus restore them to being living and moving *ideas* (cf. Lecture 1). In terms of commerce, Adam Müller happened to think that the way to remedy its drawbacks for the commonwealth, while not stifling its successful modern forms, was not simply to remove all laws controlling it (as the Physiocrats and, in his judicious fashion, Adam Smith also proposed), but to give it its place in society as a whole, tie it back into the whole complex which he named "the state," and subject it as a whole to interactions with other functions in the state.

---

[19]Müller, *ESK*, Lecture 19 (1:375). Müller was apparently unaware of the relationship in which the *Wealth of Nations* stood to the *Theory of Moral Sentiment* (1759) and other works by Smith in moral philosophy: cf. the "General Introduction" to WN by the editors, R. H. Campbell and A. S. Skinner, pp. 1–10, and the biography by the same authors, *Adam Smith* (New York: St. Martin's Press, 1982), pp. 94–108.

The state, after all, for many Romantics, should be thought of not as a machine, but as an organism.[20] Müller took this so far as to regard the state as an all-inclusive quasi-person (*ESK*, Lectures 5, 17). In the whole of his concluding Book Six, he develops variations on this theme.[21] They were meant as motives for social solidarity and a participatory society; they also lent themselves to subjugating the individuals to the aura and majesty of the state as the greater reality. Adam Müller rejected the distinction between state and society in reaction to social-contract thinking. This left his teaching bereft of adequate safeguards against the glorification of the state.

The inherent tendency of modern economic developments, which Adam Smith seemed to take for the ideal, would place the market outside of any societal constraints except those imposed on it by the sovereign for purposes of defense and public order. The new wisdom of laissez faire was to encourage this unlimited autonomy of the market—and let society at large adjust as best it might without state intervention. This is what Adam Müller saw as one-sided about even Adam Smith's description. It failed to take sufficiently into account the cultural conditions which were necessary so that commercial enterprises could be integrated into, and thus more effectively serviceable to, the state (that is identical, for Adam Müller, with organically ordered society).

The Economic Functions and Estates of the State. Müller clothed his idea finally in the garb of a fourth (business or capitalist) estate which was to take its place in the public order alongside of the three traditional estates, suitably modernized. Thus the model of a modern nation, to Adam Müller, would have four recognized estates: one engaged primarily in the cultural aspects and activities of a people, a second being in charge of the land, the third working the land and its produce into salable commodities and the fourth engaging principally in trade and commerce (Lecture 26). The sovereign and his government would stand above these estates and promote their development and interaction (drastically and exaggeratedly expressed, their "warfare") in the interests of the whole.

Not so ironically, the modern state corresponding most closely to

---

[20]Hans S. Reiss (ed.), *The Political Thought of the German Romantics 1793–1815* (New York: Macmillan, 1955), pp. 27–33 on Müller; cf. Karl Mannheim, "The History of the State as an Organism: a Sociological Analysis," in *Essays on Sociology and Social Psychology* (as above, note 12), pp. 169–182.

[21]His most striking theological formulation is no doubt the title of Lecture 34 of *ESK*, "That Christ died not only for individuals but also for states."

Adam Müller's model was Great Britain! In its peculiar circumstances, it had preserved a cultural clerisy still largely in the hands of real clergy (who staffed the universities and ran the schools, while bishops represented the first estate in parliament). It had a nobility based on great landed domains and a gentry also dedicated to agriculture. It had a large agricultural and urban force of skilled labor comprising the third estate; and to all intents and purposes, its powerful business and banking interests formed a fourth estate with its own representation in parliament defending its interests effectively.

It must be admitted, however, that no one else ever thought of the modern political economy in these terms, as far as I know, either in England or on the continent;[22] nor did Adam Müller cling to his scheme of four estates later on. Those who engaged in commerce were content to see themselves either as the third estate, representing "the (whole) people" as opposed to clergy and nobility, or strove to sink their money into land and be assimilated to the nobility.[23] Adam Müller's own subsequent political activity was in defense of agrarian, quasi-feudal nobility and to some extent of artisans in the towns.[24]

Müller saw four-fold interrelations wherever he looked in human affairs, all analogous to the basic pattern of the two pairs of opposites in the family: man and woman, age and youth (ESK, Lecture 5; cp. Lecture 19 [1:369]). Thus his first estate, the cultured or clerical, corresponds to age, the second, nobility, to the woman (fertile soil), the third, labor, to the man, and the fourth, commerce, to youth. What was practically of more significance to him, however, was the polar opposition constituted by agrarian and urban human labor, between direct unearthing of natural resources and their further processing into all kinds of marketable commodities. This resolved itself in political-economic discussions into the tension between "landed" and "moneyed" interests.

Adam Smith was no doubt the one who taught Adam Müller to

---

[22]The most notable German Idealist essay in economic theory before Müller's was The Closed Market State (1800): Johann Gottlieb Fichte, Der geschloBne Handelsstaat, edited by Hans Hirsch (Hamburg: F. Meiner, 1979). It advocated a sort of proto-socialist utopian scheme of a vocationally ordered and planned economy under the direction of intellectuals.

[23]Adam Müller, like Burke, opposed the idea of the third estate as representing "the (whole) people" in ESK, Lecture 33 and elsewhere, e.g. the citations further on in the text from Lecture 25.

[24]Langner, "Zur konservativen Position" (cf. note 12), esp. pp. 49–57 and 66–73.

notice the distinctive economic character of each type of occupation. He had a clear set of interrelated categories for understanding human economic activities and treating the problems that arise in theory and in practice. Basic to his undertaking was the recognition of the three basic "factors of production," land, labor and capital, or natural resources, the human intervention required to make them useful, and the accumulated produce, seed, tools and skills which render labor ever more productive.

Smith also sees three basic kinds of return. Corresponding to land is the *rent* that a landowner can expect for fertile acreage or well-timbered forests in his possession. Whoever works on the land or at a workbench, his own or someone else's, receives *wages* for his labor. When a person engages in trade, the return is called *profit* (*WN* I.6 [p. 69]; cp. I.xi.p.7 [p. 265]). Interest is a derivative type of revenue, owed to a person who lends previously garnered returns to another to employ; interest is also ultimately resolvable into rent, wages or profit, depending on how the borrower puts the capital to use.

With all of this, as far as it went, Adam Müller had no quarrel. But thinking in pairs of polar opposites, as was his wont, he insisted that there was a fourth original source of wealth and that it was the elaboration and accumulation of what came to be known as *human capital*. He himself called it *geistiges Kapital*, "spiritual capital" (*ESK*, Lecture 26, [2:23]. By allotting its development chiefly to the *Geistlichkeit*, his first estate, or "clerisy" (a term I borrow from his contemporary, S. T. Coleridge), he could vindicate the economic productivity of persons such as himself and Smith. Adam Smith was, after all, a university professor and then a writer supported by a patron as well as, yes, a customs assessor enforcing restraints on international trade! The taxes and fees needed to support the state were nothing else than the interest constantly accumulating on this human capital built up in the past (Lecture 27).

His criticism of Adam Smith was, as we have seen, that the latter was too exclusively concerned with *physical* capital. In truth, Adam Smith was keenly aware of the cultural conditions, education, settled habits of life and so forth, conducive to a thriving national economy, but he did not make them a part of his formally *economic* theory. It was left to Adam Müller's romantic mind to invent "this highly useful metaphor" of human capital.[25]

---

[25]Rondo Cameron, "A New View of European Industrialization," *The Economic*

Town and Country. It was axiomatic with Adam Smith that the personal liberty of citizens and their freedom to dispose of private property entirely as they wished were values to be cherished above all else. In the first part of *The Elements of Statecraft* (Lecture 8, [1:162]) Adam Müller stressed that human beings have only the *use*, not the absolute dominium, of property (a principle to be rediscovered by Neo-Thomists later in the century)—and that property is of two quite distinct kinds, land and other things. If it is immobile (land), it holds the property "owner" as much as he holds it. Müller was not speaking of serfdom here, which, like usury, he consigns tacitly to oblivion, but of "*noblesse oblige*," of special responsibilities for the natural resources of a nation. This is something that a hereditary line of owners is particularly well suited to carry out: a family may go on indefinitely; hence the present inheritor and administrator will have the incentive to treat the land as a precious heritage to be passed on undiminished in value, improved but not exploited.

Adam Müller could thus see the purpose and value in entailing land and making it difficult to sell, even though he did not go so far as expressly to defend this practice. However, he did point up the differences between the urban manufacturing sector of the economy (in the Germany of 1808, a matter of handworkers and artisans, of masters and journeymen), which might benefit by an increased pace of change and trade, and the agrarian sector, where improvements by capital investment had to respect the natural tempo of growing seasons and cycles and where the division of labor was less applicable (Smith, WN, I.1.4, p. 16; Müller, ESK, Lectures 25, 26, 29, 30). Put another way, he drew an emphatic distinction, surely of interest again in view of the ecological crisis, between goods destined for short-term consumption on the one hand and property which outlives its owner and hence becomes the vehicle for a certain social interchange between human beings past, present and future, on the other. Edmund Burke's line of thought here modified the thrust of Adam Smith's economic recommendations.

Adam Müller was constantly speaking, in a way that would hardly have been possible without Adam Smith, of increased activity and vigor in the economy. He saw the role of the government, for

---

History Review, 2d Series, 38 (1985):20. Cf. Ernst Klein, "Die Auseinandersetzungen Adam Müllers mit den wirtschaftstheoretischen und wirtschaftspolitischen Auffassungen seiner Zeit," in *Katholizismus, konservative Kapitalismuskritik und Frühsozialismus bis 1850*, ed. A. Langner, pp. 99–122.

example, not first and foremost in the control of trade, but in striving
to maintain that *balance* of economic forces in the long run which
would favor growth by intense economic activity (cf. Lectures 31
and 32). In this connection, however, he also wished to account for
the opposites that functioned in his dialectical Romantic outlook as
the other side of any phenomenon, in this case, the kind of economic
object which changes little over time: land, or, as we call it, real
estate. In his twenty-fifth Lecture,[26] after explaining and endorsing
Adam Smith's three factors of production, land, labor and capital,
he made the following remarks on the division of labor.

> How did the first and most basic differentiation of land and labor take
> place, the division of labor into farm work and town work? What was
> the security for the laborer, who relinquished work in the fields with
> its much more direct access to the prime necessities of life to take up a
> trade off the farm? The only security he could have was *time*—a power
> which political analysis until Burke completely ignored and which
> these addresses have consistently underscored. Yes, *time*, the past, or,
> as it presents itself in economic guise, *capital*. *Das Kapital*, let us
> express it more simply: the accumulation of stock over time is what
> places the individual worker in the position to follow his inclinations
> and devote himself with his particular dexterity to a special craft.

In the same lecture, Müller went on to note that England had a
particularly fortunate past that induced it to see economic life
predominantly according to the pattern of capital. Applied to model
farms, an excess of improvements brought about larger harvests and
better returns, but Adam Müller doubted that that was the secret of
Britain's success. Applied to manufactures in towns, great capital
expenditures led naturally to a great expansion of industry by the
division of labor between men and machines and between lines of
work: this was the leading paradigm of Smithian economics. Now
the German reformers wish to apply the same scheme without
adaptation to Prussia and the other states.

> In the process we have only forgotten two very important circum-
> stances: first, that the indispensable prerequisite of all British agricul-
> tural reforms has been an improportionate investment of capital; sec-
> ond, that the principle of division of labor, applied to agriculture, goes
> against the nature of this occupation.

---

[26]The next four citations are all from Müller, *ESK*, Lecture 25 (2:17–21).

It was not really agriculture, nor even skilled labor, that made Britain prosperous. It was capital, luckily preserved and prodigally expended. In all discussions of the British model, even Adam Smith's, no matter what the words said, the spirit they breathed was urban, dominated by capital, and not rural. There was nothing wrong with this, as far as the British would be concerned, but it is really only half of a balanced economy.

> The theory of the absolute *tiers-état* has insinuated itself in recent years in all British letters and sciences without causing any damage or significant loss for Great Britain itself, because an immense, well-rounded, spiritual and physical, national and individual capital is present and at work and is tacitly counted upon by every Briton who reads the one-sided systems of his nation's authors or who performs the repetitive tasks alloted to the individual by the never-ending division of labor.

It may have led to no practical disadvantages for Great Britain that Adam Smith emphasized the urban and bourgeois elements of the national economy one-sidedly. But Germany was a different case:

> "Insofar as we wish to transfer the British doctrine in its entire extent to our soil, the urban perspective that dominates it is quite unsuited to the broad flat territory that we inhabit and that we call a continent."

Nor could Germany *afford* an analogous imbalance, even if it could advance its manufacturing sector with seven-league boots. What Germany should aim for is a balance between country and town; their interplay should be promoted by an unencumbered internal market serving international trade on its own terms and not on those of Great Britain. Müller hoped after all to avoid having to compete directly with Great Britain's more advanced economy by taking fuller advantage of Germany's skills and opportunities in commerce, rather than in the mass production of goods in large factories.[27]

---

[27]When Müller was advising Metternich on economic issues a decade later (1820), he detailed the dependency relationship with Great Britain in which the German economies were caught; and he advised a cautious sort of protectionism as well as internal reforms, so that trade could be carried on to the mutual benefit of the partners, cf. *LZ*, ed. Baxa, 2:317–340 or *ESK*, 2:500–525, esp. 511–17, and Baxa, *Adam Müller* (1930), p. 106.

In the light of the debate at the moment over the use of Marxist economic analysis

IV. Conclusion: The Economics of Intangibles through Time

Adam Müller's influence was greatest with those who shared his negative assessment of the French Revolution. His own further evolution and those of the circles in which he was appreciated (primarily Austrian Catholic) tended to cross the attitudinal and ideological line from conservative to reactionary as time went on. In the Hofbauer Circle in Vienna, of which he was a part, a split between reactionaries and liberal-conservatives under the leadership of Anton Günther eventually took place.[28] It would appear as if Adam Müller continued to be honored only in the reactionary wing. This was the side that came out on top in church circles, as it happened.

When another North German socially-minded convert settled in Vienna after 1864, Karl von Vogelsang, Adam Müller's thought received renewed attention there.[29] Between the First and the Second World Wars, the Viennese economist Othmar Spann (1800–1900) celebrated Adam Müller as the founder of the corporatist tradition. Since corporatism is still acknowledged to characterize the political-economic structures of Austria and Switzerland,[30] one may surmise that Adam Müller's variation and critique of modern economic theory has had a multiform afterlife.

As to that feature of dynamic societies that Marx was later to call "class struggle," Müller's Romantic mindset allowed him to see an omnipresent role for societal conflict in many forms. He would not see it, all the same, reduced to the economic sphere alone. His solution was to harness the rivalry of groups in society by means of

---

in liberation theology, it may help to restore some sense of proportion and historical perspective to learn that Adam Müller had already posited a "dependency theory" to explain the economic relationship of Great Britain and Prussia (ESK, Lecture 19 [2:90–91]; cp. Lecture 32 [2:139]).

On an analogous issue of the presence of Marxist analysis in the 1931 encyclical, Quadragesimo anno, one should note Oswald von Nell-Breuning, "In eigener Sache," Stimmen der Zeit, 105 (1980):162–63.

[28]Rudolf Till, Hofbauer und sein Kreis (Vienna: Herold, 1951).

[29]Alexander, "Church and Society in Germany" (as above, note 4), pp. 417–422. Vogelsang was a good deal more regressive than Adam Müller, however; for example, Vogelsang denounced credit in general as involving usury.

[30]Peter J. Katzenstein, Corporatism and Change: Austria, Switzerland, and the Politics of Industry. Ithaca, NY: Cornell University Press, 1984; Philippe C. Schmitter, "A Working Bibliography on Corporatism, ca. 1800–1950," in Frederick B. Pike and Thomas Stritch (eds.), The New Corporatism: Social-Political Structures in the Iberian World (rpt. of the Review of Politics 36 [1974], no. 1; University of Notre Dame Press, 1974), pp. 128–131.

healthy restraints, so that their conflicts would be productive for the common advantage. His model for these restraints was Edmund Burke's, namely the existing traditional estates. Without doubt the existing estates or orders of society should be responsive to pressures and new developments, but they should not be destroyed on the warrant of a mere theory. Acknowledging the importance of the bourgeoisie in contemporary politics and economics, Müller wished to see them integrated into the existing order as a fourth estate; he saw this as much preferable to their conducting an unrestrained campaign outside the existing order for total domination of the state, as had happened with such tragic results in France.

Indeed, to Adam Müller, no one had yet thought of the economy in terms that were political or national enough, even though the subject was usually called political or national economy. What he was trying to supply was a thoroughgoing explanation of economic matters in terms of a social or political science (*Staatswissenschaft*), a *social* economics (*ESK*, Lecture 19 [1:373]); one moreover in which the factors of *time* and *change* would be accounted for in a Burkean-conservative spirit.

The chief concern here has been with Adam Müller's *Elements of Statecraft* in its own setting in life in Dresden and Berlin in 1809. Müller was a disciple of Adam Smith's, though a critical one. By accepting the productive role of money as capital, by acknowledging Smith's critique of the mercantile system (and of the Physiocrats' opposite extreme) and by avoiding any breath of confessionalism in his recognition that both medieval Catholic and sixteenth-century Protestant conditions were a thing of the past, he reflected the eighteenth century in which he was born. In his vision of a Christian state he was something more than that, of course, in a way looking both forward and backward at the same time.

From his Burkean conservatism and anti-revolutionary stance, as from his Romantic sensibility of paradoxical relationships in the fullness of life, came forth elements of a critique of classical economics that in their own way have become classical ("counter-classical," if I may coin a phrase; "conservative," to use the conventional one).

He insisted on the importance of "spiritual" or human capital, thus making at least one notable contribution to mainstream economic thought. He pointed out the one-sidedness of the doctrinaire free-trade approach and how its consistent application would condemn relatively backward economies to permanent dependence. He likewise weighed the advantages of more and more division of labor against its disadvantages, being one of the first to voice a concern for the deadening alienation of factory work. He challenged the presuppositions of classical economics as individualistic, as relegating sociability to a secondary and inessential sphere of human life.[31]

Seeing the trends towards an individualistic, emphatically urban, age, Adam Müller called for a balance of the urban and the rural elements in the German economy that had to develop after the wars. Not yet knowing the extent of the industrial revolution that was already indirectly affecting continental economies, he nevertheless wished to mitigate the ill effects of any revolutionary upheaval.

Catholic social thought was a long time in taking shape and has remained subject to a continuing series of surprises over dimensions of reality not previously accounted for. The cool and critical attitude towards capitalism of mainstream Roman Catholic pronouncements has no doubt been influenced by a host of historical circumstances having little or nothing to do with the intrinsic nature of capitalism and the industrialization it fostered in the nineteenth century. Granting all this, it is still the case that its pioneers, among whom I number Adam Müller, were able in imperfect ways and with a mixed record of insight, to point out some intrinsic flaws in economic liberalism. It was a start.

---

[31]Klein (above, note 25), pp. 109, 114–121.

MISSIONARY AS PHILANTHROPIST: A SOCIAL AND ECONOMIC PORTRAIT OF JOHN R. SLATTERY

William L. Portier

I. Introduction

John R. Slattery (1851–1926) has made a twofold contribution to American religious thought in general and to Catholic theology in the U.S. in particular. First, during the period between 1877 and 1900, he, for all practical purposes, directed the Catholic missionary effort to the recently emancipated American blacks. Second, in addition to his integral involvement with the history of the black Catholic community in the United States, he would eventually become one of three American Catholic priests to proclaim themselves "modernists." His embrace of "modernism," described by Pope Pius X in 1907 as "the synthesis of all heresies," explains why his story has been left untold for so many years.

As the leader of the Josephite Fathers during most of this period, Slattery was the most visible advocate and apologist for the Catholic "Negro mission" in his day. He published widely on the topic and his bibliography includes more than forty articles, many of them appearing in Isaac Hecker's monthly magazine *Catholic World*. Slattery was an intellectually honest and independent thinker who over time became disillusioned with the Catholic Church and its approach to the racial situation in this country. Part of his embrace of modernism had to do with his frustration at the church's level of support for the mission to the blacks. His version of modernism, therefore, like that of his Paulist contemporary, William Laurence Sullivan, can be viewed as a form of moralism.[1] Still, however, Slattery's had a distinctly speculative cast that stressed a conviction

---

[1] Michael B. McGarry, C.S.P., "Modernism in the United States: William Laurence Sullivan, 1872–1935," *Records of the American Catholic Historical Society of Philadelphia*, 90 (1979), 32–52.

about the incompatibility between the church's claims and those of modern science in both its biological and historical varieties.

Although my primary goal as an historical theologian is an analysis of Slattery's religious thought, I am methodologically committed to the notion that ideas can be critically understood only in the context of a thinker's concrete subjectivity in all its dimensions. A consideration of the social and economic position from which someone speaks is essential for a critical understanding of what he or she says.[2] In the late nineteenth-century immigrant Catholic Church, John Slattery's social and economic status was atypical, and that helps explain both his unusual perspective as well as the opposition which it aroused. The modest purpose of this essay is to understand Slattery's personal history as an indispensable preliminary to an exposition and critical interpretation of his religious thinking.

Even allowing for the workings of divine grace, historical theologians can still ask questions such as the following. In what social and economic setting would it make sense for a wealthy young Irish American Catholic to leave law school at Columbia for the Negro mission, and, over the strenuous objections of his father, devote his life-work to promoting the evangelization as well as the moral and social amelioration of American blacks? This question, rather than an analysis of Slattery's vision for the evangelization of American blacks or his theological modernism, provides the focus for this essay. The question will be answered in two parts. The first part will sketch a social and economic portrait of John R. Slattery. The second part will interpret his missionary career in terms of that portrait and see it as a Roman Catholic form of "Gilded Age" philanthropy.

Slattery's years as a Josephite missionary priest spanned the period between Reconstruction and the turn of the century (roughly 1877 to 1900) which historians call the Gilded Age. Taken from the title of a satirical novel which Mark Twain coauthored in 1873, the phrase *Gilded Age* suggests a certain moral and political vulgarity overlaid with a veneer of wealth.[3] From a less moralistic point of view, this was a period of industrialization, urbanization and immi-

---

[2]For a clear exposition of the thinking behind such a position, see Gregory Baum, "The Impact of Sociology on Catholic Theology" in *The Social Imperative* (New York: Paulist Press, 1979), 99–128.

[3]For a nuanced overview of the Gilded Age, see John A. Garraty, *The New Commonwealth, 1877–1890* (New York: Harper Torchbooks, 1968), chapter I. For a thorough bibliography on the period, which includes entries up to 1972, see Vincent P. DeSantis, *The Gilded Age, 1877–1896* (Northbrook, IL: AHM Publishing Corp., 1973).

gration which brought the United States into the modern era. *Laissez-faire* economics led to rapid accumulations of vast wealth for some entrepreneurs such as the Cleveland bookkeeper, John D. Rockefeller, and the Scottish telegraph clerk, Andrew Carnegie. It consigned most immigrants and minorities to a laboring class who built the railroads and smelted the iron, or as Slattery's father had done in the previous generation, hauled the gravel.[4]

Born in 1851, John R. Slattery came of age during this period in the prototypical urban center of the emerging industrial nation, New York City. His father, James Slattery, an immigrant laborer, had risen from the laboring class to the entrepreneurial ranks during the decade of the Civil War. During his years of schooling, therefore, John Slattery's experience was far removed from that of the poor laboring class. By the time of his ordination to the priesthood in 1877, at the end of Reconstruction and the beginning of the Guilded Age, the Slattery family had achieved a rank respectable status among the wealthy New York Irish. This put John Slattery and his brothers, Patrick and John, partners in construction and contracting, in a position to share in the rapid accumulation of wealth that took place in New York City during the last quarter of the nineteenth century.

II. A Social and Economic Portrait of Slattery

There is no published biography of Slattery. But his recently unearthed, unpublished autobiography provides much of the information needed to sketch his social and economic portrait.[5] In addi-

---

[4]For a view of this period from the perspective of the laboring class, see Howard Zinn, A People's History of the United States (New York: Harper Colophon Books, 1980), 206–289. Zinn argues for an emerging class consciousness among American workers which was channeled off into political conflict.

[5]The autobiography is written for the most part in French. The nearly 400 page, handwritten manuscript is located at the Bibliothèque Nationale in the papers of Albert Houtin (1867–1926), a minor French modernest and close friend of Slattery's. I am grateful to Professor Émile Poulat of Paris who told me in a letter that there was a "biographie" of Slattery in the Papiers Houtin. Houtin's own autobiography also mentions a biography of Slattery written by Houtin and entitled Un moderniste catholique américain J.-R. Slattery. The manuscript in the Papiers Houtin (NAF 15741–42) bears the simple title "Biographie de J.R. Slattery." It is written in the first person and is clearly an autobiography. See William L. Portier, "A Note on the Unpublished Biographie de J.R. Slattery in the Papiers Houtin," in Ronald Burke, Gary Lease, and George Gilmore, eds., Historiography and Modernism, prepared for the 1985 meeting of the AAR Working Group on Roman Catholic Modernism (Mobile: Spring Hill College, 1985), pp. 74–75. In subsequent notes this autobiography will be referred to as Biographie.

tion to the unpublished autobiography, there is also a published biographical sketch. It appeared in 1902, on the twenty-fifth anniversary of his ordination to the priesthood, in the Josephite fund raising magazine, *The Colored Harvest*. Although it is written in the third person, Slattery is probably the author. Passing autobiographical references in his articles and correspondence supplement these two sources. Slattery's letters are most often perfunctory and businesslike. A notable exception is a long and intimate letter to his father, asking him to establish an endowment for the training of Josephite priests. This letter, written around the beginning of March, 1895, when the country was in the midst of a prolonged economic depression, contributes significantly to our knowledge of the family's social and economic situation.

According to the opening lines of his autobiography, Slattery was born on July 16, 1851. His parents James Slattery and Margaret Shiel were born in Ireland. They were married in New York where Slattery was born.[6] Slattery described himself as "the only living birth in a family of five children."[7] The Slatterys kept their only child "in swaddling bands of the strictest sort."[8] Slattery credits his mother, who had died by the time the March 1895 letter was written, with having the profoundest impact on him. "A very devout and intelligent mother, who loved her church first, but who was fond of reading, formed me."[9] Later he would recall "the faith which a devout mother had impressed upon her only child."[10]

At the time of Slattery's birth, his father was a twenty-nine year old laborer who had yet to make his fortune. He died in October of 1905, at the age of 83, a very wealthy man.[11] The March 1895 letter mentioned above offers a glimpse of the rise of James Slattery as well as of the strain between father and son.

> Your growth in means has been parallel with my own birth and growth. Forty four years ago when I first saw the light, you were a poor

---

[6]*Biographie*, p. 1. I have been unable to locate Slattery's birth certificate or baptismal records.

[7]"John R. Slattery," *The Colored Harvest*, 3 (March, 1902), p. 306.

[8]*Biographie*, p. 1.

[9]*Ibid.*

[10]John R. Slattery, "How My Priesthood Dropped From Me," *The Independent*, 61 (Sept. 6, 1906), p. 565.

[11]On the date of James Slattery's death, see Thomas McMillan, C.S.P. to Louis B. Pastorelli, S.S.J., New York, December 25, 1926, Josephite Archives, Slattery Papers. Unless otherwise indicated, all correspondence to be cited comes from this source.

hardworking man. As your boy grew in years, you prospered in business; when he was seven, i.e. had attained the use of reason, you got the hauling of the Central Park Gravel. Ten years or so later you began the public works [illegible word] we moved in the two sections of the 84th Ave. After ten years more you bought the 84th, 83rd & 87th St. property. Throughout all these years mother was a faithful advisor and companion. Without her you would never have succeeded so well; and, since her death, you have been steadily losing ground. Under God's providence the three of us, father, mother & son have been the framers of your fortune. Yourself made it; mother saved it [illegible word]. The only part I played was the inspiration which a child furnishes to his parents. Now you and I should come to an understanding; so that I may be enabled to carry out my plans.[12]

According to this description, James Slattery advanced his economic and social position considerably during the two decades between 1858 and 1878. He was apparently engaged in contracting for municipal improvements such as parks, roads, bridges, etc. In the political environment of post-Civil War New York City, such a livelihood would have required a certain degree of political patronage.

Around 1869–70, Slattery's father "urged" him "to take an interest in his business of contracter."[13] His autobiography describes his successful bids for city contracts, presumably for improvements, for West 59th, West 56th and West 35th Sts. The account goes on to describe the payoffs necessary to get the paper work to start the job. In this connection, Slattery describes a youthful encounter with the notorious William M. "Boss" Tweed (1823–1878) of Tammany Hall, "then Commissioner of streets and in the hay day of his power."[14]

Interestingly, however, Tammany Hall was not the source of James Slattery's political patronage. "My father," Slattery wrote:

all his life long, was anti-Tammany. He was what was known as an Andrew H. Green Democrat. The two were great friends and Mr. Green called to see the old gentleman, every three months, or so, up to his end.[15]

---

[12]Slattery to "My dearest Father," no date, but internal evidence places it around early March, 1895 (Slattery's forty-fourth year).

[13]*Biographie*, p. 6.

[14]*Ibid.* On Tweed see Allen Johnson and Dumas Malone, eds., *Dictionary of American Biography*, Vol. 10 (New York: Charles Scribner's Sons, 1931, 1960), pp. 79–82. Hereafter this work will be cited as DAB.

[15]*Biographie*, p. 7. Green predeceased the elder Slattery by two years.

In 1858, the year James Slattery got the gravel contract for Central Park, Andrew H. Green (1820–1903) was a member of the recently appointed commission for the regulation and Government of Central Park. Green became comptroller of the park in 1859. It was he who layed out the northern end of Manhattan Island, suggesting various improvements such as roads, parks, bridges, etc. Boss Tweed had Green removed as comptroller in 1870. But it was during his tenure that James Slattery's contracting business began to grow. Green's former law partner, Samuel J. Tilden, was instrumental in bringing Tweed down in the Fall of 1871.[16]

The elder Slattery augmented his wealth by investing the profits from his contracting business in real estate on Manhattan's West side, in the 72nd to 86th Sts. area, between Broadway and Riverside Drive.[17] The March 1895 letter mentions some of the properties. The fact that a close friend was involved in planning the development of this area probably did not hurt James Slattery's real estate speculations.

As a moralist, John R. Slattery harbored an abiding distaste for the manner in which his father had acquired his wealth. This was the case even when, as in the March 1895 letter, he was trying to convince his father to sign over his assets to him. Later he would attribute the securing of his father's contracts to political trickery.[18]

In his old age, after his wife's death, the elder Slattery became something of a recluse. He had a residence at 218 W. 57th St., a short distance from the Paulist parish at 59th St. and 9th Ave., where he was an important benefactor. John R. Slattery's uncle Patrick lived with his wife, Margaret, and their two daughters at 320 W. 84th St. As the March 1895 letter indicates the 84th St. Slattery property was probably what we might now call a two-family dwelling and James Slattery had a residence there as well. 84th St. was John R. Slattery's mailing address during his frequent trips to New York City as a Josephite priest. Patrick Slattery also speculated in real estate. When he died in 1888, he left 1,000 acres of land in coal rich Kanawha County, West Virginia, which he had purchased in 1874.[19] Slattery's

---

[16]On Green see *DAB*, Vol. 4, pp. 535–40. I have been unable to document any connection between James Slattery's family contracting business and the present Slattery Construction Co. of New York City.

[17]Earl A. Newman, S.S.J. to Peter E. Hogan, S.S.J., New York, July 21, 1966. This letter contains Newman's account of a personal interview with the bank officer who handled the Slattery estate, James Ewart, a vice president of the Chemical Bank New York Trust Company.

[18]*Ibid*.

[19]Slattery to Robert S. Brady, New York, September 2, 1908.

widowed aunt, Margaret, was the only family member for whom he made any provision in his last will in 1925. Another uncle, John Slattery, an engineer at Blackwell's Island (probably a political patronage job) lived with his wife and daughter, Kate, at 57th St. and 7th Ave. in Manhattan.

The involvement in Democratic politics, the extended ethnic family, the migration uptown, the real estate speculation were all typical of the aspiring social class of New York Irish Catholics to which the closely-knit Slattery clan belonged.[20] By the beginning of the Gilded Age, the Slatterys were well on their way to middle class respectability. This status is evident from the descriptions contained in one of the most remarkable treasures in the Josephite Archives, the Belgian Canon Peter Benoit's diary of his journey to America in 1875. Herbert Vaughan, who was the bishop of Salford and the head of the English Foreign Mission Society sent Benoit to the U.S. to survey possible locations for the establishment of Negro missions. This religious community was known as the Mill Hill Fathers, and John R. Slattery would become a student with them. Besides some amateurish demography and social commentary, Peter Benoit provides valuable information about Slattery's family. During his New York stay, Benoit reported that Slattery's uncle John "left himself at my disposal every day to take me whither soever I wished. Benoit enjoyed the frequent hospitality on the entire Slattery family, and, on the day of his departure, John Slattery came for him in a "grand coach" and with his brother, James, loaded Benoit's luggage aboard the train.[21]

The Slatterys were located in the parish of St. Paul the Apostle where they held a family pew. Slattery described his parents as "the friends and benefactors of the Paulists." The Paulist founder, Isaac Hecker, heard Slattery's first confession.[22] The parish records provide further confirmation of the upwardly mobile social and economic status of the family. During the 1880's, the present St. Paul the Apostle Church, Hecker's dream for an American basilica, was still in the process of construction. The parish's Monthly Calendar

---

[20]For a description of Catholic life in New York during the Gilded Age, see James F. Donnelly, "Catholic New Yorkers and New York Socialists, 1870–1920," (New York: Unpublished Ph.D. dissertation, New York University, 1982), 59–75.

[21]"Diary of A Trip to America," January 6, 1875 - June 8, 1875 by Canon Peter L. Benoit, III Volumes, Mill Hill Fathers Archives, CB6 - CB7 - CB8, from a paginated transcript in the Josephite Archives, CB8, p. 335, May 28, 1875.

[22]*Biographie*, p. 4.

lists James Slattery, along with Father Hecker's flour producing, millionaire brother George Hecker, as one of the leading contributors to the St. Paul's Debt and Improvement Association for the new church.[23] In 1891 James Slattery was listed as a member of the "welcoming committee" for the St. Paul's Fair, a fundraiser. He continued to prosper and by the Spring of 1904, his son could report to his secretary, Robert S. Brady, that the elder Slattery had sold one of his houses for the sum of $102,000.[24]

As the only son among the three Slattery brothers, John R. held a special place in the family. Between 1858 and 1865, he pursued his education in the local public schools and the College of the City of New York.[25] He had begun in the local Catholic school, but only after a week his mother decided to withdraw him because of the over-crowded conditions. He learned the catechism at his mother's knee each morning before school. Later, as first in the catechism class at St. Paul's, he had the privilege of serving mass for the Paulist Fathers.[26] As he grew older, the family business continued to pros-per. Naturally it was expected that his education was preparing him to take over the family business. But despite his father's urgings, contracting, as Slattery put it, "was not to my taste."[27] His decision to become a priest, therefore, brought him into a certain tension with his family, especially with his father. The closeness of the extended family and John R.'s unique place in it as the sole male heir was not lost on Benoit in 1875. In a diary entry he asked God's blessing on the Slattery's "above all for the sacrifices they have made to God of one in whom all their affections are concentrated. . . ."[28]

After spending two years at the New York Free Academy, or the City College of New York as it came to be known during his second year there, Slattery entered St. Charles College in Ellicott City, MD to study for the priesthood. The future Americanist, Denis J. O'Con-nell, was one of his classmates here. The next year, however, a

---

[23]Monthly Calendar of the Church of St. Paul the Apostle, October, 1886 and December 1887, Paulist Archieves, New York. With its pages of advertisements for local businesses, the Monthly Calendar provides a useful resource for social histori-ans of Manhattan. I found no advertisements for Slattery Construction or contracting.

[24]Slattery to Brady, Germany, April 4, 1904.

[25]"John R. Slattery," Colored Harvest, 306. For some interesting comments on the effects of public school education, see John R. Slattery, "Scholastic Methods, Their Advantages and Disadvantages," American Ecclesiastical Review, 23 (Nov., 1900), 486–489.

[26]Biographie, p. 4.

[27]Ibid., p. 7.

[28]Benoit Diary, CB8, p. 335, May 28, 1875.

recurring eye problem flared up. His biographical sketch connects it
to a childhood bout with scarlet fever. It would bother him intermit-
tently and require periods of rest.[29] He didn't recover until 1871
when he entered Columbia College School of Law.

At this time, Professor Theodore W. Dwight (1822–1892) was the
one-man faculty at Columbia law school. Municipal law was his
specialty but he lectured on all subjects pertaining to private law.
Slattery spoke of studying under Professor Dwight. He testified that
he "loved the law," but left school abruptly five months before he
was to graduate, abandoning "the career which loomed brilliantly
before me."[30]

Both Slattery's autobiography and his published biographical
sketch provide accounts of this decision to abandon a career in law
for the Negro missions. But neither seems sufficient to explain the
dramatic reversal of direction it involved. In 1880, just three years
after Slattery's ordination, an Irish Catholic "respectable," William
Grace, was elected Mayor of New York City. Irish Catholics were
boasting their new ownership of Manhattan Island. In this changing
climate, an alumnus of Columbia Law School, Slattery would have
been in an excellent position to assume the leadership of his extended family and its business interests, building up the family
fortune. Instead he chose to spend his life as a priest, and not only
as a priest but as a missionary in the most God forsaken field. " 'If
they could go to any other mission they would not be among the
negroes,' expressed the common appreciation of them held by clerics and laity."[31]

This decision brings us to the question which is the focus of this
essay. In what social and economic framework would it make sense
for a wealthy young Irish American Catholic to leave Law school at
Columbia for the Negro mission, and, over the strenuous objections
of his father, devote his life to the evangelization and social amelioration of American blacks?

III. The Missionary as Philanthropist

In the Spring of 1872 Herbert Vaughan toured the U.S. in an effort
to raise funds and recruit candidates for his English Foreign Mission

---

[29]Colored Harvest, 306.

[30]Biographie, p. 7. On Dwight see DAB, Vol. 3, pp. 571–73.

[31]Colored Harvest, p. 306; Ibid. For a frank expression of his frustration at the plight
of the priests on the Negro missions, see Slattery to General Edward Morrell, Baltimore, January 23, 1903.

Society. Slattery heard him preach on two successive Sundays at St. Paul's, once on the Negro missions and once on St. Joseph. At the time the Englishman made little impression on Slattery until "eight or nine months later" when he had a memorable experience which served as the catalyst for his decision to commit his life to the Negro mission.

At about noon, he was returning from classes at the law school in Lafayette Place. As he came to the corner of Astor Place and Broadway, he encountered a large procession of members of the Odd Fellows Society. All of them were black. Since the parade had temporarily blocked his way, he had to stand on the corner and watch it. Narrating this episode in his autobiography, he recalled its effect on him:

> The spectacle of these poor people and the thought that the society to which they belonged was condemned by the Church moved me profoundly. The idea came to me to devote my whole life to the evangelization of this unfortunate race.[32]

From such a description it is difficult to imagine just what interior movements Slattery experienced on the corner of Astor Place and Broadway in the winter of 1872–73. It would be unwise to question without reason the strong religious motivation of Slattery's personal decision. But in a theological framework where grace is understood to work through rather than above nature, it is legitimate and useful to ask about the social and economic conditions which made Slattery's life-long identification with the religious and social interests of American blacks plausible in the society in which he lived.

The most important aspect of this setting was his standing among the *nouveau riche* Catholic immigrants. His wealthy station afforded him the luxury of viewing the parade at Astor Place and Broadway as a gathering of human beings like himself and not as an alien group of competitors seeking jobs in the labor market. The antipathy of the Irish Democrats of the industrial North to the emancipated blacks is well known. During his stay in Philadelphia, Benoit took note of "the strong antipathy which the Irish have towards the Negro when left to their natural feelings."[33] Abolitionism and the social

---

[32]*Biographie*, p. 9; cf. *Colored Harvest*, p. 306.

[33]Benoit Diary, CB6, p. 72, February 21, 1875. He continued: "This antipathy arises I am told, from the Negro being a competitor with the Irish in the labour-market." On the difficulties of integrating the interests of blacks into the labor and populist movements of the day, see H. Zinn, *A People's History of the United States*, 282–289.

cause of the Negro were identified with the anti-Catholic WASPS against whom the various ethnic groups had to contend both socially and politically. If the party of the Democrats was the party of slavery and segregation, it was also the political vehicle by which the Manhattan Irish, including James Slattery, gained entrée to the entrepreneurial success of the American dream.[34] Without drifting too far into the murky waters of psycho-biography, one could conclude that Slattery's identification with the cause of American blacks implied a certain distancing from, if not a rejection of, his ethnic Irish roots.[35]

It is not surprising then that when his family finally learned of his decision for the Negro mission, they objected. His confessor, whom he identifies as Father O'Dwyer, a Paulist and an "Irish convert," helped to arrange his entrance to the Mill Hill seminary. In what Slattery describes as a "ruse," his parents were told only that he would be a missionary. Even this was a blow to his father. His mother greeted the decision enthusiastically, but his father "experienced a great sadness about it."

> He had dreamed of a brilliant career for his only son to whom he would leave a great fortune and now this son would probably be only a humble priest, a missionary. Despite his feelings, my father gave his consent and I left for England at the beginning of 1873.[36]

His parents did not hear that his intention to be a missionary included the Negro missions until after he had been at Mill Hill for two years—probably around the time of Benoit's 1875 visit. After this Slattery was ordered home "time and time again." The simple sentence with which he closes his account of this episode conceals

---

[34]For an interesting alternative to the kind of argument put forth by Zinn (see note 4 above), see James F. Donnelly's section on "Catholics, Upward Mobility and Class Consciousness" in "Catholic New Yorkers and New York Socialists, 1870–1920," 72–75.

[35]By the time he wrote his autobiography, around 1910, Slattery had come to view his Irish past as a liability: "Again it has occurred to me many times, that to be the off-spring of a beaten race is a handicap. The Irish blood in me may have proven its worth in various fields. But the Irish are a truncated and beaten race, and this Ireland owes to Rome who to-day would be nowhere in the English-speaking world, without the Irish. Hence I started out in life beaten from the first by my Hibernian Catholicism. Nor must we forget how the Celts who, once dominated Europe, went down before imperial Rome; so too the Celtic missionaries from Ireland who converted the lands, not so many ages before ruled by their race, on their turn went down before curial Rome." *Biographie*, pp. 1–2.

[36]*Ibid.*, p. 10.

considerable pain, and also reveals something of Slattery's tempera-
ment. "He was of age and resolved to fulfill the purpose for which
he had entered Mill Hill."[37]

The conflict between father and son finds a parallel in Slattery's
rejection of the Democrats in favor of the party of the abolitionists.
In this he followed the pattern of the other Americanists, notably
Archbishop John Ireland, who were all eventually McKinley Repub-
licans. One of the most consistent and typically Republican refrains
in Slattery's writing is the plea to Northern urban laborers, especially
those in the trade unions, to grant the blacks what he termed
"competitive equality" and receive them into the unions.[38]

Slattery temporarily turned his back on the material success and
upward mobility of his father's world to identify with a marginal
group which was mostly regarded with indifference, if not complete
disdain by his own people. There is no reason to doubt the genuineness of Slattery's identification with the cause of American blacks,
but one can certainly speculate about it. In a passage written some
sixteen years after the experience on Aster Place and Broadway, and
after he had spent a decade as a missionary, Slattery reflected on the
sentiments which should motivate aspiring Josephites. The missionary's characteristic traits were specified by him as "love of truth and
a grasp of the Church's broadness." The force necessary "to impel a
soul to heroic endeavor" is "a vivid perception of universality."

> "The energy of the apostle is the personal love of our Lord Jesus Christ
> as the head of the whole human race . . . the type and perfection of
> humanity in the supernatural order."[39]

In the post-Reconstruction era, when various ideologies of Negro
inferiority were being used to legitimate the imposition of segregation patterns, Slattery's position of privilege allowed him to perceive
the systematic exclusion of blacks and to oppose it on the theological

---

[37]*Colored Harvest*, p. 306.

[38]"In the Protestant South they [the Negroes] enjoy the right of working at all trades.
Not so in the North where the church has her stronghold. The great bulk of the trade-
unionists are in many cities of the North Catholics; yet they leave no opening to the
negroes for the learning of trades." John R. Slattery, "The Catholic Negro's Complaint," *Catholic World*, 52 (December, 1890), 349. Slattery expresses similar sentiments in the following articles: "Some Aspects of the Negro Problem," *Catholic
World*, 38 (February, 1884), 609; "The Present and Future of the Negro in the United
States," *Catholic World*, 40 (December, 1884), 295; "The Negro Race: Their Condition,
Present and Future," *Catholic World*, 58 (November, 1893), 222.

[39]John R. Slattery, "An Apostolic College," *Catholic World*, 49 (July, 1889), 527.

basis of a common humanity redeemed in Christ. Although he could be harsh and demanding—Peter Hogan, a Josephite historian, has described him as "single-minded, hard headed and autocratic" and "possessed of vitriolic tongue and pen when crossed"[40]—at his best Slattery achieved a genuine oneness in Christ with those he served. It is exemplified in this passage from the address he gave at the World Columbian Congress in Chicago in 1893.

> Poverty and lowliness were characteristics of the Messias; they are two marked traits in the Negro race. They too are, as it were, 'A leper, and as one stricken by God and afflicted.' Surely, if fellow suffering creates a bond of sympathy, Our Lord and Savior Jesus Christ must deeply sympathize with and love the Negro race.[41]

But emphasis on unity and universality is often ambiguous because it is achieved at the expense of true differences. Although his position of social and economic privilege provided Slattery a peculiar vantage point from which to understand the unjust exclusion of the blacks from the American dream, it also ultimately separated him from them. This separation is illustrated in this sentimental and paternalistic description of how blacks should perceive the heroic "white Catholic missionary." In him they would see:

> a man who for the honor of God has given up all things for their sake. His celibacy, his voluntary poverty, his snapping of the ties of relationship and home, his freely living among poor strangers, his ceaseless toils for them—all these life-gifts of an educated white man would win converts to any kind of religion; much rather for a religion which enlightens the mind, warms the heart, invigorates the moral nature, purifies and elevates the whole man, pours into the soul emotions of the deepest influence while leaving it untouched by morbid excitement.[42]

---

[40]Peter E. Hogan, S.S.J., "The Role of the Josephites in the Recruitment, Education and Placement of Black Priests," from "Recruitment and Education of Indigenous Priests, Deacons and Religious for Catholic Parishes Serving Black Americans. Document prepared for presentation to the National Conference of Catholic Bishops of the United States at the authorization of the National Black Catholic Clergy Caucus," 1974, typescript, pp. 1–10, p. 4.

[41]John R. Slattery, "The Negro Race: Their Condition, Present and Future," *Catholic World*, 58 (November, 1893), 228–229.

[42]"The Catholic Church and the Colored People," *Catholic World*, 37 (June, 1883), 379. This article was written by Walter Elliott on the basis of Slattery's notes. This passage, therefore, represents Elliott's view of Slattery and his fellow missionaries. It was at Elliott's urging and encouragement that Slattery began to write for publication. See *Biographie*, pp. 83–86.

For the most part, Slattery regarded the blacks as a "childish" race in need of moral and social elevation at the hands of people like himself. However outrageous this may sound to the contemporary ear, at the beginning of the age of segregation in the U.S.,—*Plessy v. Ferguson* came down in 1896—Slattery's view of the blacks as perfectible fellow human beings to whom he was obliged by virtue of both his material and spiritual privileges, was an enlightened one.[43] It represented one of the more noble, if ambiguous, impulses of the Gilded Age, that of philanthropy.[44] In terms of his social and economic status, Slattery's career as a missionary to the freedmen is best understood as a Catholic species of philantropy. The fact that so few Catholics shared this social and economic status and thus his peculiar vantage point—the Philadelphia Drexels were a conspicuous exception—helps to explain his frustration.

In a general way, philanthropy can be understood as "voluntary benevolence," directed not only to the poor but, as the term suggests to the general welfare. Many of the institutions which we now take for granted, e.g., churches, museums, libraries, parks, not to mention colleges and hospitals, originated with the philanthropic impulses of those who had accumulated vast sums of capital during the Gilded Age. In his 1960 survey, *American Philanthropy*, Robert Bremner includes "voluntary activity in the fields of charity, religion, education, humanitarian reform, social service, war relief and foreign aid." Donations to these causes take the form of money or of service. The voluntary promotion of moral and social reform and the founding of institutions to carry on this work are important aspects of philanthropy.[45]

In more specific terms, Slattery's "voluntary benevolence" toward

---

[43]On some of the racial theories prevailing in the Gilded Age, see J.A. Garraty, *The New Commonwealth, 1877–1890*), 21. For example, the dean of the Lawrence Scientific School at Harvard, Nathaniel Southgate Shaler, described the Negro race as "unfit for an independent place in a civilized state." See "The Negro Problem," *Atlantic Monthly*, 54 (1884), 700, as cited in Edward J. Misch, "The American Bishops and the Negro From the Civil War to the Third Plenary Council of Baltimore (1865–1884)," (Rome: unpublished doctoral dissertation, Pontifical Gregorian University, Faculty of Church History, 1968), 325–26. Misch's work is indispensable for understanding the ecclesiastical context of Slattery's missionary career. For a more detailed treatment of racist ideologies in this period, see H. Shelton Smith, *In His Image, But . . . Racism in Southern Religion, 1780–1910* (Durham, N.C.: Duke University Press, 1972), especially chapters V & VI.

[44]J.A. Garraty, *The New Commonwealth, 1877–1890*, 25–28.

[45]Robert Bremner, *American Philanthropy* (Chicago: University of Chicago Press, 1960), 3–4.

American blacks can be likened to the "scientific philanthropy" Bremner describes in chapter VI of his book. Presuming a certain de facto superiority, the philanthropists sought to encourage the social advancement of the impoverished by creating institutions such as schools and libraries which individuals could use to reform and improve themselves. Slattery realized that racial prejudice complicated the situation for poor people who were also black. His writings and his efforts on behalf of integration in American Catholic seminaries testify to his opposition to racial discrimination.

As a Catholic missionary, Slattery was interested first but not solely in the salvation of souls. The very basis of his spiritual concern, his belief in a common humanity shared by blacks and whites, required him to be concerned as well with the human welfare of those whom he would evangelize. Filled with comparative statistics not only on baptisms but also on schools and other helping institutions, Slattery's numerous articles make clear that he was an active promoter of and a public apologist for, what someone of his day might have called, the moral and social uplifting of the Negro race. In the vein of Isaac Hecker, whose parish he attended from youth, Slattery was convinced that Catholicism provided the religious truth needed to satisfy the hearts and minds of both blacks and whites. "On the Catholic Church alone," he wrote, "depends the elevation and morality of the Negro race . . ."[46] Based on this belief, Slattery raised money, built churches and schools (both industrial and academic), wrote and published tirelessly, generously gave thirty years of service, and also donated considerable portions of his family fortune to the causes of the evangelization and moral and social advancement of what he would have called the Negro race.

Like St. Jerome who turned his back on the classics only to spend his life translating the Bible into the language that he loved, the equally irascible Slattery, even as he left home and fortune for the negro mission, could not escape his talent for raising and managing money. Considerable credit for the early survival and eventual success of the Josephites, in both their English and, after 1893, American forms, is due to the financial genius of John R. Slattery as a fund raiser and manager. Shortly after he arrived at St. Francis

---

[46]John R. Slattery, "The Catholic Negro's Complaint," 347–348; cf. "The Catholic Church and the Colored People," 384; "The Josephites and Their Work for the Negroes," Catholic World, 51 (April, 1890), 102–103.

Xavier Church in Baltimore in 1877, the church's $24,000 debt was handed over to him "as he had some knowledge of business."[47] By the mid-1880's, Slattery had convinced Vaughan of the need for an American seminary and apostolic college to train priests for the Negro mission. It was Slattery who secured the land and the donations to build and maintain St. Joseph's Seminary, near St. Mary's in Baltimore, and Epiphany Apostolic Church. The former was established in the Fall of 1888 and the latter a year later.[48]

Much of the money, nearly $80,000, required to purchase the buildings and run these institutions came from the fortune of Francis A. Drexel of Philadelphia, one of J.P. Morgan's banking partners, who was described by Benoit in 1875 as "fallen off from the Faith, I am told. . . ."[49] Through Mother Katharine M. Drexel (1858–1955), the foundress of the Sisters of the Blessed Sacrament and of Xavier University in New Orleans, millions of dollars of the Drexel family money would be poured into the building and maintenance of schools and other service institutions for the Negro and Indian missions. When Francis A. Drexel died in 1885, he had established a 14 million dollar trust, leaving each of his three daughters one third of its annual income. The Josephites' share of this money came through Katharine Drexel's younger sister, Louise, who had begun to contribute to Slattery's work in Richmond the year after her father's death. In 1889 Louise Drexel married Colonel Edward Morrell, a prominent Philadelphia lawyer and later a member of the U.S. House of Representatives. Maintenance of the seminaries was heavily dependent on the generosity of Louise Drexel Morrell and her husband.[50]

Even with the help of such benefactors, times were difficult. In 1893, at the beginning of the prolonged depression of the 1890's, the Paulist priest, Walter Elliott, wrote Slattery that he was glad to hear the work was going well but added:

---

[47]*Colored Harvest*, p. 307. As the biographical sketch puts it: "After groping in the dark for months, light began to break and soon the young treasurer was master of the situation."

[48]On the seminaries, see John R. Slattery, "The Seminary for the Colored Missions," *Catholic World*, 46 (January, 1888), 541–550; "An Apostolic College," *Catholic World*, 49 (July, 1889), 526–527.

[49]Benoit Diary, CB6, p. 73, February 21, 1875.

[50]See Louise Drexel Morrell and Edward Morrell to Slattery, Philadelphia, January 10, 1896 and Slattery's reply, Baltimore, March 2, 1896; cf. Edward Morrell to James Cardinal Gibbons, Philadelphia, January 5, 1903 in which Morrell threatened to withhold support from the seminaries as a result of Slattery's prolonged absence in Europe between June of 1902 and January of 1903.

> But, John, what if you should be suddenly called to paradise? Do you think it sound spiritually to just leave everything in the future to God? Can't you make some arrangement to secure the perpetuation of your work, your 'machine'?[51]

Indeed Slattery himself had been thinking along the same lines. In March of 1895, in the letter referred to above, he described himself as "laboring with many cares and living from hand to mouth," and proposed to his father the creation of the "James, Margaret and John Richard Slattery Endowment."

> By this fund over forty priests can be forever trained in St. Joseph's Seminary for our missions. Then your money will follow you into the next world and crown you there while bringing to God glory on earth, joy to many a worthy young man in his priesthood, and the salvation of innumerable souls. In our chapel, moreover, there will be placed a tablet commemorating this endowment. And every priest who stands at an altar will remember the three of us forever. This is a far higher and more lasting remembrance than the granite shafts in Westchester.[52]

His father apparently did not agree with Slattery's proposal that "these eighteen thousand dollars that you will soon receive, the use of your mortgages and property should be legally secured to me." The James, Margaret and John Richard Slattery Endowment was never established. In the meantime Slattery used at least $42,000 of his family's money in support of the missions, a sum for which he later sent Cardinal James Gibbons a bill after the latter fended off his request in 1903 to be placed *sub titulo patrimonii*.[53]

On December 20, 1904, Slattery resigned as President and member of the corporation of St. Joseph's Society for the Colored Missions, but not before outwitting the overbearing Colonel Morrell in a legal skirmish which left Slattery holding the mortgages on the properties the Morrells had purchased for the Josephite seminaries. By this maneuver the wily Slattery accomplished a certain humbling of the condescending Morrell, insured the continued existence of the Josephites which both his conduct and Edward Morrell's subsequent threats had jeopardized, and gave himself a certain financial security.

---

[51]Walter Elliott, C.S.P. to Slattery, Denham, MA, January 2, 1893.
[52]Slattery to My Dearest Father, n.d. (March, 1895), p. 4.
[53]Slattery to Gibbons, Baltimore, February 2, 1903.

In 1905 James Slattery died 'in New York and his son finally came into his inheritance. On June 15, 1906, in an Anglican church in London, England, Slattery married twenty-five year old Adele Wingate of St. Louis.[54] The following September he renounced church and priesthood in an article in The Independent of New York.[55] In subsequent years the Slatterys travelled frequently between New York and Europe with John involved in writing related to modernism. In 1909 he returned to Columbia College School of Law but there is no record that he ever received a law degree from Columbia. On April 16, 1915, he was admitted to the practice of law in the state of California.[56] Slattery died on March 6, 1926 in Monte Carlo in the state of Monaco, some say on the golf course. He is buried in the Cemetery of Monaco. Yet his philanthropic activity did not end with his death.

As if to finalize his previous break with the extended family, Slattery excluded his relatives from his will. His aunt Margaret, for whom the will provided an annuity until her death the following year, was the only exception. The remainder of his estate went to establish a 1.3 million dollar trust fund to support his wife Adele Slattery. Upon her death, the principal was to go to the New York Public Library, Astor, Tilden and Lenox Foundations.[57]

Although James Slattery's former attorney, Warner Westervelt, and nine of John R.'s cousins contested the will, it was upheld in the courts. Slattery left his estate to the New York Public Library because he wanted the people of New York to reap some profit from a fortune which had been acquired through political patronage.[58] Through wise management of her estate, Adele Slattery became wealthy in her own right. In addition to other philanthropic activities, she herself contributed over one million dollars to the New York Public Library, apart from the John R. Slattery gift. When Adele Wingate Slattery died on August 3, 1957, the principal of her estate passed, as John R. Slattery had willed, to the New York Public Library.

---

[54]The information on Adele Wingate Slattery and her marriage to John R. Slattery is taken from the minutes of the pre-trial examination, November 4, 1926, Surrogate's Court, New York County, Probate of Will of John R. Slattery, p. 1312, 1926. A copy is preserved in the Josephite Archives.

[55]John R. Slattery, "How My Priesthood Dropped From Me," The Independent, 61 (September 5, 1906), 565–571.

[56]This information is taken from my personal correspondence with the Registrar's Office of Columbia University and the State Bar of California.

[57]New York Times, June 14, 1928, p. 56, col. 2. Copies of the wills of both John R. and Adele Slattery are preserved in the Josephite Archives.

[58]Earl A. Newman, S.S.J. to Peter E. Hogan, S.S.J., New York, July 21, 1966. See note 9 above.

One of the pylons or columns in the library's main foyer lists the benefactors for the years between 1948 and 1958. Along with those of the Vincent Astor Foundation, the Carnegie Corporation of New York, and the Rockefeller Foundation, one can still read, in gilded letters, the name of John R. Slattery.

COMMON MORAL AND RELIGIOUS GROUNDS FOR UNCOMMON ECONOMIC TIMES

James F. Smurl

Introduction

Public policy disputes regarding rates charged by public utilities offer unusual opportunities to examine communities' moral, religious, and cultural understandings of the social goods they create and allocate with the aid of economic structures. The 1926 U.S. Supreme Court case of *McCardle v. The Indianapolis Water Co.* (272 U.S. 400), and the interpretations of that and similar cases by the Baptist theologian Walter Rauschenbusch, by the Roman Catholic moralist John A. Ryan, and by the Jewish social theorist Louis D. Brandeis, afford just such an occasion.

After reporting the facts and competing legal interpretations associated with the *McCardle* case, this paper will consider what Brandeis, Rauschenbusch, and Ryan had to say about this and other similar cases. In the process, some common, early twentieth-century, religio-cultural convictions and forms of moral and social reasoning about economic notions of private property and commodity exchanges will appear. The purpose of reporting the history of this case and its interpretations is not simply to describe what happened, but also to uncover early twentieth-century moral and religio-cultural norms for guiding economic activities in the interests of more important social and cultural goals—and to determine whether or not there now may be comparable understandings which should be normative.[1]

---

[1]The decision to compare the progressive era with the present is not arbitrary. As Robert Kuttner observed recently:

> The literature of economics influences Presidents, [Theodore Roosevelt and Woodrow Wilson then, and Ronald Reagan, now] even those who aren't notable readers. The 20th century is bracketed by two periods when books on economic questions mattered enormously . . .

Part of the point here is to suggest an appropriate methodology for ethical inquiries into public policies. In particular, the conclusion will be a normative proposal for the priority of equal freedom over negative liberty, and of distributive justice over freedom of contract in policies designed to regulate public utilities. The importance of methodology can be seen in public utility rate-setting disputes, which routinely raise questions which cannot be resolved by invoking what Michael Walzer calls intuitive or speculative conceptions of order (1987: 20–25). Recurrently, however, religious and other social-ethical critics respond either intuitively or speculatively to questions asking: "Who owns a public utility? Its 'product'? Who should profit, and how much so, from the sale of services to deliver such basic natural resources and human necessities as water?" The outlines of an alternative, equally serious, and arguably more appropriate, public religio-cultural methodology lies in the writings of Brandeis, Rauschenbusch, and Ryan.[2] After pursuing a version of

---

Beneath today's slick campaign symbolism, the submerged economic issues of 1988 echo earlier debates . . . [all of which] . . . are really variations on a core question that has been debated for a century: whether the free market is the solution or the problem (1988:1).

Kuttner's point is not only that books on economics and the ideas they contain have consequences; it is also that some periods in the life of a people have a sufficient number of parallels that they help us uncover some of the national community's shared, recurrent, and potentially universal, normative principles.

[2]Many of these initial points build upon three key ideas found in the works of Michael Walzer. The first is that, even though a community's understandings of social goods inevitably will be products of historically and culturally conditioned particularity—leading to warrants for caste systems and wars, for example—there remains the possibility of a stable, shared set of common human principles which are internal to cultures, and which may be reiterated across time, space, and cultures (1983: 6, 9–10, 27, 84, and 314; see also his 1977: xiii and 47). The second and related idea is that one should be reluctant to accept intuitive or speculative statements regarding what those "internal principles" might be, insisting instead that they be empirically verifiable—rather than invented or imposed (id.; see also his 1987: 20–25). The third idea is similar to one proposed by John A. Ryan—namely, that, depending on the kind of industrial outcomes to be distributed, only one of several pertinent distributive criteria may be the most pressing and pertinent one in a particular arena—as the standard of need would be in wage allocations, or that of merit and contributions in profit distributions, etc. Nonetheless, says Ryan, what is pressing in any particular area of life ought not to be made the dominant one for all spheres (1916). Walzer comes to similar conclusions from the perspective of liberal social and political theory. He contends that a community must insist on sovereignty for its different spheres of social goods, so that criteria appropriate for a sphere like commodities, for example, do not dominate all other spheres—as they would, for instance, if human rights were ignored and if we did not block the kinds of economic exchanges slavery entails (1983: 98, 100). From the same social and political perspective, Walzer encourages public discourse and a consensual process in the articulation and application of the principles one claims should govern a community's spheres of social

early twentieth-century methodology in analyzing the case of *Mc-Cardle v. The Indianapolis Water Company,* this paper will consider one of the major inferences which follows from this form of inquiry—namely, a normative conclusion that equal freedom and distributive justice are among the more pressing moral values in matters of public policy.

A. The McCardle Case

When the Indianapolis Water Company (IWC) requested an increase in rates from Indiana's Public Service Commission (PSC) in 1921 it received a favorable response. A similar request in 1923 met with a generally unfavorable reaction from the same commission. On the second occasion, the PSC denied the request on the grounds that the company's method of determining its property value for rate-making purposes was illegal. This decision then was overturned in 1924 by Indiana's U.S. District Court Judge Geiger, whose opinion in turn was upheld by a majority of the U.S. Supreme Court in 1926.

Some of the publicly significant features of this dispute can be seen both in the light of events in the 1920's, on the one hand, and with an eye to the events of the 1980's, on the other. Indiana's case was one of hundreds of similar cases contested between 1877 and 1937, a period in which public regulation came to be seen as an exercise of the police powers of the state. It was a time when courts were guided mainly by notions of relatively unrestricted private

---

goods—thereby demonstrating a confidence in "ordinary moral wisdom" (1977: 64) and a commitment to the principle of the assent of the governed (1985).

Similar points have been made recurrently in discussions of the imperative aspect of prudence as found in the Aristotelian and Thomistic traditions. For example, in *Nuclear Ethics,* David Hollenbach demonstrates why experience, political wisdom, and the historically (even dialectically) unfolding character of the moral norms pertinent to war makes their *application* ambiguous at times (1983: 21–2). A similar judgment applies equally to the more speculative as well as to intuitive *expressions* of those self-same norms. Both the history of ethics, whether theological or philosophical, and the kind of scepticism Bernard Lonergan recommended with respect to the conventional practical insights and judgments which underpin those principles (1959), prompts one to acknowledge the tentative character of many of the "governing correlations" in a community's moral principles—and most certainly in the secondary and derived forms of those principles (see also Walzer 1983: 4). Finally, note that, as William Dean pointed out in a recent paper on "Religion and the American Public Philosophy," those theorists in art and philosophy [including ethics] who "got it right by leaving behind everything that was local, particular, and historical, are now being themselves left behind—to be replaced by theories where it is impossible to talk about what anything means except as it works in the local and particular." (1988: 28–9).

property and freedom of contract. They tended to respond unfavorably toward statutes, ordinances, or administrative acts which appeared to curb these freedoms (Kelly-Harbison 1970: 526-6). In the 1980's, two decades after a spate of consumer protection acts, the environment had changed considerably. Yet, late in 1982, headlines indicated that utility rate protests had been growing since the 1973 oil embargo—and, significantly, in conjunction with a growing number of elderly and unemployed Americans. Nonetheless, in the last week of October 1982, Missouri's Public Service (an electric, gas, and water company) was the national "stock of the week" reporting a 100% increase in earnings between 1978 and 1982—thanks to earnings made possible by "rate relief." In February of 1984 new rates were approved for Indiana's Bell telephone public-utility company with estimates of a 15.5% yield on stockholders' investments, at a time when the common stock of an explicitly for-profit company like Exxon was earning 12% and that of Quaker Oats was earning 9.5%. Nonetheless, when setting these new telephone rates in 1982, the PSC said that the evidence would have justified a return as low as 14.5% and as high as 18%.

What evidence was proffered in 1982? Was it pertinent as well as accurate? How might it serve to justify the reported rates of return, and on what set of standards? These questions echo those asked throughout the dispute involving the Indianapolis Water Company in the 1920's. Valuing a public utility company's property for rate-making purposes entailed establishing a property value on the basis of which a fair and reasonable return could be assured by adjusting rates. Anything short of that would have been considered confiscatory by the courts of the day and thus a violation of constitutional protections of due process and just compensation.

In January, 1923, Indiana's PSC determined that the property value of the IWC should be set at $16,455,000. The company contended that this figure should be three quarter's of a million dollars higher in order to reflect the value added by improvements they *planned to make later* in 1923. It further contended that its previous year's 5% profit on its property value was not reasonable and that recent increases in its valuation for purposes of taxation, as well as the likelihood of an increased demand on equipment and services over the next fifteen years, necessitated a profit of better than 5%. Accordingly, the company argued for a property valuation of $17,250,000 as of January, 1923. In June of that year, the company requested a rate increase, which it amended in July to include a schedule of rates which the PSC judged would represent a 23.7% increase over the rates in effect at the time.[3] At the end of fourteen hearings in which the public and the business sectors voiced their opposition to the Water Company's request, the PSC delivered a 3-2 decision against the petition. Disputing both the method and the results of the IWC property valuation, the PSC set rates which would yield a 7% return on a property value of $15,260,400.

Before the year was out, the IWC brought suit in equity against the Commission and the City of Indianapolis. The company won a favorable decision in the U.S. District Court of Judge F. A. Geiger in 1924—so favorable, in fact, that Geiger's decision set its property value for rate-making purposes at $19,000,000, judging that it would take this amount of money to reproduce the company as of, and under conditions prevalent in January, 1924. On Judge Geiger's reading of previously established Supreme Court precedents, the pertinent rule of law required that the dominant and decisive consideration be "evidence of reproduction value and, if that means anything, it means that evidence of reproduction value at the time of the inquiry must be considered evidence of a primarily different character" (as cited 272 U.S. 400, at 422, n.5 in Brandeis' dissent from the majority opinion]).

In a subsequent hearing of a supplemental petition from the IWC, the PSC agreed to a 6.5% rate increase on the property valued at 19 million—with the result that consumers would experience a 13% increase in rates. The chairman of the PSC, Commissioner McCardle, was as unsatisfied with these results as were both the water company and its customers. He promptly appealed to the U.S. Supreme Court (McCardle v. The Indianapolis Water Company), and, in 1926, lost the appeal when the majority upheld the District Court's decision of 1924.

B. Legal Analysis of the McCardle Case

There are two major areas of *legal* dispute in this case. One centers around questions about the adequacy of the findings of fact. The other is concerned with the correct construction and application of the pertinent rules of law.

---

[3]The data above, as well as some in succeeding paragraphs, come from the Indiana public records cited in the References for this essay, and from volume 1925C of *Public Utilities Reports Annotated.*

Of all the facts pertinent in an estimate of the worth of property owned by a public utility, those indicating what it would take to reproduce the company at the time of an inquiry (spot reproduction costs) is just one index, but not necessarily the most important or decisive one. Nonetheless, this was the basis on which the court decisions turned when they held for the company. Justice Butler, writing for the majority of the Supreme Court (with Holmes joining in the result), judged the facts of the case correctly reported in the lower court's decision—namely, that it would take $19 million to reproduce the company at the time of the inquiry and that anything less than a 7% return on stockholders' investments would be confiscatory. In his conclusion, however, he stated that, while the facts of the case were sufficient to sustain the lower court's decision, they were not as specific as good practice would require (272 *U.S.* 400, at 420; 71 *L.Ed.*, 316, at 329).

In his sharply contrasting dissent, Justice Brandeis (joined by Justice Stone) argued that the facts of the case were not yet at hand. Reproduction costs are hypothetical and, when used as the decisive criterion, prompt judges to ignore other relevant facts like historical costs. Thus, in Brandeis' view, the case should have been remanded for a reexamination of the evidence. The facts of record did not justify a judgment that rates yielding a return of less than 7% would be so unreasonably low as to be confiscatory. His principal complaint, however, was that the court claimed to have made a finding of fact when it used the nineteen million dollar figure as the cost of reproduction. Willing to admit these costs were a relevant index, but not the decisive one, he argued that these costs were hypothetical, to be discovered as facts only after reproduction had occurred. Hence, on his view, no court could purport to be making a finding of fact about a matter which would require Aladdin-like clairvoyance. Still more relevant facts, like historical costs and the cost of prudent investments, had been ignored in judicial decisions in such cases (272 *U.S.* 400, at 421, 422; 423; 71 *L.Ed.*, 316, at 329, 330).

Walter Lippmann characterized the legal confusion in these judicial searches for relevant precedents as chaotic attempts to regulate public utilities in the interest of the consumer. He also thought they were mistaken attempts to reform industries by policing them through persons as ill-suited as judges were to understand the intricacies of rapidly changing industrial processes (1929: 238). Whether or not Lippmann's analysis of motives was correct, he was absolutely right about the confusion prevalent in interpreting and applying pertinent law. The majority's construction of the law in the McCardle case was illustrative. It was radically reductionist and ran counter to precedents established in the Georgia Railroad and Power Company case (262 *U.S.* 625), in which Brandeis, writing for the majority, explicitly mentioned several other factors as evidence of fair value, including historical costs and the amount prudently invested in the enterprise. Both Indiana's Judge Geiger and Supreme Court Justice Butler relied on something other than the Georgia precedent. Both relied instead on Judge McKenna's dissenting opinion in the Georgia case (262 *U.S.* 625, at 636). In the *McCardle* decision Brandeis would have opted for what he already had suggested in his concurring opinion in the Southwestern Bell Telephone case (262 *U.S.* 276, at 311)—namely, either the prudent investment standard or one which measured the cost of an equally efficient substitute company. In any event, it should not be a standard urged by utilities simply on the basis of a prospectively higher return.

C. Economic, Ethical, and Political Factors in McCardle
1. John A. Ryan

Brandeis' opinions on these cases are admixtures of economic and moral judgments (about efficiency, justice, and the like). They are mirrored in convictions expressed by Roman Catholic Monsignor John A. Ryan, who had become known affectionately as "The Right Reverend New Dealer" (Broderick, 1963), and headed up the social action department of the National Catholic Welfare Conference at the time of *McCardle*. In ways comparable to Brandeis, Ryan merged economic and ethical considerations in his social analysis of this case, and threw his political weight behind Brandeis' position (1931). Like Brandeis and several other students of economics, Ryan endorsed the prudent investment standard as the measure of the adequacy of compensation attainable from public utility rates. In his view, it should apply to railroads as well (1931: 175). He worried that the precedent set in the *McCardle* case might be applied to railroad rate cases and that its logic could be used either to prevent rate regulation entirely or to make any decrease in rates virtually impossible (147-8). Furthermore, and here differing somewhat from Brandeis, Ryan would have taken law-making in these matters out of the hands of the courts and located it in Congress and in state legislatures (175-9).

Ryan's was more than a "wedge argument", however. When expressing his concerns about the impact of these decisions on the consumers he appealed to more stringent moral principles regarding the obligation to do justice to *all* the parties involved—not simply the stockholders, and certainly not by affording them what Walter Rauschenbusch twenty years earlier characterized as unjust privileges realized by virtue of the ineffective legal control of monopolies like the public utilities (1912: 338). Ryan considered consumers were also investors—by virtue of the rates they had been paying. Thus, "to include them [the rates customers had paid] in the valuation now is to compel the consumers to pay interest on money that they have paid into the coffers of the company" (1931: 149). The effect of the policy endorsed by the courts was to allocate to consumers still further burdens, compounding those borne earlier, and doing so in ways disproportionate to the benefits the company already realized in lower operating costs attributable to the consumers' contributions to the company's going value or spot reproduction costs (*id.*).

2. The Brandeis-Ryan "duet"

Ryan's line of reasoning about the injustices these court decisions entailed accords well with the earlier expressed sensibilities of Rauschenbusch and with the concerns evident in the earlier activities of Brandeis acting as "the people's attorney" in cases involving franchises which the city of Boston and the state of Massachusetts had granted to transportation companies (Smurl 1983). His ethical analysis of the case is continuous with the Jewish and Christian traditions' concern for the disadvantaged—but in a tough-minded style more akin to that of Ryan than to that of Rauschenbusch.

No strangers to the worlds of economics, law, and politics, Ryan and Brandeis knew that hearing rate-making cases in courts of equity (as in the U.S. District Court of Indiana's Judge Geiger) implied uncertainty about the applicable law. Thus, settling these cases "on their merits" tended to leave too much room for the more purely personal economic, ethical, social, and political views of the justices.[4] Ryan in particular recognized that the way the *McCardle* case

---

[4]One should note, however, that Brandeis' style of "sociological jurisprudence" is more like that of "equity" than it is like the "scientific," formalist, "apolitical," and more purely procedural styles of jurisprudence advocated by Brandeis' contemporary, Oliver Wendell Holmes, and by many contemporary American legal scholars today (and paradigmatically in the work of Richard A. Posner).

was pleaded and decided tended to uphold a relatively unrestricted notion of private property. It equated economic value with exchange value—and thereby served to argue the priority of commutative or contractual justice, and its legal counterpart doctrine of freedom of contract, over against the social values entailed in distributive justice (1931: 155).

Ryan had seen comparable arguments made in the areas of wages, prices, and interest. He had come to appreciate the extent and the character of the resulting unjust consequences on persons who thereby became much less equally free. These latter persons were being forced to bear disproportionately larger burdens to sustain the advantages of others whose relatively unfettered quest for money was more purely self-aggrandizing. Thus, like Brandeis and Rauschenbusch, Ryan refused to accept the counsel of social despair which C. Wright Mills attributed to the value system of "The Corporate Rich," namely, "let there be no sour grapes about it from the losers" (Mills 1956: 164).

Given the ambiguity of applicable law in the 1920's, and given the way the courts construed constitutional prohibitions on the confiscation of private property without just compensation, lawyers for the utility companies sought to rest their cases firmly on the basis of the confiscation doctrine—albeit in ways counterintuitive to widely shared understandings of economic rights, values, and justice. The courts' construction of just compensation entailed several unranked measures of a "fair return on the fair value of property." But, as Ryan pointed out, the latter was "an ethical concept dependent upon a theory of right" or at least a moral relationship to be interpreted ethically (1931: 155, 178). In any case, it was neither an economic fact nor a legal rule; hence, its application required that judges fall back upon either their own or some other construction of personal and social ethics. In so doing, as in holding for the utility companies' arguments for just compensation on the basis of the reproduction value of their properties, the courts and the body of legal precedent they established in effect were claiming that "there is only one kind of value, namely, economic value, or exchange value" (id.: 155).

Similarly, the courts seemed able to imagine but one kind of justice—namely, the form which should prevail in exchanges or contracts. Since common law long had supported the notion of freedom of contract (i.e., absent any moral constraints and negatively free from legal interference), this notion was deemed applicable to the public utility cases, even though, as Ryan pointed out, the economic exchange value of utilities was determined by publicly regulated earnings (as part of a regulatory effort to control rates). In short, it was not the much-touted standard of the "higgling of the market" which determined the exchange value of public utilities (and thus their claims regarding the value of their properties for rate-making purposes). Rather, it was public regulation which ultimately determined that value. Therefore, any analogies likening the property of private companies to that of public utilities would seem to entail fatal mistakes (*id.*: 156).

Property and Distributive Justice as the Principal Moral Stakes

For Ryan, then, as for Brandeis (but also for Rauschenbusch in somewhat less systematic ways), there were two sets of ethical concepts and principles to be reappraised critically before American social policy could make good on commitments of justice and liberty for all. One was *property* and the other was *distributive justice*.

With respect to *property*, Ryan drew on Roman Catholic religious social-ethical reflection—as embodied in his earlier works *A Living Wage* (1907) and *Distributive Justice* (1916). He contrasted two conceptions of property. The more traditional one relied upon medieval conceptions and virtually equated property with an opportunity to work. In that notion, profit from property figured only slightly, if at all. Directly contradictory modern conceptions tended to equate property with capital, thus making it the principal source of unlimited, indefinite, and often arguably excessive rates of interest (1931: 169–70).[5] The older tradition rested heavily on a sense of duty and established side-constraints on freedom. Modern conceptions tended to be more egoistic, hedonistic, and utilitarian, and they leaned heavily on one-legged notions of negative freedom, without any of the older tradition's side-constraints.

This latter-day conception of property prevailed in the *McCardle* case where the legal pleading appealed mainly to considerations of commutative/exchange-type justice. Drawing upon alternative conceptions, Ryan, by contrast, asked: "Who pays?, How much?, Should they be obliged to do so?" He thereby led the discussion to seemingly

---

[5]In addition to this assessment of changing conceptions of property, one also should consider the views of Robert Dahl (1970) and Virginia Held (1984) in the late 20th century—to the effect that the ability to earn a living and "career assets" tend to be the dominant, contemporary forms of property.

ungracious considerations of the persons who profit thereby, the extent of their profits, and whether or not they are entitled to what they get.

These are some of the standard inquiries occasioned by appeals to *distributive justice*. Only implicit in most of Brandeis' dissent, these questions were made more explicit in Ryan's analysis of the IWC case. On his view, by using reproduction costs as the decisive standard of just compensation in rate-making, the court in effect had declared that public utilities are like purely private companies and that competitive concerns ought to determine their value. In short, whatever price one might have to pay to duplicate an existing utility ought to be the measure for setting customers' rates.

For Ryan public utilities should have been publicly owned in the first place; but even if privately owned, they are more public trustees than private companies. As such they are accountable for allocating public benefits and burdens and in ways which serve public, rather than private interests (1931: 171; 1916: 95–6 and 1922: 226). A publicly licensed and regulated non-competitive monopoly provid-ing water service and fire protection to the citizens and businesses of the city, the Indianapolis Water Company enjoyed some definite advantages over purely private and competitive companies of com-parable size. Principal among those underscored by Ryan is a stipu-lated rate of return on capital investment—something no private company can rely upon. In addition, there were assurances that increases in property values would remain in place despite later declines in markets, and that regulation would not reduce the companies' valuation below the number of dollars invested. In fact, it generally pegged their values higher than those conventionally assigned investments of equal security. On that basis, the use of reproduction costs as the standard for the evaluation of utility property added still further advantages to the investors, and, corre-sponding to that long list of benefits, a comparably long list of burdens to rate-payers (1931: 159, 166, 169).

In sum, from Ryan's point of view, not only was it immoral, it was also contrary to existing legal rules for courts to accord public utilities the same rights private businesses had to profit by value increases (*id.*: 166). Morally speaking, they were entitled to only a moderate gain on their investments, or, alternatively, to a just rate of interest—but not to the excessive, even rapacious, rates he perceived in the IWC case.

There is nothing in Catholic teaching which sanctions a rate of 32 per cent on a non-competitive investment, even though the rate may be legally established through some hokus-pokus called valuation as in the Indianapolis Water case (id.: 170).

With respect to distributive justice in the allocation of burdens, disadvantages, risks, costs, and losses, Ryan was generally eloquent, except perhaps on the matter of the unequal bargaining position held by consumers who must purchase a necessary "product" like water from a franchised monopoly. He trained his attention, instead, on two other unjustifiable burden allocations. Setting rates in terms of reproduction costs had the effect of allocating economic risks inequitably, giving fewer advantages to consumers than to investors (id.: 160). This created a situation in which consumers wound up paying the interest on investments they already had made in the form of payments for services (id.: 149). The burdens of consumers, therefore, were disproportionate to the benefits of investors. Morally speaking, as he had said earlier when discussing the injustices unemployment creates by allocating purchasing power unequally (1916), "governments should distribute burdens according to capacities and benefits according to needs" (1931: 217).

III.
Common Threads

Louis Brandeis, American-born son of East European Jewish immigrants, the Baptist Walter Rauschenbusch, born of immigrant German parents, and the Minnesota populist Roman Catholic John A. Ryan, from immigrant Irish stock, inhabited significantly different cultural worlds, yet at deep structural levels of story, praxis, and reasoning, they exhibited some striking commonalities. There are some more obvious coincidences in their objects of inquiry and in their basic social-ethical concepts. But the intersections between their deep roots are such as to suggest that there may be hope for building consensus on some important matters of public policy in America. This is more than what some contemporary writers in ethics and religion imagine possible and so they emphasize the "harmonizing of invariably self-interested persons." It is more, too, than what those who appear to have lost confidence in public philosophies envision when they turn instead to more sectarian enterprises.

In order first to identify some of the specifically religious-ethical elements refracted through the prism of the Indianapolis Water Company case consider the more obvious and *prima facie* similarities in the objects of inquiry and ethical concepts employed by Brandeis, Rauschenbusch, and Ryan. Though Rauschenbusch died before the case was heard, and though, of the three Brandeis' ethics are the most tacit and asystematic (hence the reason why Ryan and Rauschenbusch figured larger in preceding sections) all three writers devoted major attention to railroads, public utilities, commerce and industry in their social inquiries. The social effects of concentrations of money, power, and privilege attracted their attention regularly, perhaps because their religio-cultural ancestors had arrived in an America where opportunities were part of the promise, yet in relatively limited supply for persons with ethnic, cultural, and religious traditions similar to theirs. Bringing the resources of their traditions to bear on the practices and policies of this land of opportunity, which promised liberty and justice for all, they were commonly persuaded that economics should be scrutinized in the light of ethics. They stood vigil lest the allocation of social, economic, and political advantages serve to further the advantages of the already privileged while further disadvantaging those who were not at the same starting gate when the race began.

That the stories, practices and forms of moral reasoning which inform the Jewish and Christian religious traditions were wellsprings of this vigilance and its cognate habits of social observations is most evident in the social-ethical concepts the three shared about the nature and function of property, work, and human rights.

1. *Rauschenbusch on Property.*

With respect to property, a classic passage from Walter Rauschenbusch represents one of the common threads:

> Private property is an indispensable basis of civilization and morality. The per capita amount of it ought not to lessen; it ought to increase. But for the present the great ethical need is to reemphasize and reclaim social property rights which are forgotten or denied. Society has rights even in the most purely private property. Neither *religion,* nor *ethics,* nor *law* recognizes such a thing as an absolute private property right. *Religion* teaches that all property is a trust and the owner but a steward. *Ethics* makes the moral title to property depend on the service the

owner renders by means of it. The *law* can dispossess me under the
right of eminent domain if the community needs my property. In war
the State can commandeer anything I have, even my body. Private
property is historically an offshoot of communal property and exists
by concession and sufferance. The whole institution of private property
exists because it is for the public good that it shall exist. If in any
particular it becomes dangerous to the public welfare, it must cease.
Salus reipublicae summa lex. Religious teaching can do much to make
the partnership of the community in private property a conscious force
in public thought. The doctrine of stewardship must be backed by
knowledge of law and history, and become more than an amiable
generality (1912: 426; some emphases added; see also Ryan 1916: 358–
60 for a comparable "text").

2. Brandeis on Entitlements to Property.

Brandeis' convictions about labor as the only strict (as opposed to
presumptive) title to earnings in wages, profits, and interest, and his
related views about both New England Puritanism and American
Judaism are representative of similar concepts Ryan and Rauschenbusch employed in dealing with entitlements. From among a long
list of personal characteristics which legitimately might be called
"Puritan," Brandeis took attributes like courage, hard work, high
moral ideals, and ingenuity in overcoming obstacles to be definitive.
He thought these attributes were in decline in the New England of
the late nineteenth and early twentieth centuries and had been
replaced by more lucrative, but dishonorable, traits which may have
led to rewards for one's kin, as well as to commercial and social
success, but lacked integrity, emphasized power rather than courage,
success rather than creative labor.

These, and other of Brandeis' convictions, link his social analysis
to those of Rauschenbusch and Ryan at the level of deep structural
similarities. As a Jew he was a pilgrim but he was a Jew in America,
where Puritans had incorporated key elements of the Jewish heritage
into a Christian legacy that pervaded public morality. And in a time
when pilgrim metaphors pointed more to past than to present
accomplishments, he became something of a "Jewish Puritan"—
dedicated to pilgrim imperatives, but without the advantages which
had been cornered already by the purely nominal heirs of Puritanism
(Smurl 1983: 74–5; Gal 1980: 26, 137, 179–80).

3. Ryan on Human Rights

In the preceding analysis of ethical and political entanglements in the *McCardle* case we considered John Ryan's views on the human rights at stake in assuring that then-prevalent, legally established economic rights be respected. At this point we need only refer back to that earlier section to underscore Ryan's critically important notion that different spheres of human and social goods require priority rankings among entitlements.

CONCLUSIONS

This paper has stressed common elements in patterns of religiously grounded moral reasoning used by Brandeis, Rauschenbusch, and Ryan. But there are significant differences among their positions. Both Ryan's natural-law perspective and Brandeis' strong emphasis on public interest elements in the common law rested on an optimistic view of human nature and on the axiom that persons are equal in worth and dignity. By comparison, the role of sin and egoism in the theology of Walter Rauschenbusch, an American heir of the Protestant Reformation, prompted him to read the causes of social problems quite differently. For him "the instinct of self-interest is stronger than that of devotion to the common interest, and if the two come into conflict, the common good suffers." (1912: 272) While upholding the view that people were equal in worth, Rauschenbusch judged them still more equal in their sinfulness and in their corresponding need for redemption, so that "even men of unequal worth [can be put] on a footing of equality by the knowledge of common sin and weakness and by the faith in a common salvation." (1912: 321) In comparing forms of intracultural religious ethics, the differences are sometimes as important as the similarities.

Notwithstanding these differences, and not excluding the possibility of still others, the three figures here considered are agreed about a foursome of moral values found in the common human morality of their religious traditions. In fact-finding and in reporting, *truth-telling* is a duty owed to other persons—in public utility rate-making hearings as much as in interpersonal communications. Those licensed or franchised by government to provide public services are public trustees, obliged to *keep faith and to honor the promises* they have made. If, in the process of keeping those promises, they encounter difficulties, it is neither *beneficent* nor *just* to allocate the burdens of those difficulties disproportionately to those persons already seriously disadvantaged—particularly when the results amount to what Louis Brandeis would have characterized as gathering golden eggs from someone else's goose.

In drawing normative inferences, and in applying them to the public policy issues of their day, these three social critics shared a methodology comparable to the one Robert Handy found particularly in Rauschenbusch's work. "His method was to begin with the descriptive and the comparative, studying past and present by means of historical and sociological tools, and then to move on to the prescriptive and comparative function, both as a social prophet and as a herald of the coming kingdom." (1966: 262)

In addition to their methodological similarity, however, there is a comparable normative position—as relevant *now* as it was *then*. This position holds that:

> It is a moral failing to support freedom abstractly or to support legal forms of freedom such as contract, due process, or just compensation for the confiscation of private property in ways which burden whole classes of persons or render them less equally free while enhancing the freedoms of a privileged group protected by a public policy. Not only does such public policy reduce the freedoms of an already disadvantaged and less equally free populace, it diminishes freedom itself.

This is, in substance, an argument for the priority of human goods over economic goods, which understands economic goods only as instruments for benefitting humans and their communities, and never as ends in themselves, and which opposes using them in ways which harm persons and fundamental human goods. Finally, it also is a cogent case for claiming that, when harms to fundamental human goods become systemic, that is, when they are passed along through generations of persons insufficiently advantaged, such harms are morally intolerable. Moreover, it is claimed that the public policies which sustain and promote such harms, however unwittingly, must be renegotiated.

The *McCardle* case represents such a call for reworking critical social arrangements. It provides opportunities to reveal some perennial and recurrent convictions around which people not only can, but must, rally if the social goods which they create to meet their basic and fundamental human needs are to be faithful to their intended purposes. Exploring the nature and behavior of public utilities helps uncover (but does not invent or impose) a conception of social order. It shows that many of our shared understandings of the "ownership" of social "goods" resist turning them into commodities which are subject only to market mechanisms and standards. It uncovers moral convictions that land and other natural resources, such as air and water, should be subordinated to the common good. It shows that the bazaar, though an important part of the city, is not the whole of it (Walzer 1983); that economic systems, though essential, are nonetheless parts of larger cultural and social-political orders, whose fate depends on the moral "health" of all social goods.

Many Americans have grown accustomed to competitive, religious interest-group behaviors, to the idea that exchange value is the only economic value, and to the notion that private property is the principal and most meaningful form of ownership. Nevertheless, critical explorations like those discussed here demonstrate that we still have deep common-cultural alternatives to which we can turn in uncommon times. Those alternatives explored in this essay say not only that equal freedom is more important than negative liberty, but that the promises to be governed by commutative justice presuppose distributively just conditions. They also, and perhaps more importantly, point up the fact that many Americans believe communities cannot be morally tolerable without close and reliable connections between individuals trying to be just, common efforts for justice in common situations, and disciplined social reasoning which does the truth in justice.

References

Broderick, Francis L., 1963, *Right Reverend New Dealer John A. Ryan*, N.Y.: Macmillan.

Dahl, Robert A., 1970, *After the Revolution*. New Haven: Yale University Press.

Gal, Allon, 1980, *Brandeis of Boston*, Cambridge, MA: Harvard University Press, 1980.

Georgia Railway & Power Co. v. Railroad Commission of Georgia, 262 U.S. 625; 67 L.Ed. 1146. [1922]

Green, Ronald M., 1988, *Religion and Moral Reason*. New York: Oxford University Press.

Handy, Robert T., 1966, "Walter Rauschenbusch: An Introduction", pp. 253–263 in *The Social Gospel in America 1870–1920*, ed. by Robert T. Handy, N.Y.: Oxford.

Held, Virginia, 1980, *Property, Profits, and Economic Justice*. Belmont, CA: Wadsworth.

1984, *Rights and Goods: Justifying Social Action*. New York: The Free Press.

Hollenbach, David, 1983, *Nuclear Ethics*. NY: Paulist Press.

Indiana Public Service Commission Docket Books #21 [Mar. 7, 1923–Sept. 13, 1923], item #7080; 23 [Aug. 21, 1924–July 1, 1925], item #7781; #24 [July 2, 1925–May 5, 1926], pp. 56, 122.

"Indiana Public Service Commission re Indianapolis Water Company [No. 7080]", p. 431 ff. in *Public Utilities Reports Annotated*, vol. 1925C.

Indiana Record Center (State Library), item 65, formal case 7080, record series #81-832, box #1, location on range 54, row 6, shelf 2.

Kelly, A. H., & Harbison, W. A., 1970, *The American Constitution*, 4th ed., N.Y.: W. W. Norton & Co.

Kuttner, Robert, 1988, "Primers for Presidents," pp. 1 ff. in *The New York Times Book Review* (Sunday, October 23).

Lippmann, Walter, 1929, *A Preface to Morals*, N.Y.: Times-Life Books (1984 reprint).

Lonergan, Bernard J. F., 1958, *Insight: A Study of Human Understanding*. New York: Philosophical Library.

McCardle v. The Indianapolis Water Co., 1926, 272 *U.S.* 400; 71 *L.Ed.* 316.

Mills, C. Wright, 1956, *The Power Elite*, NY: Oxford.

Ryan, John A., 1907, *A Living Wage*, N.Y.: Macmillan.

———, 1916, *Distributive Justice*, N.Y.: Macmillan.

———, 1931, "The Ethics of Public Utility Valuation", p. 134 ff. in *Questions of the Day*, N.Y.: Books for Libraries Press, Inc., [1967 reprint].

———, and Moorhouse F. X. Millar, ed's., 1924, *The State and The Church*, New York: Macmillan, [first published in 1922].

Smurl, James F., 1983, "Allocating Public Burdens: The Social Ethics Implied in Brandeis of Boston", pp. 59–78 in *The Journal of Law and Religion*, I/1 (Summer).

State of Missouri Ex Rel., South Western Bell Telephone Co. v. Public Service Commission of Missouri, 1922, 262 *U.S.* 276; 67 *L.Ed.* 981.

Walzer, Michael, 1977, *Just and Unjust Wars: A Moral Argument with Historical Illustrations*. New York: Basic Books.

———, 1983, *Spheres of Justice: A Defense of Pluralism and Equality*. New York: Basic Books.

———, 1985, *Exodus and Revolution*. New York: Basic Books.

———, 1986, "Justice Here and Now", pp. 136–150 in *Justice and Equality: Here and Now*, Frank S. Lucash, ed., Ithaca, NY: Cornell University Press.

———, 1987, *Interpretation and Social Criticism*. Cambridge: Harvard University Press.

SCRIPTURE AND THE SOCIAL ORDER: "PARADIGMATIC CONSTRUALS" OF WALTER RAUSCHENBUSCH

William McInerny

The topic of "Religion, Economics, and the Social Order," immediately brings to my mind the life and writings of Walter Rauschenbusch. Hailed as the most brilliant and satisfying proponent of the Social Gospel movement in the United States,[1] Rauschenbusch, a pastor, professor, national lecturer and author, labored to initiate and acutalize a "social revolution" in this country. In other words, he sought to "Christianize" the American social order.[2] Rauschenbausch's vision of a new society was richly and powerfully informed by biblical paradigms regarding wealth, the poor and powerless, the equality of all persons, the unity of the human family, the moral responsibilities of persons for all other persons, and preeminently those concerning the social nature of Jesus of Nazareth's ministry and teachings. The idea of Christianizing the social order also brings to mind a contemporary movement which seeks to fuse religion, economics, and the American social order.

Under the blanket term of the "New Religious Right"[3] are some

---

[1]Reinhold Niebuhr, *An Interpretation of Christian Ethics* (New York: Harper & Brothers, 1935), preface. Niebuhr, however, mistakenly identifies Rauschenbusch as the "real founder" of the movement. The roots of the American Social Gospel reach further back into history than the life of Rauschenbusch.

[2]Walter Rauschenbusch, *Christianizing the Social Order* (New York: Macmillan Co., 1912; reprint edition, New York: Macmillan Co., 1913), pp. 124–125.

[3]The term is subject to various interpretations. See its uses in: Flo Conway and Jim Siegelman, *Holy Terror: The Fundamentalist War on America's Freedom* (New York: Doubleday & Co., 1982); Gabriel Fackre, *The Religious Right and Christian Faith* (Grand Rapids, Michigan: Eerdmans, 1982); Samuel S. Hill and Dennis E. Owen, *The New Religious Political Right* (Nashville: Abingdon Press, 1982); John L. Kater, Jr., *Christians on the Right: The Moral Majority in Perspective* (New York: Seabury, 1982); Daniel C. Maguire, *The New Subversives: Anti-Americanism of the Religious Right* (New York: Continuum, 1982).

committed groups who envision a specific social order, warranted allegedly by Scripture, and who strive to realize it by exerting pressure and power within our educational and political systems. Here the Bible functions as a revealed, normative source for various moral paradigms such as white male superiority, the natural inferiority of women, the ethical and religious inadequacies of Judaism and all other non-Christian belief systems, violence as a God-approved instrument of social change, the condemnation of homosexuals, and legitimate neglect of the nation's poor, for example.[4]

What do Rauschenbusch and the New Religious Right share in common? First, these thinkers are engaged in normative ethics and seek to spell out the inherently social nature of Christian morality. Second, they assert that Christians ought to be characterized by specific norms and traits if they are to merit the title "Christian." Both Rauschenbusch and the New Right agree that a distinctive Christian ethos is possible and mandated. Third, they acknowledge the foundational status of the biblical witness in formulating normative concepts of Christian morality. Fourth, these thinkers attempt to relate Scripture to the social and economic order by way of biblical moral paradigms. Rauschenbusch's paradigmatic construals of Scripture, however, diverge substantially from those construals invoked by some of the New Right. That observation raises intriguing questions for a Christian moralist.

In what ways should a Christian ethicist appropriate biblical materials in her or his reflections? If one criticizes some uses of Scripture in the thinking of the New Right, then that implies the existence of some other way or ways of appealing to the biblical witness that is better. If so, how is this way or these ways discerned?

The modest purpose of this paper is to explore the meaning and viability of one particular manner of relating Scripture and Christian morality: *by way of "paradigmatic construals."* For now, suffice it to say that a biblical "paradigm" is a basic model of a vision of life and of the ethos of that life, which engenders particular consistent attitudes, intentions, dispositions, values, moral sensitivities, and norms of behavior.[5] The use of biblical paradigms for relating the Bible to contemporary moral concerns is widespread[6] and particu-

---

[4]Daniel C. Maguire, *The New Subversives: Anti-Americanism of the Religious Right* (New York: Continuum, 1982), passim.

[5]James M. Gustafson, *Theology and Christian Ethics* (Philadelphia: Pilgrim Press, 1974), p. 154.

[6]For example see C. H. Dodd, *Gospel and Law: The Relation of Faith and Ethics in*

larly evident in the works of Walter Rauschenbusch. I contend that
Rauschenbusch's uses of Scripture can function as a normative guide
to ethicists who are interested, as he was, in relating Scripture to the
moral social order. The presentation of the essay's claims is divided
into three parts. First, some pressing problems facing an ethicist
who wishes to wed biblical studies and the discipline of theological
ethics are briefly discussed. Second, Rauschenbusch's insights regarding the nature of Scripture and its authority for the moral life
are examined regarding their implications for constructing biblical
paradigms. Third, Rauschenbusch's process of relating Scripture to
Christian morality is described. Given the limitations of this paper
and the staggering corpus of Rauschenbusch's writings, the following descriptions and explanations of his paradigmatic construals of
Scripture are meant only to be suggestive and by no means exhaustive.

I. Ethicists and the Bible

Christian ethicists, as "Christian" ethicists, must incorporate the
witness of sacred Scripture in their work. In so doing, ethicists must
face a tangle of questions and problems. I cannot list all these
quandries, but I can cite a few. Perhaps cross-disciplinary expertise
is the most obvious obstacle. Few theological ethicists possess the
professional, critical skills of a trained biblical scholar. The barrier
of ancient languages is formidable. Many ethicists are not capable of
examining the biblical witness in Hebrew or Greek; consequently,
the nuances and subtleties of these languages, which can greatly
influence the meaning of passages, are lost to the Christian moralist.
Ethicists may also lack adequate historical knowledge of important
religious, social, and political customs, practices, and disputes that
surrounded the composition of biblical texts. Even if one is advised
to rely on the expert work of trained biblical scholars and exegetes
the problems do not end. What should ethicists do when the experts

---

Early Christianity, Bampton Lectures in America no. 3 (New York: Columbia University Press, 1951), pp. 41, 44, 46, 51, 55, 74, 77; Richard P. McBrien, *Catholicism,* 2
vols. (Minneapolis, Minnesota: Winston Press, 1980), 2: "The Sinlessness of Jesus,"
pp. 519–20, "The Sexuality of Jesus," pp. 532–534; Rudolf Schnackenburg, *The
Moral Teaching of the New Testament,* translated by J. Holland-Smith and W. J. O'Hara
from the 2nd revised German edition (New York: Burns & Oates, 1969), pp. 25–33,
56–65, 73–81; John Howard Yoder, *The Politics of Jesus* (Grand Rapids, Michigan:
Eerdmans, 1972), pp. 118–129. This represents only a brief sampling of the available
literature which incorporates biblical moral paradigms in varying forms.

disagree? How does one judge between the positions of rival special-ists? Given even an imaginary world where universal consensus regarding the meaning of every biblical passage existed, ethicists would still grapple with questions of how to relate biblical materials to Christian moral reflection, and, in what manner of communica-tion should such relationships be expressed? These and other in-quiries are not simply matters of theoretical interest. A Christian ethicist must have recourse to Scripture. But in what way (or ways) then should this foundational source of moral insight be "tapped"? In answering that question I find the writings of Walter Rauschen-busch to be illuminating.

II. Rauschenbusch, the Bible, and Moral Paradigms

By professional training, Rauschenbusch was neither a biblical scholar or a religious ethicist; however, his biblical construals find substantial support in several contemporary methodological studies dealing with the relationships between biblical scholarship and Christian ethics. Many of the recommendations appearing in these current works were practically implemented in Rauschenbusch's writings.[7] That observation alone may be encouraging to ethicists today who lack the expertise of a professional exegete. Beyond encouraging others to a greater and a more creative use Scripture in their ethical reflections, Walter Rauschenbusch's example provides a particular pattern of reasoning that can guide one's very approach to that venture. Three factors in Rauschenbusch's method of apply-ing the Bible to Christian ethicist reflection deserve attention and imitation.

First, he was keenly attuned to the historical conditionedness of the biblical materials on the one hand, and the normative status of such materials for Christian morality on the other. He sought a way of being faithful to the historical limitations of scriptural texts as

---

[7]Bruce C. Birch and Larry L. Rasmussen, *Bible and Ethics in the Christian Life* (Minneapolis: Augsburg Publishing House, 1976), pp. 104–108 especially; Raymond E. Brown, *The Critical Meaning of the Bible* (New York: Paulist Press, 1981), of. pp. 20, 23–44; Van A. Harvey, *The Historian and the Believer* (New York: Macmillan, 1966), cf. pp. 253–258; James M. Gustafson, *Theology and Christian Ethics*, pp. 147–159; James F. Childress, "Scripture and Christian Ethics: Some Reflections on the Role of Scripture in Moral Deliberation and Justification," *Interpretation* 34 (October 1980): 371–380; Edward LeRoy Long, Jr., "The Use of the Bible in Christian Ethics: A Look at Basic Options," *Interpretation* 19 (April 1965): 149–162; C. Freeman Sleeper, "Ethics as a Context for Biblical Interpretation," *Interpretation* 22 (October 1968): 443–460.

well as to their binding force. In other words, Rauschenbusch searched out the perennially viable dimensions of Scripture amid their historically conditioned expressions (an undertaking that continues through the present).[8]

Second, Rauschenbusch distinguished between *the* gospel originally lived and preached by Jesus of Nazareth and the historical manifestation of that "good news" in the New Testament. In his thinking, Jesus of Nazareth was the ultimate, primary revelation of God's nature and will. Scripture, in contrast, is a secondary type of revelation which mediates that historical personage and his message.[9] Rauschenbusch went on to distinguish between *the* gospel of Jesus of Nazareth, its historical record in Scripture, and the different understandings of that record,

> The Gospel of Christ is one and immutable; the comprehension and expression of it in history has been of infinite variety. . . . It is on the face of it unlikely that the gospel as commonly understood by us is the whole gospel or a completely pure gospel. It is a lack of Christian humility to assume that our gospel and *the* gospel are identical.[10]

Rauschenbusch, cautioned by this historical sensitivity, searched the New Testament, particularly the synoptic gospels, for what he later termed "the constant and integral trend of biblical convictions" expressed therein. The constant, integral trend of biblical convictions constituted, for him, the authoritative dimension of Scripture.[11]

Rauschenbusch employed a variety of terms to designate the perennially viable component of Scripture he discerned. He spoke of "the mind of Christ," "Jesus' spirit," the "fundamental direction" of the Bible, and the "spirit" of biblical texts. In his vocabulary, these words denote a collective vision of what is real and valuable

---

[8]James M. Gustafson, *Theology and Ethics*, p. 151; Gerhard Kroedel, in "The Authority of the Bible," *The Ecumenical Review* 21 (April 1969): 155; Daniel C. Maguire, *The New Subversives*, p. 80; John F. X. Sheehan, "Theological Reflections on Pain," *Journal of Drug Issues* (Fall 1981), p. 428. These references are intended to be suggestive not exhaustive.

[9]Walter Rauschenbusch, "Revelation: An Exposition," *The Biblical World* 10 (August 1897): 96.

[10]Walter Rauschenbusch, "The New Evangelism," *The Independent* 61 (January–June 1904): reprinted in Robert T. Handy, ed., *The Social Gospel in America: 1870–1920*, A Library of Protestant Thought (New York: Oxford University Press, 1966), p. 324.

[11]Walter Rauschenbusch, *A Theology for the Social Gospel*, eighth printing (Nashville: Abingdon Press, 1978), p. 42.

in terms of the biblical witness. This overarching vision of reality
and value had a specific form which could be depicted and represented. Such depictions functioned as biblical paradigms in
Rauschenbusch's moral reflections. The rationale governing his recognition of scriptural moral paradigms is instructive.

Third, for Rauschenbusch, the penultimate expression of the constant, integral trends of biblically-based moral convictions resided
in the biblical portrayals of the person and teachings of Jesus
Christ.[12] In his thinking, the biblical presentations of Christ's words
and actions embodied the essential vision of meaning and value that
ought to determine and direct the moral life. Thus, Rauschenbusch
analyzed the gospel depictions of Christ and attempted to construct
the vision of moral life and meaning that governed the actions and
words of the historical Jesus. Furthermore, he sought to discover
specific attitudes, intentions, values, and norms of conduct consonant with that overall vision. In this way, particular biblical materials (stories, sayings, parables, individual scenes) could function as
basic models or objectifications of Christ's vision of life and of the
ethics animating vision. Rauschenbusch thus searched the gospels
for paradigms of the moral life that could influence and shape the
moral outlooks of contemporary Christians.[12] His investigations were
marked by recognizable steps.

III. A Process

Walter Rauschenbusch brought his intensely personal questions
and interests to biblical materials, especially the gospels. He wished
to discover what, if anything, the Scriptures contained about the
important pressing social topics of his day such as wealth and
property. Did consistent trends of biblical thought regarding these
subjects exist? Did the depictions of Jesus Christ in the New Testament show consistent attitudes or insights about them? In this way,
Rauschenbusch's search for biblical paradigms was grounded in his
agenda of social concerns. Yet, he did not restrict his investigations
to that agenda alone, however. He also employed descriptive and
historical exegesis (as he understood it) to uncover the moral teachings of the biblical documents themselves, their major themes and

---

[12]Walter Rauschenbusch, "Does the New Testament Provide a Definite and Permanent Church Policy?" *Twenty-Second Annual Session of the Baptist Congress* (New
York: Baptist Congress Publishing Company, 1904), p. 114.

emphases.[13] This twofold manner of addressing Scripture led to a second step.

In the actual process of relating Scripture to Christian morality, Rauschenbusch made appeals to the redacted level of biblical materials—the form in which the texts now stand before us. At times he wrote about what Jesus said when he preached the Sermon on the Mount; or he described the manner in which Jesus responded to a rich person who approached him one day; or about what other biblical characters did, said, or experienced on given occasions. Such statements do not betray a naive biblicism. In Matthew's gospel, at the redacted-story level, Jesus does preach the Sermon on the Mount; in Mark's gospel and others, the character Jesus does address a rich man with specific words and with a recorded attitude (Mk. 10:21). Relating and redepicting the actions and words of biblical figures as they speak and move as *characters* in a scene or story is not the same as claiming that in history, at a given time and place, the very actions recorded occurred or that the exact same words were actually spoken.

When Rauschenbusch incorporated biblical materials paradigmatically in his work, he ordinarily referred to specific scenes or stories. To spell out the exemplary dimensions of these passages he executed what I term a literary-historical-moral process of analysis. This constitutes a third important step in Rauschenbusch's procedure of relating Scripture and the moral life.

The type of analysis identified was guided by certain assumptions.[14] Human actions can be signs; they can embody and express one's vision of life, one's moral character, one's deepest convictions. The same is true for the words we speak. Furthermore, one's vision, moral character, and convictions ordinarily engender actions and words consonant with them. Would it not be possible, within limits, to work *backward* from recorded or reported human actions and sayings to the factors governing that behavior and speech? Such a process would involve a good deal of inference, but these inferences could be checked and warranted to an extent. Thus, in analyzing

---

[13]Walter Rauschenbusch, "Social Ideas in the New Testament," *The Treasury* 17 (June 1899): 155.

[14]See Walter Rauschenbusch, *Christianity and the Social Crisis* (New York: Macmillan, 1907; reprint edition New York: Macmillan, 1912), pp. 308, 309, 349, 351–352; "Revelation an Exposition," p. 101; *The Righteousness of the Kingdom*, ed., Max L. Stackhouse, foreward by Robert T. Handy (Nashville: Abingdon Press, 1968), pp. 75, 81, 119, 121, 130, 142.

specific biblical passages, Rauschenbusch intended to distill the moral values, character, attitudes, intentions, and convictions that could account for the behavior and words of biblical figures. Biblical visions of the moral life thus discerned could be appropriated and fused into the moral horizon of contemporary Christians. Rauschenbusch sought to shape and influence others by his usages of Scripture at the most fundamental level: the ways in which they envisioned reality and moral values.[15]

If Rauschenbusch were to infer a moral vision on the basis of select biblical materials, then, at the redacted level of such passages, he had to scrutinize the specific elements of those texts. The literary dimension of his analysis took the following form. He identified the major characters involved in the passage; the circumstances of the scene or story; the setting of the scene or story; the actions that the characters performed and the words they spoke; the manner in which behavior and speech were executed; the implicit and explicit relationships between the characters; the meaning and significance of numbers if stated; spatial relationships between persons and between objects; and any other pertinent details presented. He then went on to isolate issues such as wealth, poverty, the social status of characters and so on, if these were evident. The literary stage of Rauschenbusch's analysis rendered the core elements from which a vision of the moral life would be drawn.

Having completed this stage, Rauschenbusch brought his historical knowledge to the fore to shed further light on the individual parts of the biblical passage under study. He reasoned that it was necessary to understand, as far as possible, the historical background and context of the passage and its contents in order to understand fully the significance of the actions and words and attitudes expressed therein.[16] For example, if Pharisees were characters in a story then one needed to know who such people were in Jewish society, what were their beliefs, customs, functions, and so on. If a leper or a poor person was involved, then one should learn as much as possible about what being a leper or a beggar meant within their social settings, what hopes did they have, how did society treat them, and so on. Historical information of this sort not only illuminates the passage, it also helps set limits on the types of inferences

---

[15]Walter Rauschenbusch, *Righteousness of the Kingdom*, pp. 74, 75, 101, 115, 142; *Christianity and the Social Crisis*, p. 308.

[16]Walter Rauschenbusch, "The Influence of Historical Studies on Theology, *The American Journal of Theology* 11 (January 1907); 112–115, 117.

that could legitimately be drawn on the basis of the passage and its contents.

After an historical analysis of the literary elements of a text, Rauschenbusch embarked upon the most venturesome task of construing biblical materials paradigmatically. The next stage of the process entailed a creative, imaginative construction of the moral vision governing the actions and words of biblical figures within a given story or scene. At this point, Rauschenbusch attempted to move from the actual elements of a biblical passage to discern what the actions and words of the main characters might signify in terms of moral vision, character, attitudes, intentions, and convictions. Unfortunately, Rauschenbusch's works don't give the details regarding this process. He left no record of his mind's journey as he moved from the level of *what is* in the passage to the level of *what it might signify* morally. Rather his works offer only the conclusions of his thought process, and not its specific steps.

Intriguingly, contemporary authors such as James M. Gustafson and Bruce C. Birch and Larry L. Rasmussen, explore the use of biblical paradigms and also do not spell out, specifically, the process involved which moves them from the level of *what is* in the biblical passage at its literary and historical dimensions, to *what it might signify* in moral terms.[17] Perhaps the process transcends precise articulation. In any event, I submit that the process is governed by at least one important guideline: human actions, attitudes, and words within a particular context are subject to a somewhat open but definitely limited range of interpretations. An illustration of this principle can make its meaning clearer.

Consider the following situation. Two friends, one living in South Bend, Indiana and the other in Dublin, Ireland, meet at O'Hare International Airport after a separation of some five years. Upon seeing one another both extend their arms and hands, and initial handshakes quickly merge into an embrace. Given even the sparse details of these circumstances, what can the actions of the two friends signify? The meaning of greetings by handshake and embrace, particularly between males, in the 1980's can be interpreted as signs of affection, restored communion between persons, joy, and so on. These meanings constitute the "somewhat" openness of the described actions to interpretation—no one understanding of the

---

[17]James M. Gustafson, *Theology and Ethics*, pp. 154–155; Bruce C. Birch and Larry L. Rasmussen, *Bible and Ethics*, pp. 105–106.

actions may completely explain their meaning; nonetheless, a meaningful comprehension of the situation is possible. On the other hand,
given the historical setting of the 1980's and the circumstances
related, one would be hard pressed to show that handshakes and
hugs are signs of hatred, malcontent, sorrow, disdain, and the like.
Within reason, the behavior described in the example is open only
to so many interpretations. The limits to such explanations are set
by the situation itself and a consideration of who is involved, at
what time, where, what motives are entailed, are there viable alternative actions that could have taken place just as well, what are the
foreseeable effects of the actions and/or words? for example. Addi-
tionally, one's overall knowledge of the historical practices, customs,
beliefs, in short one's comprehension of the social situation in which
the situation takes place helps define the perimeters of responsible
discernment.

Determining the scope and range of possible, reasonable, meanings signified by the actions and words within a specific set of
circumstances that are reported or written requires literary, historical, and moral sensitivity as well as the courage to be imaginative.
All these traits find concrete expression in the paradigmatic construals of Walter Rauschenbusch.

Rauschenbusch discerned visions of the moral life grounded in
biblical paradigms. To what end did he relate his findings? How did
he communicate the insights thus gained?

A primary aim of Rauschenbusch's uses of Scripture was to reshape, re-orient the moral horizon of his audience. He strove to give
others a new way of seeing themselves, others, and society—a way
of seeing that was biblically grounded. An everpresent pastoral and
social goal of Rauschenbusch's was the transformation of the moral
character of his readers. On the basis of a transformed moral vision
and character, he believed new socially sensitive, ethical attitudes,
intentions, and norms would flow and find expression in personal
and social action. When relating Scripture to Christian social morality, Rauschenbusch intended to inspire, challenge, and motivate his
audience to action. To this end he communicated his understandings
of biblical moral paradigms in a delightful variety of forms.

Walter Rauschenbusch engaged in bible storytelling. He advocated
storytelling as an important manner of conveying the "spirit" of
biblical texts. In so doing, he would incorporate historical insights
and information in the actual narration. He also rendered the moral
characters of biblical personages. Rauschenbusch composed "free

renderings" of familiar scriptural passages. He rephrased biblical materials in terms of contemporary language, idioms, and circumstances; thus he attempted to juxtapose the core vision of specific biblical texts with present-day experiences. Rauschenbusch also expressed biblical moral paradigms in the forms of topic collages and social principles. All of these were vehicles for communicating the moral vision of biblical paradigms.

As stated at the beginning of this paper, this presentation and explanation of Rauschenbusch's paradigmatic construals is suggestive and not exhaustive. A thorough investigation of his uses of Scripture ought to include an examination of his personal history, religious consciousness, his sensitivity and appreciation of beauty and especially children, his understanding of the Bible as simultaneously a religious and historical text, his concept of exegesis, and his understanding of Christian morality. All these factors were part of his biblical construals. Nonetheless, this examination has explored the meaning and viability of construing Scripture paradigmatically. We in our time can profit greatly from the life-long work of Walter Rauschenbusch. We disregard his accomplishments in this area at the risk of our own impoverishment.

Paradigmatic construals of Scripture can be recommended to contemporary ethicists and religious educators as useful ways of relating the Bible and Christian social morality for at least six reasons:

1. The formation and development of moral character is a foundational goal of Christian ethics. Biblical paradigms by their nature are aimed at character formation.

2. The use of biblical paradigms demands the exercise of creative moral imagination. Indeed, they intend to capture the imagination in such a way that one's way of seeing the totality of experience is altered.[18]

3. The literary analysis required by this usage of Scripture can be learned readily. If one can read a novel or any complex piece of literature and identify major characters, plots, and so on, then one is capable of learning this type of literary criticism. Biblical commentaries and other research tools are easily accessible to aid one in the historical analysis required.

---

[18]cf. Van. A. Harvey, *The Historian and the Believer* (New York: Macmillan, 1966), pp. 253–258.

4. Paradigmatic construals offer a bridge from the biblical texts to contemporary ethical reflection. All manner of biblical stories, scenes, and sayings *can* function as paradigms; consequently, a responsible selection among the available options is required. The process of selection ought to include one's present moral system. The following question cannot be legitimately avoided: Does the paradigm further a more humane life and the quest for justice? If one answers yes, then the position advancing that claim needs to be brought forth. When we pronounce judgment regarding what helps or hinders the pursuit of a more humane life, we necessarily engage in the art-science of ethics.

5. Paradigmatic construals resonate well with the very nature of much of the gospel materials.[19]

6. Finally, this manner of construing Scripture allows one to incorporate critical, historical exegesis but forces one to go beyond the results of that kind of analysis.

Paradigmatic construals thus offer us a viable, creative, accessible model of wedding the seemingly divergent disciplines of theological ethics and biblical studies.

---

[19]See Guenther Bornkamm's explanation of pericopae in *Jesus of Nazareth*, translated by Irene and Fraser McLuskey and James Robinson (New York: Harper & Row, 1975), p. 25.

Part Four

CHURCH PERSPECTIVES

LIBERATION THEOLOGY AND THE VATICAN: AN ASSESSMENT

Arthur F. McGovern

Controversy has, for some time, surrounded liberation theology in Latin America. The Vatican document (issued by Cardinal Joseph Ratzinger in September 1984 for the Congregation for the Doctrine of the Faith),[1] far from resolving the controversy, only added more fuel. In this paper I would like to highlight the major criticisms made of liberation theology and to assess their validity. To assess adequately the whole of liberation theology would require a far more extensive study.[2]

Background: The Catholic Church and Liberation Theology

At its inception, in the 1960s, liberation theology could find strong support for its positions in many documents of the Roman Catholic Church. Liberation theology placed great emphasis on the Church's mission to work for the transformation of this world and to challenge injustice. Vatican II and the 1971 Bishops' Synod on "Justice in the World" strongly affirmed these concerns. Liberation theology stressed two meanings of "liberation" in the Latin American context: "liberation" in a theological sense meant that God acts in history to save His people not just from personal sin but from physical bondage and oppression; "liberation" in a political-economic sense linked freedom from poverty and oppression to liberating Latin American

---

[1]"Instruction on Certain Aspects of the Theology of Liberation," issued by the Sacred Congregation for the Doctrine of the Faith", issued September 3, 1984, printed in the *National Catholic Reporter*, September 21, 1984. Citations will be indicated in the main text of the essay, using the paragraph numbers given in the document.

[2]My own earlier and fuller assessment is given in McGovern, *Marxism: An American Christian Perspective* (Maryknoll, N.Y.: Orbis, 1980), chapter 5, "Liberation Theology in Latin America."

peoples from "dependency" on foreign economies. The Latin American bishops at Medellin (1968) affirmed both of these meanings. The bishops spoke of God sending His son "that he might come to liberate" all people from the slavery to which sin had subjected them, from hunger, misery and oppression. The bishops implied the second sense of liberation in their criticisms of international imperialism and by placing the principal guilt for the economic dependence of Latin American countries on foreign monopolistic powers.[3] Pope Paul VI's *Populorum Progressio* (1967) lent added support to the charges that rich nations contribute to the poverty of underdeveloped nations. Even liberation theology's use of Marxist analysis could claim some legitimacy by referring to Pope Paul VI's distinctions (in *Octogesima Adveniens*, 1971) about different meanings of Marxism,[4] and to Bishop Helder Camara's call for a theological synthesis of Marxism and Christianity.

But conflict was not long in coming. It emerged most sharply in the early 1970s with the formation of the Christians for Socialism in Chile, after the election of a Marxist president, Salvador Allende. The bishops in Chile adopted a position of neutrality. The Christians for Socialism actively supported the new socialism and sharply criticized the bishops for their cautious neutrality. The conflict led finally to a formal condemnation of the Christians for Socialism by the bishops. Their statement merits attention for it anticipated, point by point, all the major criticisms which the Vatican document would make ten years later. The Christians for Socialism, said the Chilean bishops, reduce Christianity to one dimension, the political. They treat the Marxist method of analysis as an "indisputable science"; they describe all social changes in terms of class struggle; they reduce all opposing views to "bourgeois" ideology. They seek to create their own Church, their own parallel magisterium, in the name of true Christianity.[5]

The 1970s witnessed the growing influence of liberation theology in Latin America and in other parts of the world. Gustavo Gutierrez's *A Theology of Liberation* (1971; 1973 in English) became a focal

---

[3]The Medellin documents can be found in Joseph Gremillon, ed., *The Gospel of Peace and Justice* (Maryknoll, N.Y.: Orbis, 1976). On Jesus as liberator, confer "Justice", No. 3, p. 446; on criticisms of dependency confer "Peace", No. 9, p. 457.

[4]"Octogesima Adveniens", n. 33, also in Gremillion, *The Gospel of Peace and Justice*.

[5]The Chilean bishops' document is given in John Eagleson, ed., *Christians and Socialism* (Orbis, 1975), Document 19. Confer also, McGovern, *Marxism*, ch. 6 on Chile.

point of study, complemented by the work of many other theologians (e.g. Juan Luis Segundo, Hugo Assmann, Jon Sobrino, Leonardo Boff, Segundo Galilea). Great numbers of priests and religious incorporated a "liberation theology perspective" into their ministry; thousands of base communities reflected on the Bible from this same perspective. Some critics viewed liberation theology as a passing fad, but it has become deeply embedded in the life of many sectors of the Church in Latin America. Its influence has been profound. The biblical section of the current U.S. bishops' pastoral letter on the U .S. economy owes much to the themes stressed in liberation theology; the commitment to "faith and justice" in my own Society of Jesus' 32nd Congregation was inspired and prompted to a great extent by Jesuits from Latin America and other Third World areas. But opposition to liberation theology also remained strong, in Latin America led by Bishop Lopez Trujillo and Roger Vekemans, S. J., and in Europe by some German theologians. An attempt was made by Bishop Lopez Trujillo to have liberation theology condemned at Puebla (1979), but it failed. The Puebla documents, though they lacked the forcefulness of the earlier Medellin statements, reinforced the "preferential option for the poor" and supported base communities. Vatican opposition to liberation theology was, I suspect, greatly intensified by Pope John Paul II's visit to Nicaragua where a "popular church" was perceived to be in conflict with the bishops and the hierarchical church.

The Vatican (Ratzinger) document was issued in September 1984. It stated a very limited and precise purpose: to draw attention to "the deviations and risks of deviation, damaging to the faith and to Christian living, that are brought about by certain forms of liberation theology which use, in an insufficiently critical manner, concepts borrowed from various currents of Marxist thought" (From the Introduction). But *what* liberation theologians were meant to be included under these "certain forms" (they are not cited in the document itself)? One's assessment of the fairness and accuracy of the Vatican criticisms depends greatly on determining whom they were targetted against. If the document is taken simply as a warning about the ways in which liberation theology can be popularly adopted and used (e.g. the Christians for Socialism in Chile), many of the criticisms I find to be well-taken. If the document was meant to criticize and even delegitimize the major liberation theologians, its criticisms do not appear to me to be accurate or fair. Unfortunately, I think the latter was the intent of the document. I base this conclusion on

several facts or reports: that an earlier address by Ratzinger, critizing
liberation theology, *did* cite Gutierrez, Sobrino and Boff[6]; that Ratzinger sent the Peruvian bishops a list of charges against Gutierrez;
that Sobrino and Boff were called to Rome, and that Boff was
eventually silenced.

With this background and these preliminary comments, I will now
proceed with my overview, discussing liberation theology under the
heading of three groups of criticisms which I find most prominent
in the Vatican document: use of the Bible, use of Marxism, and
criticisms of the Church.

I. Use of the Bible

The starting point of liberation theology is not simply the Bible,
but the Bible in the context of a troubling historical situation, the
fact that the vast majority of people in Latin America live in poverty,
a poverty that often appears linked to unjust and oppressive structures. All of the issues raised by liberation theologians—about the
Bible, about social analysis, about the Church's role—result from
confrontations with this situation. Given this situation, liberation
theologians questioned their faith: does the Bible, God's revelation,
speak to conditions of human poverty and oppression, and if so,
what does it tell us of God's concerns?

Liberation theologians believe that God has indeed spoken, and
spoken forcefully, to the problems of the poor. In the Old Testament
(the Exodus), God acted in behalf of the poor to liberate them, not
just from personal sin but from servitude and oppression. The
prophets (e.g. Isaiah, Jeremiah, Amos, Hosea) repeatedly denounced
injustices against the poor. In the New Testament, Jesus identified
himself with the poor both in words (e.g. Luke 4, the Beatitudes, Mt
25) and in actions (by associating with the outcasts of society). Jesus,
in preaching of the "Kingdom of God," held out to the poor a vision
of the kind of world God intended, where all would be treated with
dignity, compassion and justice. Liberation theologians argue also
that Jesus' denunciations of the rich, and of ruling religious leaders,
contain strong political statements which led ultimately to his
condemnation and death. To be a follower of Jesus, then, means to
continue his mission, to work with and for the poor, and to strive
for the Kingdom he envisioned.

---

[6]An address by Cardinal Joseph Ratzinger appeared originally in 30 Giorni, March
1984, and was published by *Catholicism in Crisis*, September 1984.

The Vatican document acknowledges much that liberation theology says about revelation, that "liberation" is a legitimate theological theme, that God does defend the poor and affirm aspirations for justice. But it criticizes "certain forms" of liberation theology on two main scores: that liberation theology reduces faith to politics, making changes in this world its whole focus, and that it emphasizes social sin to the neglect of personal sin. On the first score the document charges that: the political dimension in Scripture is made into "the principal or exclusive component" leading to "a reductionist reading of the Bible" (X, 5); "every affirmation of faith or theology is subordinated to a political criterion" (IX, 6); "Faith in the Incarnate World . . . is denied" and "an exclusively political interpretation is thus given to the death of Jesus" (X, 11–12); it tends also to identify the 'Kingdom of God' with human liberation movements (VIII, 3).

In respect to the second charge, the document asserts that liberation must be seen as first and foremost a liberation from the radical slavery of sin, with other forms as consequences and by-products. But some "put liberation from sin in second place and so fail to give it the primary importance it is due" (Introduction; cf. also IV, 2, 12). Related to this is the charge that sin and evil, in liberation theology, are localized principally or even uniquely in bad social situations and not in the root of evil, which is personal sin (IV, 14–15).

To assess these charges is difficult, as noted before, when no specific texts or theologians are cited. My own reading of major liberation theologians leads to different conclusions. The urgency of addressing social issues, and giving them primacy of concern, are indeed stressed in liberation theology. But giving prime attention to a problem is not the equivalent of "reducing" the gospel to politics. Some Christian activisits may indeed substitute politics for faith, and hence a warning against this may be in place, but most liberation theologians clearly place politics in the context of a greater faith life.[7] Quite frankly, I frequently use liberation theology as spiritual reading, as an enrichment of my own faith and prayer; I could not

---

[7]Even in Gutierrez, A Theology of Liberation (Orbis, 1973) one finds a spirituality that includes a stress on prayer, the gratuitous of grace, the need for conversion, etc. (cf. especially, pp. 203–208), and far more on spirituality in such works as his We Drink From Our Own Wells (Orbis, 1984); confer also Segundo Galilea, Following Jesus (Orbis, 1981). And in Jon Sobrino, The True Church and the Poor (Orbis, 1984), the need for love and reconciliation at all levels of life (marriages, friendships) is explicitly stated. "The reign of God embraces the totality of human relationships" (p. 76).

do this if I found it only political. As to other charges, Sobrino has
written about the political sense of Jesus' death, but "exclusively"
as political? And where does one find in liberation theology that
"faith in the Incarnate Word is denied?"

Some Christian activists may indeed try to identify the Kingdom
of God with some specific liberation movement (I found this to be
true at times in Nicaragua and in reading Christians for Socialism
statements in Chile). But liberation theologians I have found to
distinguish carefully between the Kingdom as "gift" and human
efforts. The role of grace, moreover, is seen as essential in the human
efforts as well.[8] Should not the "Kingdom of God" be a Christian
vision guiding the work of trying to transform society? If the Vatican
statement that "God, and no man, has the power to change the
situations of sufferings" (III, 5) is to be taken literally, then what are
we to make of John Paul II's encyclical on work and all previous
social encyclicals?

Related to this issue of human efforts toward social change are the
Vatican's comments about sinful social structures. Liberation theologians may merit some criticism in speaking of the creation of a
"new man" through changing social structures; (even this, however,
does not deny the need for moral conversion and certainly does not
assume a materialist determinism of social attitudes). But the Vatican
document, while admitting evil structures which need to be
changed, appears to treat the change as coming only through inner
conversion of those in power (IV, 15; XI, 8). The source of injustice,
says the document, lies in the heart of men. "Therefore it is only by
making an appeal to the moral potential of the person and to the
constant need for interior conversion that social change will be
brought about which will truly be in the service of man" (XI, 8). The
weakness of past Church social teachings (in my opinion) lay in
their reliance on moral appeals to those in power. But significant
changes, including moral changes of attitude, often follow upon
changes in structures rather than waiting for moral changes in the
guilty parties. Thus the legal structures of segregation had to be
changed in the United States for better racial attitudes to develop,
and workers' unions had to be fought for before most capitalists
would pay just wages. The Church itself does not place all its hopes
on moral conversion alone, as in its efforts to change laws regarding
legalized abortion, or invoking Church laws and discipline to re-

---

[8]Sobrino, *The True Church*, ch. 3.

move priests from political office (rather than waiting for the conversion of those involved).

II. The Use of Marxism

Faced by the issue of poverty and oppression, liberation theologians asked what are the causes of poverty in Latin America? They saw the need for a "scientific analysis" of the causes. Marxism, along with non-Marxist versions of the "dependency" theory, appeared to provide an answer by focusing on the exploitation of the poor by wealthy elites and foreign investors. Liberation theology has borrowed other related concepts from Marxism as well: a stress on the need for action (praxis), a critique of ideologies (including ideological aspects of religion) which justify the status quo, and the idea of class struggle.

The Vatican document charges that liberation theology (again, the bad kind) adopts Marxism uncritically and allows the theology to become "captive" to Marxist ideology. The more specific charges are these. First, liberation theology accepts uncritically the Marxist claim to offer the correct "scientific" analysis of conditions in Latin America. Thus liberation theology adds to its description of conditions of injustice a "pathos which borrows its language from Marxism, wrongly presented as though it were scientific language" (VII, 12). By adopting the Marxist analysis exclusively it falls into simplifications which prevent any real rigorous study of the causes of poverty (VII, 11). Second, liberation theologians are misguided in thinking that Marxist analysis can be separated from the rest of its ideology (atheism, materialism, violence, etc.). "No separation of the parts of this epistemologically unique complex is possible" (VII, 6). If you start with the analysis you end up with the whole of Marxist ideology. Third, liberation theologians make this Marxist analysis the guiding force of "praxis" which then becomes the sole criterion of truth, such that anyone not involved in this praxis cannot be expected to know, judge, or act upon the truth (VIII, 1–5). Fourth, the main praxis called for by liberation theology is one of class struggle, which leads to hatred and violence. Liberation theology, says the Vatican document, accepts the idea that class struggle is "the fundamental law of history . . . the driving force of history" (X, 2–3). It also falls into a disastrous confusion of the biblical poor with the proletariat of Marx (IX, 10). Those who accept class struggle are led to hatred and to "systematic and deliberate recourse to blind violence" (IX, 5, 7). Finally, in adopting Marxist class struggle, liberation theologians fail to recognize the consequences of Marxist socialism, viz. totalitarian regimes which deny human freedoms (IX, 10). Again the target of these charges is not clear, though Ratzinger's earlier address would suggest that Gutierrez is a major offender.

As a series of potential dangers in the use of Marxism, and as a criticism of the way some Christian activists have uncritically appropriated Marxism, the Vatican document can serve as a useful critique. But if its intention is to offer an accurate picture of what most theologians hold, it fails because it "reads into" liberation theology far more than is actually said, and it fails to recognize the points on which liberation theologians themselves criticize Marxist ideology.

Liberation theologians do seem too often to identify social science or social analysis with Marxism, and to accept its claim to be scientific. Thus, for example, Jose Miguez Bonino states that Marxism "offers a scientific, verifiable, and efficacious way to articulate love historically."[9] Luiz Gomez de Souza, addressing an ecumenical conference on base communities, stressed the need for objective analysis to guide actions but then claimed "For that we need a method of scientific analysis, and Marxism is the scientific method the people's movements possess to understand their practices."[10] In Mexico and Nicaragua, I read Christian catechisms which used a popular form of Marxist method as the basic tool of analysis. (The catechisms show a tree with its trunk as economics, its limbs as political, and its leaves as ideology—a picture clearly intended to present Marx's analysis of economics determining the superstructure of society.) Many sympathetic critics of liberation theology have urged them to broaden their method of analysis and to challenge the adequacy of Marxist analysis.

Some American critics (e.g. Michael Novak) have criticized liberation theology's reliance on "dependency theory."[11] But on this score, the Vatican seems rather to agree with liberation theology's analysis, at least if the descriptive accounts could be stripped of references to Marxist analysis. In surprisingly strong language the

---

[9]Jose Miguez Bonino, *Christians and Marxists: The Mutual Challenge to Revolution* (Grand Rapids, Mich.: Eerdmans, 1976), p. 115. But Miguez Bonino (a Protestant theologian) also warns against blind acceptance of Marxist analysis and ideology.

[10]Luis A. Gomez de Souza, "Structures and Mechanisms of Domination", in *The Challenge of Basic Christian Communities*, ed. Sergio Torres and John Eagleson (Orbis, 1981), p. 13.

[11]Michael Novak, "The Case Against Liberation Theology,"in *The New York Times Magazine*, Sunday, October 21, 1984.

Vatican document refers to the "seizure of the vast majority of wealth by an oligarchy of owners bereft of social consciousness . . . military dictators making a mockery of elemental human rights . . . the savage practices of some foreign capital interests" (VII, 12). Such a statement, ironically, would be attributed to Marxists if the source were not known. So, too, would many charges made by John Paul II against rich nations dominating poor ones. Yet the Church seems unwilling to admit that many of its own critiques of injustice coincide with Marxist charges. Marxist analysis may indeed be blind to other factors that have caused Latin American poverty (e.g. lack of a strong work ethic, lack of entrepreneurship, lack of property distribution needed to make even free enterprise possible). But factors which support Marxist analysis are all too evident also: in Nicaragua, prior to 1979, the control of the largest businesses and 30% of the land by the Somoza family; in El Salvador, poor landless peasants forced to work for $1–$2 a day, while the twenty leading families accumulated wealth estimated at $70–$300 million per family; in Chile, foreign-owned copper companies taking over $10 billion in profits, with profit rates as high as 52% of investment.

On the separation of Marxist analysis from Marxist ideology, it can be argued that most Marxists (Marxist-Leninists) do build their analysis on materialist philosophical principles. But many independent Marxist scholars do not, and certainly a Christian can separate the two, just as Christian psychiatrists have learned to use Freudian analysis without accepting Freud's views on religion. Moreover, liberation theologians do challenge reductionist tendencies in Marxism, especially in respect to religion where Marx's analysis failed to recognize the true nature of religious belief. That elements of Marxist analysis can be borrowed without becoming captive to Marxist ideology is evident in John Paul II's, 1981 encyclical *Laborem Exercens* which clearly uses a Marxist problematic and Marxist concepts while challenging Marxist conclusions and solutions.

Regarding the issue of "praxis" as a criterion of truth, some activist groups have argued that only those who use Marxist scientific analysis as a guide, and become actively engaged in revolutionary struggles, are on the side of truth and the gospel. J. Guadalupe Carney's *To Be a Revolutionary* (Harper & Row, 1985) expresses this conviction. I would challenge it. Even from a practical standpoint, it is difficult to see how Marxist "science" and "praxis" can serve as criteria for truth since Marxists disagree sharply among themselves as to correct strategies and tactics of social change. In respect to

Christians, the Vatican is certainly right in affirming that political commitments should never involve surrendering or suspending all critical and ethical judgments about the movement to which one is committed. But do liberation *theologians* argue that we *should* suspend all critical and ethical considerations in opting for the poor?

Finally let me comment on the issue of class struggle. Gutierrez would appear to be the target of Vatican critics (and more specifically his 1971 work with little reference to all the change and process of development in his work). Gutierrez does say (1971) that Latin American countries are marked by class antagonisms; but so do numerous non-Marxist historians recognize the dominance of wealthy elites in many Latin American countries. What I do not find in Gutierrez are the Marxist statements attributed to liberation theology in the Vatican document, that "class struggle is the fundamental law of history" or the "driving force of history." Gutierrez and other liberation theologians do argue that the Church must opt for the poor in their struggle. I would fault them for not making explicit the moral norms which must govern such an engagement, but I certainly do not find Gutierrez calling for the tactics which the Vatican attaches to advocacy of class struggle, viz. hatred of class enemies and systematic recourse to violence.

III. Criticisms of the Church

Confronted by the poverty of the masses in Latin America, liberation theologians have raised a third question. What has the Church done in response? Especially in the early years of liberation theology, many sharp criticisms were directed against the Church itself. It had long been aligned with the rich land-owning class in Latin America. It had done little to voice concern for the poor. Most of its educational efforts involved the upper or middle classes. Its piety seemed to fit all too well the Marxist critique of religion: pacify the poor with promises of eternal life and downplay the insignificance of this life or the need for social change. The social teachings of the Church were seen by some groups as too reformist and as relying only on top-down "moral conversion" of the rich and powerful. In recent years, Leonardo Boff has directed sharp criticisms at the internal government of the Church as well, charging that all spiritual power and authority is invested in a top-down hierarchy, and arguing that the Church does not fulfill, in its own practices, what it calls for in society (e.g. respect for the dignity of its own members, shared decision-making, a breakdown in concentration of power).

While Marxism receives the greatest stress in the Vatican document, the issue of Church authority may well be the most fundamental concern for the Vatican. At least Pope John Paul II appears to have the restoration of Church authority and discipline as an overriding concern. The Vatican document, in tones that suggest almost a personal note of hurt, strikes out at the criticisms made against the Church by liberation theology. "The social doctrine of the Church is rejected with disdain" (X, 4). The hierarchy is discredited in advance as belonging to the class of oppressors (IX, 3; X, 1). It is difficult, not to say impossible, to dialogue with some liberation theologians (X, 3).

A second Church concern voiced in the document regards the "popular church". Liberation theology is charged with opposing a church of the poor to the hierarchical church, by promoting its ideas in base communities whose people lack the theological preparation and capacity to discern (X, 13; XI, 15).

Liberation theologians, and popular movements inspired by them, have at times been excessive in criticisms of the Church (just as criticisms against liberation theologians have been excessive). Some groups (e.g. Christians for Socialism in Chile, 1972) have disdained Church social teachings. But what the document does not acknowledge is any sense of the deep faith and loyalty of most liberation theologians: their efforts to work with bishops at Puebla; the great efforts made by Gutierrez's summer schools in Lima to study and promote the social teachings of the Church, including those of John Paul II; the dedication of a Jon Sobrino remaining in El Salvador, at great risk, to aid Bishop Rivera y Damas; the close bonds between Leonardo Boff and many of the Brazilian hierarchy, etc.

Conclusion

There are many legitimate criticisms that can be made of liberation theology, though most of the criticisms are most applicable to early writings in liberation theology and to activist groups. Some of the criticisms of the Church have been excessive. There is (or was) a "tendency" to demand unquestioned commitment and to reject all divergent views as "bourgeois", too much reliance on Marxist analysis, and too much faith in economic socialism with insufficient attention paid to political freedoms. But the Vatican document fails to give a truly balanced and objective account of liberation theology. It sees Marxism only in terms of a monolithic Marxist-Leninism, and consequently does not recognize the degree to which liberation theology can and does include "critical" uses of Marxism. It reads into liberation theology positions which are not expressed (or at least which I have not found), for example: that class struggle is the driving force of history, a denial of the Incarnation, an identification of the biblical poor with a Marxist proletariat, that all class struggle involves hatred and violence.

But above all the *tone* of the document is disheartening (even more so considering its insistence on reconciliation and love over class struggle). While it acknowledges the dedication of many Christians who work with the poor, little or no credit is given to liberation theologians for the many theological insights and developments they have contributed to the Church, and the document shows no appreciation for the deep faith, love and loyalty that has inspired the works of so many. They are treated almost as "class enemies."

We do not do justice to liberation theology if we simply accept it romantically without question or criticism. But it deserves to be presented as fairly, objectively, and caringly as possible to arrive at the truth. This I have tried to do, but I am keenly aware of my own limitations and the influence of my own values in the assessments I have made.

MAKING THE POOR THE RICH: RHETORIC VS. STRATEGY IN THE PASTORAL LETTER ON THE ECONOMY

Rebecca Chopp

The first draft of the Pastoral Letter on Catholic Social Teaching and the U.S. Economy relates the long tradition of Catholic social teaching to the reality of poverty in the United States. Attempting to follow the Second Vatican Council's mandate to discern the times, the letter is a plea to measure American society by the option of the poor and to reform our practices both nationally and internationally in light of human dignity and common good. On the whole, the letter is a call for a progressive reform, believing in both the necessity and possibility that Americans can and will correct their ways.

The main strategy of the letter rests on the correctivist principle of the option for the poor formulated by a substantial reinterpretation of the church's social teaching, theological foundations, and a description of the present situation of the U.S. economy. Four themes contribute to and ground the correctivist tendency of this letter. First, continuing the trajectory of the Roman Catholic social teaching since the Second Vatican Council, the foundational notion of human dignity is constituted through appeals to the common good. The importance of the integral relation between human dignity and common good is twofold: (a) it suggests a new social anthropology and (b) it allows for the ground of human rights to be formulated through the realization of human activity.

Second, the Bishops argue the need of rights in the social-economic realm. The Bishops offer a strong case for the right to economic activity not only to meet basic subsistence needs for the full realization of the human person and the human community. In light of the relation of economic rights to the foundation of human dignity and the common good, the bishops introduce the measure of the

option of the poor. How a society treats its poor is a just measure of
its own realization of human dignity and common good.[1]

Third, the Bishops read the Christian tradition in light of an option
for the poor, suggesting that the Bible points to a vision of human
life that is not vaguely religious, but substantively just. The convenantal community is judged by how it treats the poor, creation and
justice are integrally linked, life is not only created in solidarity but
through Christ is recreated in a solidarity with those who suffer. The
Christian tradition, therefore, reveals an option for the poor as a
measure of fidelity and loyalty to God.[2]

Fourth, the Bishops construct a careful and powerful presentation
of the facts of poverty and poverty's interdependency with other
parisitic problems in American life. Poverty affects ethnic minorities
far more than it does whites: 1 out of 8 whites, 1 out of 3 blacks and
1 out of 4 hispanics and Native Americans are poor. Black income is
55% of white income. Female heads of family now have a rate of
poverty 6 times that of 2 parent families.[3] The Bishops force us to
look beyond our borders; half the world's population lives in countries where the per capita income is now the average of $400 and
less.[4] The descriptive option for the poor shocks us into the recognition that most human beings in our world are poor.

The interblending of these four themes is powerful: we are asked
to look anew at how we distribute our resources and how we measure
our lives. These themes demonstrate that we must change our ways:
we must begin what the Bishops call a new American experiment to
correct the pervasive problem of poverty. But, I want to argue that
this text deconstructs itself by demanding a far more radical reconstruction than the letter's correctivist strategy provides, for what the
Bishops actually present in this letter demands a radical critique of
the epistemic principles and of the social structures of American
life. While other critics, locating themselves outside the document,
argue for the Bishops to offer a more radical critique and reform, I
contend that the document itself calls for its own deconstruction:
the rhetorical argument demands more than the strategy offers.
Specifically, the option of the poor introduces a radical principle

---

[1]For a history of the development of the "option for the poor" in Vatican social
teaching see, Donal Dorr, Option for the Poor: A Hundred Years of Vatican Social
Teaching (Dublin: Gil and MacMillan; Maryknoll: Orbis Books, 1983).
[2]Para. 196.
[3]Para. 198.
[4]Para. 274.

that calls not for a correction within a fundamentally secure social order but a principle that requires the reconstruction of the basic practices and systems of that social order.[5] My argument can be summarized as a question: how is the option of the poor to be read? I want to suggest that the text must be read not from the general principle of human dignity which the option for the poor measures; but from the poor which are—despite the Bishops' strategy—everywhere present in this document.[6] Furthermore if we are to be true to the rhetorical argument of this text, the Bishops' proposed American experiment will depend—like its predecessor—upon a revolution. This revolution will not be against a king across but amongst the drowning sea of our own individualism and consumerism. The weapons of this revolution will have to be, at least in part, a critical theory of American culture and a reconstructive social theory of the intercontextuality of social practices and institutions in the economy. Let me offer my rhetorical reading of the option of the poor in three central areas.

First, to begin with the description of poverty—which comes last in the strategy of the letter. The actual facts present an overwhelming place to stand: between 1969 and 1978 one-fourth of the American populace lived in families receiving welfare in any one year[7]; 20% of the Americans receive 70% of the income while the bottom 40%— nearly half—receive 13% of the income.[8] In the global economy, the option for the poor means the option for most of the people of the world: 800 million people live in conditions of what the Bishops call *absolute* poverty.[9] Descriptively speaking, the option for the poor is not a derivative principle, but an interruptive fact—it is the place where most human subjects struggle to merely survive.

---

[5]Gregory Baum has made a similar sounding point concerning the Canadian Bishops Letter on the Economy, see "The Shift in Catholic Social Teaching," *Ethics and Economics; Canada's Catholic Bishops on the Economic Crisis*, Gregory Baum and Duncan Cameron (Toronto: James Lorimer & Co., 1984). Baum does not offer a rhetorical reading of the document, but argues the option for the poor depends on a general shift to liberation theology in Catholic social teaching. Our points parallel only because we both argue that internal to the document the option for the poor demands a radical reconstruction of the polis.

[6]The correctivist strategy makes this not a document *of* the poor but a document *for* the poor. Nevertheless, in the theological interpretations and the description of the situation of poverty, the poor tempt what the Latin American theologians would call an "irruption" into the document. See, for instance, Gustavo Gutierrez, *The Power of the Poor in History: Selected Writings*, trans. Robert R. Barr (Maryknoll: Orbis Press, 1983)

[7]Para. 221.

[8]Para. 202.

[9]Para. 274.

Second, the theological interpretations attempts to make the case for the foundation of human dignity in communal solidarity whereby the poor become the measure of justice and fidelity in a community. But the theological reconstruction also suggests far more than this conclusion. Note first, that though the Bishops entitle the first section of the biblical perspectives on economic life, "Creation, Covenant and Community," in reality the section flows as covenant, community, creation, recreation, and eschatology.[10] These five movements are filled in with the content of justice, liberation and freedom. The Bishops, for instance, don't talk about just any covenant or any community, but a covenant and community formed in light of a liberation from slavery. Accordingly, the paradigm of communal experience and of God's action, that the letter offers, is one of liberation. The convenantal community is not based on a derivative principle of the option for the poor but on a transformative vision of a liberating God acting in history. Or, note the Christology of the theological reconstruction: Jesus is not introduced in the text as a kind of universal incarnation of human dignity,—a yes to the fact that life is,—but as a definitive model of how life must be. Jesus serves as the paradigm for both Christian and social activity: "Indeed, the option for the poor is the social and ecclesiological counterpart of the emptying (kenosis) of Jesus in the incarnation."[11] The theology of the pastoral letter focuses substantively not on general human dignity and common good, but on justice, liberation, conversion, repentance judgment, and freedom; it forces the non-identity of tradition and vision; and it offers a transforming vision not only of a corrective movement of distributive justice but of new ways of being and doing in history.

Third, on occasion the letter itself calls for a far more radical reformation of the social order and the cultural ethos than a correction of particular economic practices and social institutions would entail. For instance, the Bishops speak of the need for a new political will and criticize both America's punitive attitude toward the poor and its excessive consumerism. The Bishops, no matter what their intentional strategy of the letter, talk not only in the language of mere correction, but also in the rhetoric of struggle, challenge, crisis, and conversion. Thus, language, facts, and the reading of tradition all introduce a far more critical meaning into the option for the

---

[10]Para. 27–40.
[11]Para. 54.

poor—a position of critique and transformation of the values, consciousness, and social practices of our country. From this option of the poor, the letter's strategy must be criticized at two fundamental points.

First, the fundamental construct of the human subject as constituted through "meaningful" work.[12] The very possibility of work for all can be questioned: is the expansion of our economy really infinite? Can the status of all jobs in any economy be inherently fulfilling? What about those who cannot work—such as the elderly— are they left to be "un-realized?" In this letter, the Bishops never question their own definition of work or the assumption that work is somewhow definitive of human being. Perhaps what needs to be criticized, as theologian Johann Baptist Metz has indicated, is the notion that the value of the human subject is equal to the work a person provides.[13] Related to this is the need for a stronger critique of values of consumerism—a critique of the poverty of affluence and of the apatheic consciousness that bourgeois consumerism demands. Most problematically of all, the anthropological construct of the pastoral letter never questions the need to make the poor the rich and hence, a certain objectification of the poor occurs. Indeed, the poor once again prove their functional usefulness to the rest of us, this time as a measure of our fidelity to God and of human solidarity.

Secondly, the option of the poor interrupts an ideological construal of the common good. The pastoral letter assumes that its corrective strategy will be readily accepted for Americans, we are to believe, can come to a reasoned conclusion and a cultural consensus to change our ways. But at least since Max Weber, there has been an ongoing critique of the resources for change in bourgeois rationality.[14] Indeed, through modernity there has been a critique of the very potentiality of technological rationality to prevent any such cultural consensus in the polis.

We must, of course, recognize a theoretical problem behind this letter that may be a particularly thorny problem for the Bishops, a problem that poses more difficulties than an anthropological construct, the objectification of the poor, or any naive assumptions of

---

[12]Hannah Arendt, *The Human Condition* (Chicago: The University of Chicago Press, 1958).

[13]Johann Baptist Metz, *Faith in History and Society: Toward a Practical Fundamental Theology*, trans. David Smith (New York: The Seabury Press, 1980), p. 35, p. 101.

[14]Max Weber, *The Protestant Ethic and the Spirit of Capitalism*, trans. Talcott Parsons (New York: Charles Scribner's Sons, 1958).

the growth of the economy. This is the relation of faith and reason in the Roman Catholic tradition of human rights.[15] The traditional Roman Catholic teaching of human rights was based on the natural law with the assumption that natural law and revelation yielded the same essential perspective. With Vatican II's recognition of cultural pluralism and the historicism of knowledge, the relationship of revelation and reason changes so that revelation grounds the depth of human person in ontology, and human reason or culture thus fills in the content of the foundation which revelation grounds. It is this paradigm that the first draft of the pastoral letter follows.

Obviously, the fundamental condition for this paradigm is that culture must be able to provide such a content to human rights. Thus, in this document, the Bishops refer back to a general solidarity of the American people or a collective fabric of moral ethos. The critical problem however, is that this content is either not there at all, or so distorted, that it cannot yield the substance of a common good.[16] An appeal to the common good will not solve the problem if there is no generally-agreed upon content or if the content is as radically distorted as rhetoric of the pastoral letter suggests. Therefore, the appeal to the common good must be developed by a critical interpretation of the common good via a reconstruction of social practices and institutions in the American economy, unless the Bishops intend to argue—as surely they must not—that making the poor rich is the best we can offer.

To discern these times through the option of the poor we need not only a formal foundation for moral claims, but some substantive content and transforming vision of the common good. To do this, the Bishops will, as I have suggested, have to revise the tradition of human rights. They must delve into areas of critical theory and of reconstructive social theory. They also have the possibility, indeed the mandate, to follow the example of an uniquely American tradition, the tradition of social theologians such as Reinhold Neibuhr and Martin Luther King, Jr., who used the biblical vision to critique and transform the reason and experience of our culture. For as in the

---

[15]For an excellent history of the Roman Catholic human rights tradition see David Hollenbach, *Claims in Conflict: Receiving and Renewing the Catholic Human Rights Tradition* (New York: Paulist Press, 1979).

[16]See, for example, Alastair MacIntrye. *After Virtue: A Study in Moral Theory* (Notre Dame, IN: University of Notre Dame Press, 1981) and Robert N. Bellah, et. al., *Habits of the Heart: Individualism and Commitment in American Life* (Berkeley, University of California Press, 1985).

days of Niebuhr and the days of King, the common good is not well among the American people and a change of heart and a change of mind is desperately needed before we, the American people, can correct our ways.

EPISCOPAL TEACHING AUTHORITY ON MATTERS
OF WAR AND ECONOMICS

James Heft

American Catholic Church historians emphasize that from the foundation of the Republic, Catholic bishops made a distinction between the spiritual authority of the pope, to which American Catholics were subject, and the temporal matters, in which they were free to do whatever was necessary for good citizenship. In 1826, Bishop John England told Congress that American Catholics wished to be just like their fellow citizens except in matters of religion.[1] In 1960, John F. Kennedy assured a group of nervous Protestant clergymen that his own Catholicism would in no way influence the exercise of his duties as president. Religion and politics would be kept separate. Or, as it was put on the eve of the 1980 presidential election by the title of an editorial that appeared in the *New York Times*, "Private Religion, Public Morality."

But times have changed considerably, especially in the last few years. Both England and Kennedy would be forced to rethink their statements now that the American Bishops have published a pastoral letter on the morality of nuclear war and are currently preparing one on the economy. The public reaction has been intense and disparate.[2] Among Catholics, some are thrilled by what they perceive as a new style of leadership, one marked by humility and courage and the free admission of its fallibility. Others are appalled that the leadership of their Church is teaching through an episcopal conference when it has no authority to do so. Still others believe that although the conference may issue letters, they should only outline

---

[1]David J. O'Brien, "American Catholics and American Society," in *Catholics and Nuclear War*, p. 18, ed. by Philip J. Murnion (Crossroads: New York, 1983).

[2]See "Notes on Moral Theology: The Bishops and the U.S. Economy" by David Hollenbach, in *Theological Studies*, 46(1985), p. 102.

principles, leaving their application to those with the competence to apply them. Finally, some few are disappointed in the tentative character of the conference statements, and would have preferred clear and binding statements, the sort that would have enhanced, they believe, the authority of the bishops.

The purpose of this paper is to reflect on three points: first, the teaching authority that bishops may legitimately exercise on matters of morality that have to do with war and economics; second, the kind of teaching authority that episcopal conferences may exercise in such matters; and third, the ecclesiological significance of the process the American bishops have engaged in to draw up these pastoral letters. In other words, using more technical language, I will consider what bishops can teach about authoritatively, that is, the object of teaching authority; then the way in which bishops in national conferences can teach, that is, the subject of teaching authority; and finally, the role of the *sensus fidelium* in the formulation of authoritative teaching.

1. *About What Can Bishops Teach Authoritatively?*

In their 1983 pastoral letter on war and peace, the U.S. Bishops explained that they would "address many concrete questions concerning the arms race, contemporary warfare, weapons systems and negotiating strategies." But they immediately added:

> We do not intend that our treatment of each of these issues carry the same moral authority as our statement of universal moral principles and formal Church teaching. Indeed, we stress here at the beginning that not every statement in this letter has the same moral authority. At times, we assert universally binding moral principles (e.g., non-combatant immunity and proportionality). At still other times we reaffirm statements of recent popes and the teaching of Vatican II. Again, at other times we apply moral principles to specific cases (par. 9).

They then proceeded to explain that when they apply moral principles, they make "prudential judgments" based on specific circumstances which not only can change, but which people of good will can interpret differently. While admitting that their moral judgments in such specific cases (e.g., their treatment of "no first use") therefore do not bind in conscience, the bishops nevertheless ask that they be given "serious attention and consideration" (par. 10).

I shall limit myself to asking one question about these carefully nuanced statements of the bishops: at what level of authority are "universally binding moral principles" taught? In other words, could a person for good reasons dissent from such a "universally binding moral principle"? Put in another way, could a Catholic support the saturation bombing of civilian populations believing that such a tactic would in the long run save more lives? Put in still another way, can "universally binding moral principles" be taught infallibly, in which case no dissent may be possible without sacrificing one's identity as a Catholic Christian?

The first conciliar discussion of the object of pastoral teaching authority took place at the Council of Trent (1545–1563) where the role of the bishops was said to include the preaching to their people of the faith that must be believed and put into practice. The bishops used the phrase *res fidei et morum*, which, according to Francis Sullivan, "indicates that while some matters of faith are simply to be believed, others are to be both believed and put into practice."[3] At Trent, the Gospel was described as *"fontem omnis et salutaris veritatis et morum disciplinae."* Thus, the Gospel is understood as the source of all saving truth and *disciplina morum* is understood best not as "moral discipline," as a literal translation would have it, but as instruction or teaching (*disciplina*) about *morum* or practices, which includes how we are to live and act and worship as Christians.[4] At Trent, *disciplina morum* included more than teaching about morals; it included as well matters of custom and ecclesiastical and liturgical discipline. Thus, the phrase *res fidei et morum* is best translated as "matters pertaining to (Christian) faith and practice."[5]

A more thorough discussion of the object of episcopal teaching authority took place at Vatican I (1869–1870). There it became clear in the discussion about the object of papal infallibility, that is, about matters of faith and morals, that there existed both a direct and an indirect object. In the official *expositio*, Bishop Gasser, in the name of the deputation of the faith, explained it this way:

---

[3]Francis A. Sullivan, *Magisterium: Teaching Authority in the Catholic Church* (Paulist Press, New York, 1983), p. 128.

[4]Maurice Bevenot, "Faith and Morals in the Councils of Trent and Vatican I," in (*Heythrop Journal*), 3(1962), pp. 15–30.

[5]Sullivan, p. 128. He explains that he insists "on the word 'Christian' to bring out the fact that for Trent, not only the 'salutary truth' but also the *disciplina morum* has the Gospel as its source."

As I said before, since other truths, which in themselves may not be revealed, are more or less intimately bound up with revealed dogmas, they are necessary to protect, to expound correctly and to define efficaciously in all its integrity the deposit of faith. Truths of this nature belong to dogmatic facts insofar as without these it is not possible to protect and expound the deposit of faith, truths, I repeat, that do not belong directly to the deposit of faith, but are necessary for its protection.[6]

According to Gasser then, infallibility extends first to those truths which are revealed, and then to those which are not directly revealed, but which are necessarily connected to revelation. The bishops of Vatican I had disagreed over the precise content of the indirect object of infallibility. They had agreed as to how those truths should be connected. Some of the bishops wanted the secondary object defined as "those things connected with the deposit of revelation," but others objected that this was too vague and could be interpreted to include almost anything. Gasser explained that it included only those truths necessarily connected to revelation. He noted the teaching of theologians that infallibility concerned only revealed truths, while other definitions were only "theologically certain."[7]

Vatican Council II (1962–1965) did not attempt to clarify further the secondary object of infallibility (see *Lumen Gentium*, art. 25), and since the Council the only official statement to touch upon the matter was *Mysterium Ecclesiae* of 24 June 1973 which restated the secondary object of infallibility in slightly different terms: "things without which the deposit cannot be properly safeguarded and explained" (*sine quibus hoc depositum rite nequit custo diri et exponi*).[8] Sullivan concludes his discussion of this matter in this way:

While the fact that there is a secondary object of infallibility is held by most Catholic theologians to be certain, there is by no means unanimity with regard to what is contained in this object. I think it would be fair to say that many manuals of ecclesiology prior to Vatican II reflected the broad description of the secondary object as 'truths connected with revelation.' The current trend would be to limit this object to what is

---

[6]Mansi. 52:1226.

[7]Mansi. 52:1316–1317. See also Gustave Thils, *Infaillibilité pontificale: Source, conditions, limites* (Gembloux: J. Duculot, 1969), p. 246; also Sullivan, p. 133.

[8]*AAS*, 65 (1973), p. 401.

strictly required in order that the magisterium might be able to defend
and explain the Gospel.[9]

Another way in which theologians have taken up this question is
to ask whether the magisterium is able to teach infallibly about
questions of natural law. After examining relevant portions of Gasser's official commentary on the texts of Vatican I, and after comparing a relevant portion of a *schema* proposed at Vatican II for the
document on the Church with the final approved text, and after
analyzing portions of the minority report of the commission of
experts appointed by Pope Paul VI to study the question of birth
control, Sullivan concludes that particular norms of natural law are
not the object of infallible teaching.[10] Catholic theologians have come
to this conclusion not only because of the particular complexity of
moral problems facing us today, but also because the Gospel often
provides light rather than specific solutions for which Christians, as
well as others, must search long and hard.[11] Finally, if the particular
norms of the natural law are not to be included within the framework
provided by Vatican I for the object of infallible teaching, basic
principles of the natural law are, even though it "does not seem that
any such moral principle has ever been solemnly defined."[12]

In the light of these considerations, I now return to my original
question. What conclusions can be drawn? Can "universally binding
moral principles" be taught infallibly? If Sullivan is correct, the
answer would seem to be yes, but only if we are talking about basic
principles of natural law, and specifically about those which have
been revealed to us "for the sake of our salvation." The United States
bishops illustrate what they mean by "universally binding moral
principles" by citing as examples the principles of non-combatant

---

[9]Sullivan, p. 134.

[10]Sullivan, pp. 140–147. For a spirited argument against Sullivan's conclusion and
for the possibility of defining infallibly particular norms of natural law, see Germain
Grisez, "Infallibility and Specific Moral Norms" in *The Thomist* 49 (1985), pp. 248–
287. Grisez argues that adultery and abortion could be infallibly condemned. His
disagreement with Sullivan concerns the teaching on contraception. Our concern in
this article, of course, is moral principles that have to do with war and economics.

[11]Sullivan, p. 151.

[12]Sullivan, p. 149. Sullivan explains: "Catholic moralists generally agree that those
basic norms of the natural law which have also been revealed to us 'for the sake of
our salvation' could be infallibly taught, either by solemn definition or by the
universal ordinary magisterium" (p. 149). I suspect that moral theologians would
have as difficult a time agreeing upon a list of basic and particular norms of natural
law as dogmatic theologians would have in agreeing upon a list of infallibly defined
dogmas.

immunity and proportionality, principles that require in their application the evaluation of complex specific circumstances, evaluations
which in many instances could be legitimately disparate. This fact
alone would seem to rule out the possibility that these principles
could bind consciences, at least in their application, in the way in
which basic principles of the natural law could bind. I will leave it
to the moral theologians to enumerate and distinguish between basic
principles of the natural law which could be infallibly taught, and
the particular norms of the natural law which can not. The very fact
that moral theologians have not done this indicates the difficulties
inherent in formulating moral principles that can be defined infallibly. Moreover, it would also be necessary to show that these principles, even before their application, have been revealed to us "for the
sake of our salvation." No dogmatic theologian has, to my knowledge, ever attempted to demonstrate that.

2. With What Kind of Teaching Authority Can Episcopal Conferences Teach?

I have just established that particular norms of the natural law, the
sorts of norms which would be most often employed in discussions
about the morality of war and economic justice, can not be a part of
the secondary object of the infallible magisterium. I now turn to my
second question: with what kind of authority can episcopal conferences treat matters of war and economics? It is commonly held in
Catholic ecclesiology that the teaching authority of the hierarchy
may be exercised in one of two ways: on the one hand, in an
"extraordinary" way when a doctrine is defined by an ecumenical
council, or by a pope speaking *ex cathedra*, or, on the other hand, in
an "ordinary" way when a doctrine is taught by an individual bishop
in his local church (see *Lumen Gentium*, article 25). The authority
of teaching, *mandatum docendi*, is exercised legitimately therefore
in either an extraordinary or an ordinary manner.

When the American bishops went to Rome in 1983 to discuss
their pastoral on the morality of nuclear war, Cardinal Ratzinger
said: "A bishops' conference as such does not have a *mandatum
docendi* (a mandate to teach). This belongs only to individual
bishops or to the college of bishops with the Pope." Compared to
the teaching prerogatives of individual bishops, Ratzinger said that
"national conferences have no theological base."[13] Moreover, he

---

[13]See *The Tablet*, December 8, 1984, p. 1223; also see *Newsweek*, December 31,
1984, p. 63.

stated that such conferences are merely practical expedients that run the danger of undercutting by bureaucracy and anonymity the personal teaching authority of individual bishops.

Several points need to be made in view of the remarks of Cardinal Ratzinger. First, Vatican II acknowledged and encouraged the establishment of limited expressions of collegiality. At the end of Article 23 of *Lumen Gentium*, for example, it is stated that modern episcopal conferences can contribute fruitful assistance in the development of a deeper collegial sense.[14] Articles 37 and 38 of the *Decree on the Bishops' Pastoral Office (Christus Dominus)* underscore the importance of episcopal conferences by likening them to the synods, provincial councils and plenary councils that achieved so much good in the early Church. Concerning the teaching authority of episcopal conferences, article 753 of the new Code of Canon law states:

> "Although they do not enjoy infallible teaching authority, the bishops in communion with the head and members of the college, whether as individuals or gathered in conferences of bishops or in particular counsils, are authentic teachers and instructors of the faith for the faithful entrusted to their care."

Article 753 appears in the section of the Code that deals with the Church's teaching function. There is, therefore, in recent official statements of the Catholic Church, a theological base for episcopal conferences exercising a legitimate role as authentic teachers.

There is also strong historical precedent for episcopal conferences that teach with authority. Particular councils have contributed in significant ways to the development of doctrine. One needs only to recall, among many possible examples from the early Church, that the provincial council of Carthage issued in 418 the first decrees on the subject of original sin, and that the council of Orange condemned in 529 semi-Pelagianism, and from more recent history, that the episcopal conferences of Latin America have issued important statements at Medellin in 1968 and at Puebla in 1979. In view of this, it

---

[14]Article 23 of *Lumen Gentium* speaks of episcopal conferences as helpful ways to develop a "collegiate spirit" (*collegialis affectus*), a phrase that has led, in the words of Charles Murphy, to a distinction between "effective and affective" collegiality: " 'effective' referring to the exercise of supreme power in strictly collegiate acts; 'affective' describing more of an atmosphere of mutual co-operation, assistance and love among the bishops" (see "Collegiality: An Essay Toward Better Understanding," in *Theological Studies*, 46 (1985), p. 40).

would be difficult, in the opinion of Avery Dulles, "to defend the view that there is no teaching authority between the universal magisterium of the popes and ecumenical councils, at the one extreme, and that of the individual bishop in his own diocese at the other."[15] After explaining that episcopal conferences do not, according to Vatican II, exercise a magisterium in the strict sense, Archbishop James Hickey of Washington, D.C. spoke about the impact of the teaching of episcopal conferences while addressing a meeting of the American bishops at Collegeville in June of 1982:

> . . . one would have to be quite blind and deaf to reality if he denied that the statements of episcopal conferences do have an effective impact on the pastoral life of local dioceses and beyond. How many have not relied on the pastoral letters of episcopal conferences to find pastoral solutions to burning moral issues? How many times are priests and people not referred to the teaching of our conference and of other conferences? Many of the pastoral letters of conferences play an important role in the life of the Church. We have to admit, then, that the conference offers a most effective vehicle nationally for our teaching office.[16]

It is of course important that national episcopal conferences avoid nationalism which would weaken the unity of the universal church.[17] Moreover, they are not to substitute for the voice of the

---

[15]Avery Dulles, "Bishops' Conference Documents: What Doctrinal Authority?," in *Origins*, Jan. 24, 1985, Vol. 14, #32, p. 530. Since Ratzinger's statements in December of 1984 concerning episcopal conferences, Dulles and a few other theologians have cited Ratzinger's article published twenty years ago in the first volume of *Concilium* (Paulist Press, 1965) on "The Pastoral Implications of Episcopal Collegiality" in which the then young German theologian and *peritus* of Vatican II argued for a more effective exercise of collegiality through episcopal conferences.

[16]Sullivan, pp. 121–122.

[17]Henri deLubac, among others has written about this danger. See his *Particular Churches and the Universal Church* (San Francisco: Ignatius Press, 1982). Dulles notes that in this regard "a test case arose in 1983, when several national hierarchies were simultaneously preparing divergent statements on war and peace. The Holy See intervened and called an international meeting at which some of the problems were thrashed out before the American pastoral was put into final form. Even so, however, there were significant differences of approach between the American, French and German statements" (*Origins, art. cit.*, p. 533). In an article published a few months earlier, Dulles remarked that "the issuance of diverse statements by different hierarchies may be an excellent way to initiate dialogue with a view to reaching an ultimate consensus" ("The Teaching Authority of Bishops' Conferences," in *America*, June 11, 1983, p. 454). Concerning the differences of approach among the pastorals on the American, French and German Bishops on war and peace, see my article, "Do the European and American Bishops Agree?," in *The Catechist*, October, 1984, pp. 20–23.

individual bishop, but rather to strength it by providing a coherent framework within which complex issues may be addressed more effectively.[18]

It should be clear then that episcopal conferences do have solid historical and theological bases. It is also clear that they exercise a legitimate and authentic teaching authority. One question, however, remains: in the strict sense, do they have a *mandatum docendi?* Some theologians, including Cardinal Ratzinger, have answered negatively, and have based their response on what they maintain is a strict reading of the documents of Vatican II and the new code of Canon Law. They state that episcopal conferences are not given the capacity to engage in "truly collegial acts," acts that are given only to the pope united with the bishops in a council, or to all the bishops dispersed throughout the world but acting in union with one another and the pope.[19]

In response to such an argument, it needs to be remembered that one of the rules for the strict reading of any official document of the Church is never to assume that an answer has been given by a text to a question which was not raised when the text was formulated. At Vatican II there was no discussion of whether episcopal conferences had a *mandatum docendi.* The Council encouraged the establishment of episocpal conferences. Now that they have been established and are having a definite impact on the life of the Church, the question of whether they have a *mandatum docendi* naturally arises. The question is an open question. If one bishop teaching in union with other bishops and the pope has a *mandatum docendi*, it seems to me reasonable that even more so an episcopal conference which teaches in union with other bishops and the pope should have a *mandatum docendi.* An episcopal conference does not, of course, have "the authority proper to the whole episcopal college together with the pope."[20] Nevertheless, as canon 753 of the new Code states,

---

[18]Bishops James Malone, "The Intersection of Public Opinion and Public Policy," in *Origins*, Nov. 29, 1984, vol. 14, #24, p. 388. In a recent personal letter to me, Archbishop Pilarczyk explained that the authority of episcopal conferences "is a kind of joint but voluntary one, that is, each bishop must somehow make his own that which the Conference produces. To support such a theory, I point out that during one of my first meetings, when we were discussing capital punishment, one bishop got up and said that he believed in the appropriateness of capital punishment, and that if the Conference took a position against it he would publicly oppose that position in his see. Moreover, the ethical guidelines for Catholic health care facilities demand promulgation by the individual bishop in his diocese" (quoted with permission).

[19]See, for example, Charles Murphy's recent article in *Theological Studies* (note 14).

[20]Sullivan, p. 122.

the bishops, individually or gathered in conference, are "authentic teachers and instructors of the faith for the faithful entrusted to their care." Indeed, we may come to conclude that episcopal conferences exercise a *mandatum docendi* situated somewhere midway between that exercised by the individual bishop and that exercised by the bishops and pope gathered in council.

3. The Expanded Role Given to the Sensus Fidelium.

The establishment in the last twenty years of both episcopal conferences and the international synod of bishops has created promising forms of collaboration among the hierarchy. One of the most significant dimensions of the way in which the U.S. episcopal conference has chosen to work is the process it used to draft the pastoral letter on nuclear war and is using again to draft its letter on economics. The committees responsible for drafting these letters have consulted a wide variety of people. Preliminary drafts were made public so that criticisms could be made and suggestions offered with a view to preparing a second draft which again would be criticized and discussed before submission for a final vote— article by article—to the members of the episcopal conference. Several comments should be made about this process. I shall limit myself to three: first, the way it indicates a new role for the laity; second, the way it calls for more persuasive teaching; and third, the way it points out the importance of non-infallible teaching.

Without ever defining what infallibility actually is, the bishops of Vatican I did say that it was the same infallibility that belongs to the Church as a whole. We know that the consultation of the laity through their bishops played an important role in the definition of the two Marian Dogmas.[21] The bishops of Vatican II made it even clearer that the infallibility of the pope and bishops had to be related to the *sensus fidei* possessed by the entire people of God:

> The body of the faithful as a whole, anointed as they are by the Holy
> One (cf. 1 Jn. 2:20, 27), cannot err in matters of belief. Thanks to a
> supernatural sense of the faith which characterizes the People as a
> whole, it manifests this unerring quality when, 'from the bishops down
> to the last member of the laity,' it shows universal agreement in matters
> of faith and morals. For by this sense of faith which is aroused and

---

[21]James Heft, "Papal Infallibility and the Marian Dogmas," in *Marian Studies*, 33 (1982), pp. 59–63; reprinted in *One in Christ*, 18 (1982), pp. 309–340.

sustained by the Spirit of truth, God's People accepts not the word of men but the very Word of God (cf. 1 Th. 2:13). It clings without fail to the faith once delivered to the saints (cf. Jude 3), penetrates it more deeply by accurate insights, and applies it more thoroughly to life.[22]

It is important to note the four effects of the *sensus fidei* mentioned in the article: (1) the people accept the Word of God for what it really is; (2) they adhere to the true faith without ever falling away from it; (3) they are enabled to penetrate more deeply and elucidate more clearly that revelation; and (4) they are able to apply the Word of God more thoroughly to life. When we consider the issues of the morality of war and economic justice, it should be evident that the competencies of the laity must play a central role in the shaping of these teachings, especially if these teachings are going to include applications. It also seems evident that the bishops responsible for overseeing ("episcopacy") the drafting of such documents will need to depend upon the competencies of the laity to grasp more clearly and with greater insight the ways in which the Gospel is to be applied to these modern complex matters.[23]

Closely related to the *sensus fidei* is the *sensus fidelium*. if the *sensus fidei* is more of a subjective quality of believers, the *sensus fidelium* carries a more objective meaning which refers not to the believers but to what they believe. The importance of the *sensus fidelium* was pointed out by Newman when he showed how it was precisely the laity who had faithfully clung to the truth in the face of the Arian crisis. It is the recognition of the importance of that same *sensus fidelium*, that moved another English cardinal, George Basil Hume, to speak on 29 September 1980 at the International Synod of Bishops on the Familay about the necessity of consulting the laity on such matters. He explained that the prophetic mission of husbands and wives is based on their experience as married people "and on an understanding of the sacrament of marriage of which they can speak with their own authority." Both their experience and their understanding constitute, the Cardinal suggested, "an authentic *fons theologiae* from which we, the pastors, and indeed the whole Church, can draw."[24]

Many theologians who write today about consulting the laity write

---

[22]*Lumen Gentium*, article 12.
[23]*Lumen Gentium*, article 37.
[24]G. B. Hume, "Development of Marriage Teaching," in *Origins*, Oct. 16, 1980, Vol. 10, #18, p. 276.

also about the way in which teachings acquire authority through
their reception.[25] There is a tendency in our democratic society to
reduce the matter of consulting the laity to the taking of a majority
vote or the settling for the least common denominator. At the other
extreme is the perception common among non-Catholics, and unfortunately among not a few Catholics as well, that papal and episcopal
statements acquire their authority only because popes and bishops
make them, and not also because the statements are true. Neither
democracy nor autocracy exemplifies the process by which teaching
acquires authority in the Catholic tradition. There is rather a subtle
but important interplay, yet to be sufficiently worked out by theologians, between, on the one hand, formal (who says it) and material
authority (what is said), and on the other hand, the way in which
the acceptance of a teaching affects its authority. Suffice it here to
say that important insights into this complex matter will be found
in a deeper grasp on the nature and function of the *sensus fidelium*.

A second new emphasis in the Church is the need for more
persuasive teaching. There has been in the last 25 years a shift away
from an emphasis upon formal authority to one on material authority.[26] This becomes all the more necessary when we are dealing with

[25]On the idea of reception, see Yves Congar, "La 'reception' comme realite eccle-
siologique," *Revue des sciences philosophiques et theologiques*, 56 (1972), pp. 369—
402; Aloys Grillmeier, "Konzil und Reception. Methodische Bemerkungen zu einem
Thema der ökumenischen Diskussion," *Theologie und Philosophie*, 45 (1970), pp.
321–352; Edward Kilmartin, "Reception in History: An Ecclesiological Phenomenon
and its Significance," *Journal of Ecumenical Studies*, 21 (1984), pp. 34–54; and
Margaret O'Gara, "Infallibility in the Ecumenical Crucible," *One in Christ*, 20 (1984),
pp. 325–345.

[26]Not all members of the Church represent the shift from formal to material
authority. In an article entitled "The Sources of Conscience" that appeared in the
Notre Dame Magazine (vol. 13, Winter 1984/85, pp. 20—23), James Burtchaell has
pointed out the irony of how Archibishop (now Cardinal) John O'Connor and
Governor Mario Cuomo, as well as Geraldine Ferraro, all agree completely on the
source of authority for their quite different stands on abortion: both depend on formal
more than material authority. The bishop sees his obligation as pastor discharged
when he reiterates the official Catholic teaching on the matter. He once referred the
entire matter to a higher authority: "So Geraldine Ferraro doesn't have a problem with
me. If she has a problem, it's with the pope." Burtchaell comments: "The Archibishop
gives the global impression that within the Catholic Church, moral edicts are officially
asserted by bishops. The bishops formulate doctrines to which, as a matter of loyalty,
all Catholics are expected to conform, and fail to do so at their peril." Governor
Cuomo says essentially the same: namely, that to be a Catholic is to believe the core
dogmas of our faith, one of which condemns abortion. As a Catholic, one might
accept that Church law. Burtchaell explains: "The Church does not have a law on
abortion, anymore than it has a law on embezzlement or a law on gossip or a law on
child abuse. It does have a wisdom on these matters. And that wisdom, if it has any

moral matters that depend to a considerable extent upon the inter-pretation of the natural law, such as is the case with matters of war and economics. As Sullivan explains, "When the (moral) norm itself is said to be discoverable by human reasoning, it would be a mistake to rely too heavily on merely formal authority in proposing it for acceptance by thinking people."[27] The more people are consulted, the more the final result embodies the wisdom of the community, the more likely it is to be accepted by that community.

A third aspect of the new situation in the Church in North America is the discovery of the value of fallible teaching authority. In the past, most Catholics expected their bishops and the pope to speak infallibly or to remain silent. The new dialogical mode of proceeding employed by the American bishops in drafting their most recent pastoral letters openly calls for help and expects to learn a good deal through the process. The bishops in using this method have stated that some of their conclusions may be wrong and expect and respect divergent opinions on matters of application. This mode of operating is perplexing for those who prefer their bishops to speak in absolute ways or to remain silent. We all need to recognize that in many of

---

sense behind it, should be accessible to others whose grounding is not in our faith." And again: "Any moral conviction that is taken on faith alone is no conviction at all, but only a sectarian mystery that should not be let outside to roam the streets and threaten people."

[27]Sullivan, p. 165. To ask for more persuasive reasoning in areas of morality related to the natural law is not to demand proof, nor is it to assume that what the natural law requires in particular cases is always obvious. Note the sobering remarks of Fr. Bede Griffiths, O.S.B.: "Is it not time for the Catholic Church to reconsider the respect which is due to the pronouncements of the Roman magisterium on matters which are outside the sphere of divine revelation? The Pope has declared that the morality of contraception is a matter of natural law, that is, of natural reason. It is obvious that neither the Pope nor the Roman Curia has any monopoly on natural reason, and in this matter the majority of theologians and educated lay people disagree with his view. In the same way, the Pope has said that the present system of nuclear deterrence is "morally acceptable" under certain circumstances, whereas many would hold that it is totally unacceptable under all circumstances. These are but two instances in which there is disagreement about the application of the natural law at the present time. In the past there have been many occasions on which the Roman magisterium has been proved to have been wrong on matters of politics and economics and science and history and morality. Even in matters which concern the Bible and the liturgy, which come nearer to the sphere of divine revelation, the Roman magisterium has had to admit that it was mistaken. Above all, on the question of the relation between the different Christian churches and between Christianity and other religions, it has proved to have been seriously mistaken. To confuse such pronouncements with statements which belong properly to the sphere of divine revelation, on which the Church has a real claim to speak with authority, can only lead to discrediting the Catholic Church in the eyes of other Christians and of the rest of the world" (The Tablet, "Letters to the Editor," September 1, 1984, p. 850).

the most important areas of our life we must rely upon discernment rather than infallibility to indicate for us the right way to live. In 1967, the German bishops put the matter well:

> . . . human life, even at a wholly general level, must always be lived 'by doing one's best according to one's lights and by recognised principles which, while at the theoretical level they cannot be recognised as absolutely certain, nevertheless command our respect in the 'here and now' as valid norms of thinking and acting because in the existing circumstances they are the best that can be found. This is something that everyone recognises from the concrete experience of his own life. Every doctor in his diagnoses, every statesman in the political judgments he arrives at on particular situations and the decisions he bases on these, is aware of this fact. The Church too in her doctrine and practice cannot always and in every case allow herself to be caught in the dilemma of either arriving at a doctrinal decision which is ultimately binding or simply being silent and leaving everything to the free opinion of the individual. In order to maintain the true and ultimate substance of the faith she must, even at the risk of error in points of detail, give expression to doctrinal detectives which have a certain degree of binding force, and yet, since they are not *de fide* definitions, involve a certain element of the provisional even to the point of being capable of including error. Otherwise it would be quite impossible for her to preach or interpret her faith as a decisive force in real life or to apply it to each new situation in human life as it arises. In such a case the position of the individual Christian in regard to the Church is analogous to that of a man who knows that he is bound to accept the decision of a specialist even while recognising that it is not infallible.[28]

The bishops can not afford to remain silent about matters on which they can not speak infallibly. How specific they should become in what they say may well be debated.[29] Whether they should speak at all should be ovious from what has been written here.

---

[28]Sullivan, pp. 156–157.

[29]I agree with Brian Benestad (*The Pursuit of a Just Social Order Policy Statements of the U.S. Catholic Bishop, 1966–1980* [Washington, D.C.: Ethics and Public Policy Center, 1982]) who distinguishes between social teaching and policy statements, and recommends that the bishops limit themselves to the former unless it is clear that only one policy is consistent with the Gospel. Avery Dulles, who agrees with Benestad on this matter, puts it this way: "When they (the bishops) issues politically controversial statements, they tend to divide the Christian community along political lines and to marginalize persons whose faith and morals are above reproach. In their peace pastoral the bishops attempted to distinguish between their doctrinal teaching and their policy judgments, but this distinction was overlooked in much of the discussion. Generally speaking, I believe, the episcopal conference should devote itself primarily

4. Conclusion

I have concluded that bishops can teach infallibly only on the basic principles and not the particular norms of the natural law. I noted that it is commonly agreed that no such basic principles of the natural law have ever been infallibly defined. Secondly I concluded that episcopal conferences have in fact had powerful impacts through their teaching activity, and have in the process recreated in the Church a variety of expressions of collegial cooperation and activity. And while the question of whether they ought to have a *mandatum docendi* remains open, I have argued that in fact they should. Finally I have described three new developments in the interaction between the hierarchy and the laity: a more important role for the laity, an emphasis on more persuasive teaching and a deeper appreciation of the value of non-infallible teaching authority. These developments are, of course, causing a good deal of confusion within the Church, something not unexpected when there is a change in the way of doing things. With the new initiatives of the bishops and the greater involvement of the laity addressing issues that in fact constitute the structures of everyday life for all citizens, the *sensus fidelium* will be called upon more than ever to penetrate the Gospel and apply it more thoroughly to life as it is actually experienced and lived.

---

to teaching, leaving the concrete applications, where these are not obvious, to lay persons regularly engaged in secular affairs. Where they do feel obliged to make specific policy statements, they should clearly identify them as such" (in *Origins*, Jan. 24, 1985, Vol. 14, #32, p. 533).

CONTRIBUTORS

Stephen J. Casey is associate professor of social ethics in the department of theology and religious studies at the University of Scranton.

Rebecca S. Chopp teaches systematic theology at the Candler School of Theology, Emory University, Atlanta.

Joseph F. Gower teaches courses in religion and culture in the department of theology at Saint Joseph's University, Philadelphia.

James L. Heft is a member of the religious studies department at the University of Dayton where he teaches Roman Catholic studies.

Joseph A. La Barge teaches courses in social ethics and Catholic studies in the religion department at Bucknell University.

Arthur F. McGovern is professor of philosophy at the University of Detroit and offers a course in Marxism and Christianity.

Anne McGuire teaches courses in New Testament and early Christian literature at Haverford College.

William F. McInerny is a member of the department of theology and religious studies at Rockhurst College, Kansas City.

Paul Misner offers courses in the history of Christianity in the theology department of Marquette University.

Ronald E. Modras is professor of systematic theology in St. Louis University's department of theological studies.

William L. Portier teaches courses in American Catholic thought at Mount St. Mary's College, Emmitsburg, MD.

James F. Smurl is professor of comparative and social ethics in the religious studies department of Indiana University-Purdue University at Indianapolis.

Douglas E. Sturm is professor of religious ethics and of legal and political thought in the department of religion at Bucknell University.

Andrew F. Tallon teaches philosophy of religion and ethics in the department of philosophy at Marquette University.

Leonard J. Weber offers courses in religious ethics and medical ethics in the department of religious studies at Mercy College of Detroit.